To Konrad and Lori Schaum
Fritz Marti

RELIGION AND PHILOSOPHY:

COLLECTED PAPERS

Fritz Marti

University Press of America

Copyright © 1979 by

University Press of America, Inc.™

4710 Auth Place, S.E., Washington D.C. 20023

All rights reserved

Printed in the United States of America

ISBN: 0-8191-0702-6

Library of Congress Catalog Card Number: 78-68801

PREFACE

For many years I harbored the notion of republishing a number of my papers which appeared in print, mostly as a document for my children and for old friends and former students. Now I am happy to dedicate this collection to all of them.

On my own part I am pleasantly surprised to discover that, in a way, the papers cohere in content and make a book.

I thank the following journals and publishers for their permission to reprint the papers here listed by number.

Faith and Freedom, Liverpool, England	VI	Summer	1953
Harper	IV		1947
Herder	IX		1968
The Journal of Religion, Chicago	III	January	1946
The Modern Schoolman, St. Louis	XIII	November	1977
Rentsch Verlag, Erlenbach-Zürich	V		1946
The Review of Religion, New York	I	January	1937
	II	November	1942
The Southern Journal of Philosophy	VIII	Spring	1969
	X	Spring	1970
	XII	Winter	1975
Studies in Romanticism, Boston	VII	Winter	1964

The Proceedings of the 1974 Lewis and Clark Philosophy Conference, edited by T. P. M. Solon, at Godfrey, Illinois, were never copyrighted and I retained the copyright.

South Bend, Indiana, All Saints Day 1978   F. M.

i

BIOGRAPHIC NOTE

I was born January 1, 1894 and attended the municipal elementary school in Winterthur, Switzerland. My college preparatory school was the scientific branch of the municipal Gymnasium at Bern, from which I graduated in 1913.

After some work in a machine factory, I had my basic infantry training in spring 1914. I did the regular war time duty 1914-18. 1915-23 I served in the Motor Transportation Corps, eventually as company commander and technical instructor. 1922-23 I was manager of the Electric Cable Railway Bern-Gurten.

I studied mechanical engineering at the Swiss Federal Institute of Technology in Zürich from 1915 to 1918, when I changed to philosophy which I studied at the Universities of Zürich and Bern. I made my doctorate at Bern in 1922.

In 1923 I came to the University of Oregon and later taught at Goucher College, Haverford College and Hollins College where I also had the assignment of starting an art department. 1935 I went to the University of Maryland to start its department of philosophy and to introduce courses in the history of art. I also taught such courses in the Graduate School of the U.S. Department of Agriculture, in the National Gallery. 1943-44 I was a visiting professor at the University of Chicago. In 1946 I was called to Marietta College in Ohio as head of philosophy and lecturer on art history. Later I taught at Antioch College, Hiram College, Washington University and finally at Southern Illinois University which gave me the title of Professor Emeritus in 1973. I retired in 1974 and in 1976 settled in South Bend.

In 1937 I married Gertrude Austin, a pianist and private school music director. We have five daughters and a son. For the sake of our six we started a private preparatory school, the Berglihof School, on our 135 acre farm at Lower Salem, Ohio, where for a decade we were subsistence farmers. 1956 we transferred the school, as The Marti School, to Dayton, Ohio, where we soon had 120 pupils, from Kindergarten through twelfth grade, with seven full time and seven part time teachers.

Mrs. Marti made her B.A. at the University of Dayton and her M.A. at Western Reserve University. She was an Assistant and Associate Professor of French at Southern Illinois University in Edwardsville and retired in 1976. Her vegetable garden is feeding us, and she is making jewelry.

Our son is a carpenter and cabinet-maker and has designed and built many houses. All our daughters have master's degrees, two a Ph.D. They are teaching, from kindergarten to graduate school, subjects like psychology, Russian and sculpture. The four who are married have each two children.

INTRODUCTION

Philosophy comes packaged in human individuals. Death will dispose of the wrappings. However, the philosophical content could never attain its verbal form without the living responsibility of the author. Furthermore, barring incurable laziness, the individual cannot help following his calling. He hopes to mature in his human pursuit. Therefore one may reasonably look for continuity and consistence of problem and motif in his writings. To be sure one may find ramblings and deviations, for a human being is not a book.

Half a century of academic teaching more and more impressed on my mind the pathetic need for philosophical guidance felt by very many of my students who were baffled by the verbiage of religion. They could not drop the matter, the way college students drop a course they think they cannot handle. Religion rankles for, in our present age, young people are seldom taught how to guide their own thinking in matters not strictly secular. I never met a single student who, in church or school, had become familiar with the old warnings. As long ago as a millennium and a half, Augustine warned against the literal use of secular analogies. If God were "up there", he said, "the birds would beat us to Him" (Commentary on Psalm 130:12). He also said that "as long as we cannot inhere in the eternal, let us at least expel from the spectacle of our mind all nugatory and deceptive games" played with words (On True Religion, 50:98).

It is not merely a matter of language. We need to revise our thinking. For instance, in popular parlance, the word myth is too frequently used as a synonym for fake. Our schools and churches do not point out that myths can be possessive powers and that they exert that power even in our proudly enlightened age. Even manmade myths exert that power, like the Nazi myth of the German race or that Marxist myth of a classless society. These, to be sure, are faked myths. But the great historical myths were never manmade. They came upon me like dreams. But men realized that they could not call them mere dreams and so put them out of the way. They felt the superhuman power and presence of their gods.

Giambattista Vico in 1725 and Carl Gustav Jung in our time drew attention to the profound significance of myth in human life. This significance used to be acknowledged, and there were words for it, like revelation and sacred story. But nowadays, to look only in Christendom, most Christians resent the very phrase Christian myth, for they take it as a slur.

Philosophy endeavors to say in nonmythological language what can be prosaically told of the poetic expressions of religion. It does not intend to nor can it abolish the myth.

But it wants to remove the obstacle of nugatory objectification and ossification of the great images that constitute myth. Religion and philosophy go together. If they separate, it is to their own detriment. This is what the title of my book is hinting at.

The theme of the book can be stated simply. I take the liberty of borrowing a well known sentence of Kant and writing a variation or application of it. Kant lived 1724-1804. In the Critique of Pure Reason he wrote (page B 75, Norman Kemp Smith translation 93): "Thoughts without content are empty, intuitions without concepts are blind." My book would like to make clear that philosophy without religion is empty, and religious experience without philosophic verification is blind.

Kant's first Critique was published in 1781. Fiftysix years earlier, one year before Kant's birth, Giambattista Vico brought out the first edition of his Scienza Nuova, the "new science" that made clear the dignity of religious language which is naturally mythological, speaking in "fantastic terms."

After all, every religion insists that at least its own myth be taken seriously and be not set aside as fantasy. Nor are serious intentions enough. What is needed is the discipline of historical information and philosophical critique based on insight.

In the introduction to his Philosophy of Religion(XI,15) Hegel said "faith too is knowledge, but an immediate knowledge." All such knowledge becomes mediated as soon as it is put in words. An adequate wording depends on the mental purity of the receiving knower and on his poetic conscientiousness. For sometimes only poetic words can do justice to the message received.

If we take the figurative words literally - which is precisely what sheer ratiocination is likely to do - we are in danger of becoming victims of superstition.

Common sense, not acquainted with philosophical discipline, takes ratiocination for reason and therefore endeavors to protect religious knowledge from all "reason." The main difficulty of college teaching springs from a preparatory schooling which has not led its pupils beyond the common sense notion that ratiocination is all there is to reason. That may lead to adding religion to the curriculum, as if religiosity were a mere subject like spelling or arithmetic, and not the very core of all really human teaching.

Our problem is to retain the living truth which the myth conceals as well as reveals. Endangered not by reason but by rationalism, myth is in dire need of both, concealment as well as revelation. Then only does revelation not stand naked, at the mercy of cold ratiocination.

I. The first paper is really programmatic. It barely touches on many topics which some of the other papers elaborate, some times years after 1937.

II. A presidential address may rightly make bold to express the speaker's view of the state of the nation. In 1942 I looked at things more optimistically than now. Then, at the height of the war, there seemed to be hope we might be taught a lesson. Yet I saw dangers, and my diagnosis would seem to hold still. "The separation between science and religion, between thought and faith (I did say separation, not distinction) vitiated our educational system. It made us fear fundamental issues" (26). And it still seems "more political to acknowledge a sovereignty of the vulgar in matters of religion" (30). On the other hand, I would no longer say that colleges show no inclination to unlock the medicine chest of philosophic knowledge for religiously perplexed students. They no longer merely leave students "to their own devices or put them off with the advice to participate in the activities of denominational student clubs" (31).

III. Of course the trouble was and still is the habit of identifying faith and belief. I have no evidence that my second presidential address had any perceptible effect. Maybe I should not so blithely have used the chameleon word faith. After my talk a hearer asked me had I no other word. I replied, yes, the word health, insofar as it can signify that gift of basic health which persists through all kinds of infections and afflictions. The Swiss psychiatrist Balthasar Staehelin uses the word <u>Urvertrauen</u>, basic trust, that is, the deep sense of having a place and personal assignment in this world, in short, the feeling that we are wanted. Beliefs are only intellectual endeavors to give voice to this being at home, "here and in heaven."

IV. I do believe it is the lack of this gift which causes so many misunderstandings or the lack of understanding among individuals, groups and nations. If we were keenly aware of the semantic and historical relativity of beliefs, we could talk with and thereby love our enemies. Too many minds lack a sense of history. For all of us, at least in our early growing years, "myths are required as our solid ground" (45). But myth must mature and become up to date thought, attainable by historical study. "As yet, the multitudes are not historically minded" (46). Nor are many of their intellectual and spiritual leaders. <u>Where are the teachers? - Mine was Fritz Medicus.</u>

> I did not delete the footnote 2 on pages 49 and 50. My late friend Walter Farrell, O.P., whose early death I still regret, seeing things from his place, called "great religious truths" what I, with all due respect, called myths.

V. Every section of this book can be called an occasional paper. My birthday present to Medicus was an especially solemn occasion. Once in my life it was given to me to write good language, this time German, and that is the reason why I include the original version in this collection. I trust the reader who has German will sense the solemnity.

VI. For Augustine God was surely the truth (<u>veritas</u>, - Carl Gustav Jung would say significantly feminine) which is the best of teachers (<u>magistra</u>) by teaching us inwardly (On Free Will, II,ii,4). Augustine says: "Behold and see, if you can, that God is truth. Ask not <u>what</u> is truth; for immediately the mists of corporeal images and the clouds of phantasms will put themselves in the way and will disturb the calm which at the first moment shone forth for you, when I said truth" (On the Trinity VIII,ii,3. See Przywara: An Augustine Synthesis, 247, p. 133, Harper Torchbook 35, 1958). The first move of human consciousness is away from God, said Schelling (XI,186). In that manner God is put far away, turned into a strange idol. I should call it the original sin. Neither intellectually nor religiously can we any longer tolerate the deification of God. An innermost awareness of this should be, so I believe, the ultimate goal of teaching and catechization.

VII. Among truly modern philosophers we should consult Schelling who said that "to speak of God as a probability is a true blasphemy" (90). "The existence of God is an empirical truth, nay it is the ground of all experience" (90). "Man in his original being has no other meaning but to be the nature which posits God" (93). However it is difficult to understand Schelling if one is ignorant of all findings of Kant, or if one has been taught to misread Kant.

VIII. The longer the more my college teaching has made me aware of the didactic need for Kant's distinction between ratiocination (Verstand) which deals with the conditional, and reason (Vernunft) which, in this conditional world of ours, seeks the unconditional (Critique of Pure Reason, B364; Smith translation 306). Religion seeks God, but an ostensibly religious ratiocination seeks <u>a</u> God, that is, a hypothetical entity for which one must then seek proof. It forgets that there are many such gods, no matter what is the length of time during which they rule. This sentence of mine is not couched in Kant's language but it rests on his contribution to metaphysics.

IX. It was my teacher who made me aware of both, the conditional nature of human history and the unconditional challenge of the super-temporal. For readers who know German, my Vienna paper gives samples of the language of Medicus.

X. If my mosaic of quotations from Medicus does not cohere everywhere like a jigsaw puzzle, the reader can at least ponder the pieces. It may be helpful to remind him that Medicus consistently keeps in mind Kant's distinction between reason and ratiocination. The two are not separated. Reason needs ratiocination as a tool for being articulate and clear. On the other hand, while a rationalist may believe he can do with ratiocination alone, which deals with the conditional, he should realize that even the cogency of his conditional conclusions is unconditional in its binding strength. Moreover the distinction is manifest in the fact that ratiocination can be managed and used at will. It serves the evil minded as well as the man who seeks the good. Medicus borrows Rudolf Eucken's suggestive expression that ratiocination (Verstand) "hovers freely" (p. 42, On Being Human; Ungar, New York 1973). Medicus also says: "Our intelligence is what we have, and each one has his own. But reason has us: we are held fast and supported by its superindividual necessity" (ib.78; Medicus uses Schelling's phrase, VII,149; see below 177 and note 54).

XI. It may seem far fetched to look in Aquinas for corroboration of Kant, and it would surely have astonished Kant who had grown up in the Enlightenment. But both thinkers are keenly aware that it is the reason which has us which alone leads to the unconditional. Notwithstanding the apparently decisive difference in language and intellectual stance, the two are also clearly aware that "in God essence or whatness is nothing else than being" (136), as Aquinas puts it, or as Kant says, the idea of God is a postulate of regulative dignity, that is, it does not refer us to a conditional object (137).

XII. One very instructive way to Kant leads through young Schelling whose early works of 1794-95 (see my book, The Unconditional in Human Knowledge, Bucknell University Press 1979) show his struggle toward that unity of theoretical and practical reason which even the last of Kant's three Critiques had called a "must" but not made entirely clear. (See below 154 and note 12.)

XIII. Again it may seem too far a quest to go back to Augustine in order to show that the findings of Kant and his successors, especially of Schelling, are nothing entirely novel and, as I believe, are simply more mature formulations of insights into the core of human religiosity. I was led to this epistemological query by the literary fact that the search for proofs of the existence of God continues in our days, as if Schelling had never pointed out that proof leads into the field of the conditional. To be sure this search originates only in rationalist minds. Yet they still have the main say in our century, above all in our school curricula, from kindergarten and catechization well into graduate school.

The question as to the possibility of man knowing God is legitimate. The rationalist as well as the materialist, believing that God is a transcendent object, must deny the possibility. Affirmative answers can be given only by thinkers who know that all objects are conditional, thinkers like Augustine, Kant and Schelling. Let the reader weigh their answers, but let him not forget that the idea of God is no moot matter. Schelling said, "the insane one who will deny it, gives it voice without knowing he does, for he cannot reasonably connect any two concepts except in this idea" (177 and note 54). And Augustine wrote in his Soliloquies (I,1,2) "Whatever can love loves God, knowingly or unwittingly." These are no dogmatic assertions, although what is needed for understanding them is the discipline of philosophic reflection. It must be learned and it can be taught. And that brings us back to the question of our homes and schools.

TABLE OF CONTENTS

Preface.. i

Biographic Note.. ii

Introduction... iii

I   Religion and "Natural History".............. 1937   1

II   Religion, Philosophy and the College........ 1942   9

III   Faith versus Belief......................... 1945   33

IV   Abutments and Piers for Bridges of Cultural Understanding. 1945   45

V   Göttermacht und Gottesfreiheit.............. 1946   57

VI   The power of the gods and the freedom of God. 1953   71

VII   Schelling on God and Man.................... 1964   83

VIII   Kant's Contribution to Metaphysics.......... 1965   95

IX   Fritz Medicus (1876-1956)................... 1968   103

X   Fritz Medicus Full version in English....... 1970   113

XI   Aquinas and Kant on the Identity of Essence and Existence... 1974   125

XII   Young Schelling and Kant.................... 1975   151

XIII   Theological Epistemology in Augustine, Kant and Schelling....... 1976   165

Epilogue... 181

Index.. 185

The dates given above indicate the time when the papers were either first read or else published.

RELIGION AND "NATURAL HISTORY"

IN SCHELLING's unfinished book *Die Weltalter*, presumably written before 1814, we find the following passage: "What could occupy God before he created the world? This is a question which is so natural that even children will ask it. And indeed, it seems necessary to conceive of a duration of that as yet inarticulate state of things, provided that creation is to be thought of as a free act. Still, upon closer scrutiny, the concept of such a duration appears as unthinkable, since eternity, in itself and by itself, has no duration. Only time has duration, in contrast with eternity. Hence, that eternity before the world vanishes immediately into nothing or, what is the same, into a mere moment. The teachers usually find a way out of the difficulty by dodging the question. But leaving without answer such questions which strike even a child, is the very cause of the general lack of faith." (307)[1]

If, according to Schelling, the obviously false conception of eternity as duration causes a lack of faith, our apologists must not expect a great revival to result from a restatement of the obvious. To be true, that erroneous conception of eternity must be corrected. But a more pernicious though less obvious error is involved. It is the misconception of creation. The persistence of this error would seem to explain the insistent yet sterile occupation of some theologians with cosmology. These theological cosmologists wish to revive faith by means of erecting their theology on a naturalistic basis. We might remind them, of course, that the faith thus attained would have to be Stoic rather than Christian.

However, I have no mind to contribute to ecclesiastical apologetics. Nor am I at all inclined to set up any private theism or pantheism, after the fashion which accompanies periods of enlightenment, like ours. I share the eschatological feeling of the children of enlightenment, and it makes me wary of both traditional and invented answers offered in the uncritical terms of naïve questions. Yet, I do not follow

[1] Page references are to volume VIII of Schelling's works (J. G. Cotta, Stuttgart und Augsburg, 1861).

the fanatics of enlightenment who would make us believe that all naïve questions are unphilosophical. And the childlike question about what happened before creation strikes me as being pregnant with problems which cut at the very root of our knowledge of nature. I here propose to deal, in part at least, with the deep meaning of the very conception of creation.

To me, it means the undoing of the notion of reality as a sequence of events which simply supersede each other, either irrationally, or after the pattern of mechanistic laws in which time is a mere parameter. I do not mean to say that, in the historical development of human thought, irrationalism or mechanism came first and the conception of creation arose as a correction of them. I merely hold that creation means either divine arbitrariness within a nature dependent on this very foundation, and therefore basically unreal, or it means that in nature itself there is a growth of the new from the old—that the old is not merely superseded but made into the past of the new which thus alone comes to pass. I do not deny that the first and childish one of these two meanings can be found in religion, but it is my thesis that the second and only justifiable meaning is what redeems religion, in this controversy about creation.

However, I am anticipating, and I will start my argument with an analysis of the conception of acts of God. I cannot dismiss as thoughtless the naïve notion of acts of God, in nature. This notion, I believe, is not originally limited to calamities such as floods and plagues. No doubt, the phrase, acts of God, is also used by thoughtless people who would be called religious—people who conceive of God as a cosmic stage-manager, an odd job man, a scavenger, and eventually a scapegoat. Such notions, most impious as they are, still do pass for religion, since there are still people who seem to believe that using the name of God is a proof of religiosity. We may even find those notions in the minds of genuinely religious people, and then they meet with our forbearance. For the essence of genuine religiosity lies beyond such notions; it lies in man's sense of the eternal in reality. And it is the *eternal* in nature which the man of true piety means when he speaks of acts of God.

According to this phrase and conception, whatever is, in nature, is a fact, in the root sense of the word: factum. It has been done, by God.

Unphilosophical minds interpret this conception in a merely temporal sense, taking the acts of God as contingent events in time. This is a twofold misinterpretation. An act of God is nothing contingent; it is eternal. And eternity is not a matter of time, although time may prove to depend on eternity.

There is, in ecclesiastical parlance, an ostensible synonym for the eternal: the everlasting. And rash interpreters jump to the conclusion that the everlasting explains what the eternal means. The opposite is true. Even Platonism would point out that duration must be explained in terms of the timeless. But the Christian era felt that timeless ideas could never account for the historical reality of the temporal. The assumption of an arbitrary and therefore inexplicable act of a Demiurge who shapes the temporal world after the pattern of the timeless idea will never account for the simple and majestic dignity of nature. Nature simply is. It is not a contingent occurrence in an otherwise empty time. Nor is time a merely accidental attribute of nature. Nature is genuinely temporal. Somehow, it must be historical. And it is this historical character of nature to which the phrase, acts of God, must refer.

Acts of God are not contingent events in an indifferent time. No true act is contingent. And whatever the qualification act *of God* may signify, we ought to grant, at least, that the word *act* might prove significant if taken philosophically, not anthropomorphically.

An act, properly speaking, is no mere event, nor is it arbitrary. Very naïve people believe that they act freely when they act arbitrarily, when they do as they please. Even a naturalistic philosophy would remind them that this good pleasure of theirs is not, in turn, 'as they please,' but is conditioned by their own past about which they merely forget. Arbitrariness simply means to yield unawares to the past. Thus, arbitrariness has the appearance of a contingent event.

To act, however, means precisely to do away with contingency. It means to do what is meet and, thus, to overcome the past. Our true acts do not spring from nothing, they rest on our past. Yet, without our action, the past would persist as it was. It would modify the present, but it would not be modified and made into a real past which is no longer what it was. To act means to posit a past, to set it down as past, and thus to overcome it. Overcoming the past means freedom,—

real freedom, not that apparent liberty to do as we please. Freedom and necessity are one and the same. And this identity constitutes the realm of the spirit, the realm of our history, and hence—I think—the realm of nature.

True enough, neither naturalistic thought, nor religious words can reach this reality of which we may speak in terms borrowed from Schelling, saying that real is what has a "decided past" and, hence, a "true present" (259).

For naturalistic thought, whose enthusiasm has been voiced most intensely, perhaps, by Anaximandros, the present merely supplants the past and is in turn supplanted by the future. Naturalism may speak of evolution and progress; yet it cannot conceive of historical life. Life deposits the past by means of positing it (if I may thus render the double meaning of the Hegelian term 'aufheben'); the past is kept alive by doing away with it. This dialectical reality does not enter into naturalistic notions. But it does enter into the speculative conceptions of religion. It is my thesis that the conceptions of creation, and of acts of God, would be meaningless unless they referred to this nature of historical reality, and hence, I believe, to the historical character of nature, to an actual "natural history."

But these religious conceptions must be understood philosophically. Often the words creation and acts of God are taken for mere anthropomorphisms, by both infidels and shallow believers alike. The latter may even hope to benefit by God's arbitrary power over nature, expecting him to arrange things more pleasantly for them. They are fundamentally impious, since they do not humbly accept their station as creatures. They literally lack religion, if the word 'religio' means to own the ties that hold us within the whole of creation by means of our nature, which is what constitutes our human task. Genuine religion binds us back into our own nature, and thus, into nature at large. In the words of tradition, religion tells us to acknowledge that we are creatures, and it summons us to be of good cheer, as creatures. Truly, if we can gain this simple confidence in our own place, we are attaining the happiness of the good life.

Those men whom we call sound, and solid, and genuine, and real, have that basic confidence in themselves, in their own substance—that confidence which shows a unity of spirit and nature. For, man's substantial decisions spring from his nature, although they cannot be called decisions, nor are they his, unless this nature has acquired the dignity of a decided past. I quote a few sentences from *Die Weltalter* (259): "A man who has not overcome himself has no past, or rather, he never gets out of his past, he lives in it all the time. . . . Only a man who has the strength to tear himself away from himself (from what is subordinate in him)—only such an one is capable of making a past for himself, and he alone enjoys a true present and looks forward to a genuine future." Schelling continues: "Even these ethical considerations will make clear that no present is possible but what rests upon a decided past, and no past but what underlies a present, as overcome by it." And indeed, I should say, it is not merely an ethical matter. Although our freedom demands that our nature become our past, and the spirit our present, the very relation of present to past implies that we cannot live in spirit alone. We must have confidence in our nature, which is not of our making. We must trust in God, says religion. And the words on our coins might be taken as a true expression of a sense of creature dignity, if it were permissible to forget about the thoughtlessness which is impotent to master the words of the past, and which repeats them slavishly, instead of making them voice the free present.

The past, by itself, would enslave us, being no past but a haunting presence. But if we master it, it proves to be what is concrete in our freedom. And our past is not of the spirit alone. 'Genius is born,' we say. And without roots in human nature, there would never be personalities 'making history.' History is made by making a past out of the merely natural. If the natural were not thus mastered, we should call it unnatural, abnormal. Human nature finds its norm in becoming the decided past of a true present. And this relation of past and present is neither a mere temporal sequence, nor a timeless law. It is the mastery of time, and of the temporal. It is what may properly be called the eternal.

Only in such mastery can man find reality. Only in history. Thus, history is the realm where things really happen. History is no contingent and arbitrary play moving on a heavenly stage. It is reality, happening in the midst of nature, and from nature. Man's nature, then, need not be torn from the context of nature at large. Man is a creature, and his history springs from nature. But his nature becomes real, and human, only in his history. And what we call history, in the sense of historical knowledge, proves to be the real 'natural science' about man. In human history, human nature finds itself, its actual reality. Now, if the nature of man is no unnatural exemption from nature at large, must we not ask whether nature as such can be at all exempt from the relation of past and present? Must not nature as such have its history? And is not the essence of science 'natural history'?

I have no ready answer to this question. It strikes me, though, that perhaps a man as keenly natural and as much master of himself as Socrates, may have been speaking very much to the point when, taking his cue from Anaxagoras, he made the claim that nature must find its reality in 'Nous.' Socrates seems to have taken this to mean that the method even of natural science must be teleological. Meanwhile, we have learned from the scientific impotence of traditional theology that the teleological interpretation of the relation of present to past is inadequate. The prefixed ends of teleology would appear to establish a real dependence of the present on the future, but they cannot furnish a ground for the present in the past. They are, therefore, just as unilateral and unsatisfactory as the antecedents on which mechanism rests everything. Neither mechanism nor teleology can know of a time in which things really happen. Neither has access to nature, to the nature which underlies history. Nor can they comprehend history, that is the rise of the spirit, which finds itself as having a real past.

According to Schelling, nature is the past of God.[2] Obviously not a past that is dead, and done for, but, as Schelling says, an "eternal past" (254). "God, with respect to his highest self, *is* not revealed, he is revealing himself; he is not real, he becomes real. This, in order that he appear as the freest of all beings (*das allerfreieste Wesen*)." (308)

Perhaps, I should apologize for resting my case here, since such sentences as the ones just quoted sound like theological dogmas, and since I cannot claim them as my own decided past. This much is certain, both the naturalistic theorist and the non-speculative religious thinker are bound to miss the living continuity of history. To them

---

[2] "Nature is an abyss of the past." (243)—"The claim of an eternally posited past in God himself." (197 and 254)—"We do not know God in any way but in relation to an eternal nature subordinated to him." (259)—*Et passim.*

it must appear as a matter of contingency—as a riddle. Contingent events occur in an indifferent and therefore abstract time, and they require a deterministic and therefore endless explanation. Its endlessness can be done away with only in appearance and by dogmatic decree. This, incidentally, is why the religious dogmatist feels that the endless tale of naturalism gives him a fine chance to finish the story. Mythological thinking mistakes finished stories for living history.

But conscientious religiosity corrects the stories which the religions tell about the plan of nature and of history. Truly religious sense feels that creation is act, that nature is historical. What is implicit in that religious sense of reality, philosophy makes explicit and applicable in science and history. The problem of a nature that is not only of the books and laboratories calls for a recognition of history. And real history, in turn, demands the "religio" of spirit and nature, the spirit's recollection of the nature from which it takes its issue.

RELIGION, PHILOSOPHY, AND THE COLLEGE*

It was in October, 1923, just about a month after my departure from Switzerland when, on the Old Oregon campus, the profoundly human, wise, and wiry elderly scholar, George Rebec, who had invited and was befriending me, took me to a ritual I had never heard of, the academic assembly. A goodly number of students and a portion of the faculty had gathered to hear a message delivered in person by a gentleman who, I was told, held the office of President of the University, a position also unknown to me. Before the President spoke he amazed me by ceding the platform to a man of the cloth, for the invocation which, I believe to remember, was offered in a very perfunctory manner. It was not this manner, however, which shocked me. I was upset by the performance as such. I had just come from academic surroundings in which the belief prevailed that, of the two institutions, the church and the university, the latter was the loftier. Consequently, I believed, it would be quite possible though not usual to have a scholar give higher consecration to an ecclesiastic function, but to have a clergyman in his clerical capacity elevate an academic function seemed a contradiction in terms.

I had no anticlerical rancors. My persuasion was antiecclesiastic. For me, the university—the *universitas literarum*, or rather the *universitas idearum*—was the only conceivable church, the ἐκκλησία καθολική. I took the word ἐκκλησία in its root sense of an "open assembly," and, taking seriously the wholeness asserted by the terse adjective καθολική, I found none of the churches spiritually all-embracing or catholic. The university, however, seemed to be the properly organized public assembly of men bent upon the truth, as the church visible, embracing not only the holy orders on the campus but holding in its fold every inhabitant of the land, and as the church spiritual, being the repository of every truth without exception. In contrast, it appeared to be the very nature of the denominational churches to make exceptions, putting doctrine before inquiry. That some seem to prefer popularity to both, doctrine and inquiry, I had not then discovered. Nor had I become

---

* Presidential Address, delivered April 3, 1942, in Nashville, Tennessee at the 37th annual meeting of the Southern Society for Philosophy and Psychology.

sufficiently aware of the inherent shortcomings of all organizations, especially of academic organizations. My antiecclesiasticism simply expressed an inordinate confidence in the efficacy of organization.

My intransigeance of twenty years ago put me in line with the all-American principle of separating public schools and churches. I had read about this separation before I came to this country. I was astonished to find that the principle was not rigidly adhered to in public schools, particularly in state institutions of higher learning.

I was not quite so unworldly as not to understand that there is a problem. A substantial part of the people feel that serious undertakings like education demand a recognition of their religious bearings. Most of them are satisfied with a ritual recognition, hence the custom of invocations and benedictions before and after school celebrations. As for considering the feelings of unbelievers, the presumption seems to be that the shorter the ritual the less offensive it should prove in the eyes of such outsiders. The minority can be expected to submit gracefully to the habits of the majority. Ours is a civilization of tolerant and kindly compromise.

The problem has a religious side, however, a side not amenable to compromise. I will state it briefly. Either all education is religious education, as Croce said in 1923, and as I believe, or it is not.

If it is not, then invocations and benedictions are mere appendages to school functions explicable only as concessions to the apparent demands of public opinion. In plain English, people are welcome to bring to commencements and similar celebrations not only their infants but also their divines, at least in token samples. To my way of feeling, such a concession shows anything else but true respect for religion. A strict separation of scholastic and religious rites would be much more respectful, if education had nothing to do with religion.

If, however, religion is at the very core of education, then this innermost essence must be given voice, implicitly at least, every hour of school, and it must be explicitly voiced at those occasions when faculty and student body are assembled, or when, following the admirable American tradition, the academic citizenry and their outside relatives and friends have come together to celebrate the school as an educational enterprise.

To express the religious ties of education seems to be an uncomplicated matter in a denominational school which, without unfairness, may rest its actions on the assumption of a common faith. But in our day of very mixed constituencies of public schools, there is hardly a more embarrassing task than that of voicing the religiosity of education, in the classroom or in open assembly. To put it in old words, who can live up to the summons of Paul: "Let your speech, while always attractive, be seasoned with salt, that you may know how you ought to answer each one"? (Col. 4: 6). For, the listeners do have questions.

The cultural history of this country has been of a kind to lead many, possibly the majority, to identify religion with ecclesiasticism. As a consequence, the dissenters, or a large number of them, conceive of themselves as non-religious. In their eyes, the official appearance of a clergyman on a school platform appears as a concession to their church-minded contemporaries. And in their ears, the phraseology of ecclesiastical tradition does not seem to be seasoned with the salt of thought, nor does it seem to have the flavor of all-embracing wisdom. How are their unspoken questions to be answered? And how is the answer that is fit for them to be fit simultaneously for the ears of the conformists? Simultaneously, I say, for a speaker who would first address the left and then turn to the right with a different speech would give the impression that he was desirous of carrying water on both shoulders, and therefore under suspicion of political aims; he would be suspect of lacking the candor required for voicing whatever is deeply religious.

There are moments when one cannot help but feel that it is not considered quite proper for a philosopher to make so much as a reference to religious depths. Such moments are symptomatic of an aged condition in our culture; they are indicative of the fact that the language of traditional religion has lost the vitality with which it would assail everyone. Our religious situation is in need of revival.

However, revivalism will do no longer. Our mood is too serious for a mere turning over of the leaf and beginning anew, simply repeating all the old words. Nor can we afford any longer to put down on the new page the naturalistic formulae which, earlier in our century, imbued many a modernist and, sad to remember, too many teachers with the feeling that religion was overcome for good, or that it was reduced to its scientific ingredients. Such scientism now proves to be of a kind with revivalism, being the mere reverse of it.

If I say, with such assurance, that we have become older, I have in mind numbers of the young people who, in my classroom and in my office, have expressed their unwillingness and inability to go back, their bewilderment with the scientistic panaceas, and their desire to know. We are in need of philosophical knowledge, and there is no use in deploring our age. "When philosophy paints its gray upon gray," said Hegel, "a form of life has become old, and with gray upon gray life cannot be rejuvenated, it can only be known; the owl of Minerva begins its flight only at dusk."

The religious people may not know Hegel, but they sense the impossibility of spiritual rejuvenation by philosophy alone. Not knowing philosophy, they may jump to the conclusion that they can do without it, nay, that philosophy is detrimental to the religious quest. They never heard of, or they have forgotten about all the times in history when philosophy did become efficacious, not indeed as a substitute for religion, but as a tutor.

It is my belief that ours is such a time, a time of checking and deepening, a period of potential rejuvenation. Actual rejuvenation is not to be had at will. It is a gift of Providence. But the gift is not bestowed upon the unprepared. Rejuvenation does not come upon an unwilling man. We must set our will on the things that are meet to do. We must align ourselves with all those who offer the best help, though they be long dead. We must profit from the merits of those whom the heaven of history harbors.

We can profit only if we live up to the foremost duty of our age, the duty of translating and retranslating. For we are no longer unilingual, neither in speech nor in thought. No longer can we abide by a single set of terms, or be satisfied with but one language. Nor are there any true findings, no matter how refined and recondite, which do not become the concern of ordinary public opinion, implicitly or explicitly. Our time, however, demands of us to be explicit. Those who still endeavor to muddle through are no longer of any use; they are through, except for their nuisance value. Our time demands clear-cut commitments.

We must be explicit. That means we must recognize the shortcomings of all verbal formulations. We must distinguish between wordings and meanings. The ever fermenting wine of truth cannot be kept in old skins. We must translate the old wordings in order to regain the old meanings. If by translation and retranslation we regain them, these old meanings prove to be new; what the dead once thought turns out to be our own most intimate thought.

And here is the apparent paradox. Any attempt on our part to be original merely makes us obsolete, and fatuously ineffective. Our efficacy springs from our faithfulness in rethinking the old thoughts. Almost everyone is willing to concede the truth of this in the field of the sciences, where mere originality is identical with arbitrary fancy, and where genuine originality springs from faithful attention to the facts. The truth is not so easily conceded in philosophical matters. For most of us have been brought up to believe that philosophical ideas are nothing but arbitrary theories, and to disbelieve any assertion that there is a substantial continuity of philosophical problems and solutions.

This disbelief has its reasons. It rests on the remnants of old beliefs, religious beliefs which once were experienced as the very foundation of life. These beliefs were not the product of explicit thinking; in fact, their efficacy was only enhanced by the implicitness of their meaning. In comparison with such fundamental beliefs, the explicitness of philosophy appeared ephemeral. The verdicts of philosophy rule only the day, and their power over the future depends on the adequate rewording they must receive from future thinkers. Philosophy therefore looked as if it were sheer verbalization, empty ratiocination, void of a substance commensurable with the substance of belief whose very words last throughout their epoch.

Moreover, in so far as belief has to be articulate in order to be conscious belief, its articulateness is that of simple enunciations, sententious sayings, apparently obvious tenets, utterances in the form of an honest witness report. It was the natural assumption, therefore, that the reports of other witnesses would be commensurate. In fact, the witnesses would corroborate each other's beliefs. Compared with this unanimity among the believers, the concert of the philosophers appeared as nothing but discord. For the enunciations, the sentences, the utterances of the philosophers seem to express diametrically opposed views. In philosophy, the very problems demand, ever so often, to be rethought so fundamentally that the consecutive formulations seem to be at odds. The trained student will see the *perennis philosophia*. To the outsider, however, the history of philosophy seems nothing but an orderless sequence of odd opinions, not only lacking continuity of presentation, but lacking it because of a lack of substantial foundations.

Psychologically speaking, philosophy seemed to lack roots in the subconscious. It appeared as a matter of mere consciousness, and therefore of mere ideology. Belief, on the contrary, had made man whole, reaching down into the unfathomable depths of his soul, and rising up into articulate creeds and confessions. Philosophy seemed to be a matter of the mind only, of a mind detached from reality. Belief appeared more realistic. It appears realistic even to those who have lost it.

It is realistic because it reaches below the surface of the merely conscious. It reveals our depths. Belief is no mere conscious construction. One does not invent the terms of it. They come upon us. In this very sense of being discovered, not made up, belief is mythological. No myth can be invented. None of the great myths of humanity were mere poetry, though the poet in man was needed to give them clear voice.

It is not within the power of peoples or of individuals—says Schelling—"to abstain from mythological notions, to accept them or to reject them. For they do not *come* from without, they are *in* men, and men are not aware how. For these notions come from the interior of consciousness, and they present themselves in consciousness with a necessity which leaves no room for any doubt about their truth."[1]

1. *F. W. J. Schellings sämmtliche Werke.* Zweite Abtheilung. Erster Band. *Einleitung in die Philosophie der Mythologie.* (Stuttgart und Augsburg, 1856) p. 194. I also translate the following passages, by way of expounding the one translated above, in the text. "Mythology is not explicable as a merely ideal relationship between consciousness and some object" (p. 77). "To be sure, mythology has no reality *outside* of consciousness. But although it occurs only in determinations of consciousness, that is in images *(Vorstellungen)*, yet this *occurrence*, this *very succession of images*, as a succession, can not in turn be merely *imagined*, it must *really* have taken place, it must have come to pass actually, in consciousness. This real succession is not made by mythology, mythology is made by it" (pp. 124 f). "Former explanations used to assume that somehow mythology was an *invention*. In order to be done with such explanations, and in order to express very definitely that which is independent of all invention, nay that which is *the contrary of all invention* ... we must say: mythology comes to pass by *a necessary process* (necessary in consciousness), a process whose origin is lost and hides in the super-historical, a process whose particular traits consciousness may resist, but whose entirety it can neither stop nor much less reverse" (p. 193). "No individual trait of mythology, only the process as a whole is truth" (p. 211). "With this result in mind, one may even ask whether mythological images could ever have been *meant*, that is, whether they could ever have been the object meant when we say 'I mean this,' the object taken for true by a free act. . . . Mythological images are neither invented nor freely accepted. Being products of a process which is independent of thought and will, they were of unequivocal and unavoidable reality. Peoples as well as individuals are only tools of this process which they can not survey, and which they serve without understanding it" (Here follows the sentence quoted in my text).

Men live by myths. We moderns are loath to admit this, for we have not quite gotten behind us the rationalism of the Enlightenment which, from its intellectualistic detachment, looked upon everything mythological as merely primitive. Even Giambattista Vico, the early eighteenth century thinker who was profoundly suspicious of a certain vacuity he sensed in rationalism, and who on that account bent his mind on the investigation of mythology, looking for the realistic meaning of myth—even Vico speaks as if man could definitely outgrow the mythologizing childhood of his mind. "The first men, being the babes of mankind, and being unable to form intelligible concepts of things, were in natural need of fashioning poetic notions, which are imaginative genders or universals."[2]

For all I know, our suspicions about the imaginative forms of thinking may have roots not only in rationalism but in the iconoclasm of the Reformation. Notwithstanding its reactionary appearances—and even its essence is reactionary in one respect—one aspect of the Reformation is modern: the demand for explicit consciousness, the demand that the implicit meaning of religious imagery ought not turn into the dead ritualism of idolatry. Iconoclasm expresses this demand most crudely. Calvinism articulates it in terms of legalism and even of casuistry. The reactionary concepts of the reformers were unfit to bring about a redeeming explicitness. Nay, they repressed the subconscious which demanded redemption in explicit terms. But the demand was there— "every man his own priest," said Luther—and it marks modernity.

We need to become articulate about our own situation. Ours is not an angelic existence. Angels, being by definition pure spirits, could be in need only of determining their own lucid place in the spiritual realm, which is wholly transparent. Our lot is to rise from obscurity. We too need orientation, we need to know our place. But first of all we need articulateness. We are unable to resign ourselves to a vegetative existence. Nor can we remain in a brooding condition of mind, forever befogged by the numb stirrings in our soul. We need some kind of language, some terms in which to say who we are. We must come forward from noncommittal obscurity, and commit ourselves. But such committal dare not be arbitrary guesswork; it must be somehow revelatory of our actual condition. To commit ourselves arbitrarily would mean to cast ourselves in characters not our own. Such personifications would

2. *La Scienza Nuova* (ed. Nicolini, Bari, 1928) Vol. I, p. 91, Article xlix, no. 209.

retain the impersonality of an actor's role, which is not to be mistaken for his own personality. Our committal must be personal. It must truthfully articulate the condition we are in, the condition of creatures, of beings who reach for the light *de profundis*. The depth of our souls must enter into our commitments. The genuine articulations of ourselves, therefore, retain something of the ineffable darkness from which we rise. None of our true commitments are translatable into rationalistic formulae.

Now, the rationalist is not wrong when the ineffability of the expressions stemming from our subconscious disturbs him, and when he makes bold to postulate a liberation from this bondage to darkness. He is wrong only in so far as he expects a total transfiguration of our being. We are not gods who have never known darkness. It is precisely our task to *know* our own darkness. We must transfigure our subconscious origin, but we cannot transcend it.

This transfiguration which is the very task of man, is not a mere sublimation. To sublimate our nature is to desert it, or to falsify it, no matter in what subtle manner. What we need is not sublimation but wholeness. And we cannot be made whole if we lack the humility of acknowledging our nature, while transfiguring it.

Our nature is not apart from our historical condition. We are our very selves not as abstract spirits, but as these concrete selves who have a calling, who are to do what we alone are fit to do in our historical circumstances.—Fichte once answered the question about the real nature of things by saying that things *are* what we ought to make of them.[3] In this sense we too are like Fichte's things: we *are* the ones into whom we ought to make ourselves. We make ourselves responsible for what we are to be. We do not acquiesce in our natural conditions; we are historical beings. We posit history by acknowledging our factual condition as our task. Our potential tasks are our very substance. And it is this substance which must be acknowledged in the terms which articulate our very selves.

Our first self-articulations are imaginative, not conceptual. Vico said that, "by necessity of human nature, poetic speech was born before prosaic." Thus "the imaginative universals were born before the reasoned universals of philosophy." And it was not "the remote wisdom of

3. *Grundlage der gesammten Wissenschaftslehre.* 1794 (*Sämmtliche Werke.* Vol. I, p. 286).

great and rare philosophers," not the reasoned but the imaginative universal which constituted "the common wisdom of the legislators who founded mankind."[4] We may condense Vico's statements, saying that it is the imaginative act, the act of poetry which raises man to the level of humanity. Ποιεῖν means to posit, and man does posit himself as human, that is, as an historical being, as soon as he attains as much as an imaginative position in the scheme of things—as soon as he finds his myth. I say, an imaginative, not a merely imagined position.

Whereas, in the derogatory sense of the word mythology, mythological figures are fictitious characters, merely imagined entities, man's first self-articulation is myth in a quite different sense. The myths in terms of which we come to recognize ourselves as in a mirror, are not fictitious but realistic, they are no mere poetic inventions. They have been called revelations. They are not fanciful fashionings out of nothing. They reveal something. They reveal unto us who we are.[5]

And since we are not apart from our historical condition, it is possible that we can recognize ourselves in the imagery of the same myth in which our fathers and our contemporaries recognized and recognize themselves. It is possible that a whole age find its own basic truth in a genuine myth. This is possible *if* the myth be genuine, that is, if it be found, not made up—revealed, not invented. This finding of a true myth, this coming of a revelation is not a matter of arbitrary will. It is not a matter of will at all, except in so far as will means the perseverance of waiting, and the resistance to what is arbitrary and therefore "not of God." The bringers of humanity's great myths have always emphasized that they were sent, that they spake not of themselves, that, far from advancing imperious schemes of priestcraft, they themselves were subject to the power of their message. The great religions came to pass through profound piety, not by political nor even by statesmanly will. Only when a myth had come into existence could the political minded as well as the great statesmen make use of it.

It is a sign of the shallowest misunderstanding of the nature of myth when certain uprooted individuals try to create a new myth at will— like the Nazi theorist Rosenberg—or when others, driven by the dismal lack of bearings, attempt a deliberate conversion of themselves or of others. Wilful endeavors to believe are a sign of decadence, a sign

4. *La Scienza Nuova* (ed. Nicolini, 1928) Vol. I, p. 195, no. 460; p. 151, no. 384.
5. Compare above, note 1, especially Schelling's sentence from pp. 124 f.

that an age nears its end, that an epoch is in transition. Ours is such a time.

Historical epochs are marked by the myths in which the men of each epoch find the revelation of their own being. A genuine myth creates an age. The myth of a people—said Schelling—"is not due to their history. On the contrary, their history is determined by their mythology. Or rather, the mythology does not *determine*, it *is* the destiny of a people (just as the character of a man is his destiny)."[6]—Every great myth creates an historical epoch. Ours is the Christian.

Ever since the Enlightenment, there have been voices expressing an opinion that the Christian epoch has come to its end, or is approaching it. In Nietzsche's *Zarathustra,* only the old hermit in the wilderness has not heard what all the world knows, that the old God is dead. And when the Nazis—whose nihilism Nietzsche fortold and detested— endeavor to substitute for the Christian God a god, or a whole set of gods of their own making, they merely conform, in their own crude and popular manner, to the mood of the pet victims of their diatribes, the mood of those liberals who not only find themselves outside of the Christian faith, but who have lost the sense of being descendants of Christianity, and therefore the sense of gratitude to the Christian myth. The Nazis identify this kind of liberalism with all liberalism. This is natural, for they hate their own sire and magnify him into a demon. The elder sons of the same sire, the Marxists, assume that man can live without religion. "Religion is opium for the people." The Nazis have the slight merit of being conscious of the need of myths, whereas the Communists are the more genuine myth-makers: they cater to the need without admitting it, when they bring forward their own eschatology, their own version of the final state of things, their own Millennium. All such artificialities reveal the emptiness of men who are mythless. Into the vacuum of their souls pseudo-myths keep entering, but they fill them only with passions instead of peace.

Mythological epochs do not end abruptly. Nietzsche has his Zarathustra say that gods die many deaths, and one of Zarathustra's guests holds that "Death, for gods, is but a prepossession." In another book, Nietzsche relates the legend that the shadow of Buddha could be seen, in a certain cavern, for centuries after the Master's death. A mythological epoch is not comparable to the lifetime of an individual. What is

6. *Op. cit.*, p. 65.

more, great myths have the capacity of rejuvenation, entering substantially into newer myths. Thus, at about the time of the Babylonian exile and probably on account of it, Jehovah lost the traits of a tribal deity and showed himself as a universal God of justice. Similarly, this Jewish God revealed himself, under the New Dispensation, as the Christian Trinity.

It is not necessary to assume that we stand between the times, in the sense of having Christianity behind us, and something else ahead. It is quite possible that ours is an age of purification, from which our successors will emerge with a deeper insight into and therefore a firmer faith in Christianity. But it does not seem to be a baseless assumption if we speak of a time of spiritual crisis in which we live. In this sense, we do stand between the times. And such intermediary periods are marked by certain temptations and certain corresponding duties.

A man lost in the apparent vacuum between the times looks back upon the realm of myth as upon an incubus. He is easily seduced to believe that the time of all myth is past and will never return. In his eyes, myth marks the childhood of man. Man's task is to outgrow it. Only as a trait of actual or belated childhood will myth survive in individuals. This view, it seems, is shared by large numbers of our contemporaries. It is the view of rationalism and individualism.

Opposed to it is the view of those who prefer irrationalism, and who hanker for authority. Theirs are nostalgic souls. They too have lost the old faith, but they try to convince themselves, spasmodically, that they have not. Nothing can shock them more profoundly than the encounter with an actual faith, a faith strong enough gladly to submit to the scrutiny of reason, and confident enough not to need for support the dead props of authoritarian command.

In the man of strong faith, the epoch of the old myth survives even in a time of transition, and the man of weak faith should pray that he be made strong. He will remain weak just as long as he assumes that strength rests on thoughtlessness. In the recent film *So Green Was My Valley*, the young parson says to the lame boy: "When you pray, think. Do not wallow like a hog in religious sentiment." Sentimentality springs from weakness and begets weakness. Strong faith is thoughtful, though its thoughts are symbolical and not argumentative, substantial, not formalistic.

Formalism and argumentativeness are merely the opposite of, and therefore akin to, weak and sentimental faith. And just as there are men of weak faith and men of strong, so, among the unbelievers, the rationalists are weak, and the strong stand on more substantial ground than argumentation. However, this substance is not irrational. Irrationalism is only the reverse of formalism. And the formalist lacks what Richard Kroner, referring to Hegel, called piety of thought.[7] This piety demands that we watch and wait and prefer suspense to submissiveness. Intellectual conscience will not let a man submit to doctrines which to him have no symbolic personal significance. Therefore the pious unbeliever's prayer is mute, a quest *de profundis.*

My teacher, Medicus, used to say that there is only one legitimate prayer: the prayer for the presence of God. The word prayer is akin to the Sanskrit word *prcchati* which, according to the dictionary, means to ask for, but also simply to ask, to inquire. The German verb *fragen* comes from the same root. To pray for the presence of God, when mythological words are not available, means to raise the question about the very meaning of the phrase "presence of God." It means to inquire into the reality of that presence. For, spiritual reality *is* meaning. The peculiar piety of those who stand between the times but are not lost on that account, is the piety of thought.

If prayer and thought are separated, prayer becomes superstitious, and thought becomes argumentative.

Superstition takes literally what the myth proclaims. Owing to its task of annunciating the whole man, conscious and subconscious, myth has the power of poetic unity. Sensing this unifying power, superstition fastens upon the poetry of the myth as upon its essence. It mistakes the poetic unity for reality.[8] Thus, superstition becomes impervious to the non-literal symbolic sense of the myth. Instead of an analogy it posits an identity, and it lapses into idolatry. Likewise, argumentative thinking is tied to the verbal expression but, being without poetic sense, it misses the inner unity of the myth. Therefore this thinking either argues legalistically for, or it debates rationalistically against the myth. It becomes either apologetics or iconoclasm.

The logic of true faith is not argumentative. The true believer is aware of the symbolic character of his myth. He realizes that the myth

---

7. *Hegel. Zum 100. Todestage.* (Tübingen, 1932) p. 23.
8. Vico: "The human mind is naturally inclined, owing to the senses, to see itself outside, in the body, and it finds much difficulty in understanding itself by means of reflection." *Op. cit.*, p. 95, no. 236.

embodies fundamental reality and genuine truth. He feels keenly that the expressions of the myth are not mere arguments thought up to serve as intellectualistic props in order to support ulterior tenets. He feels that the mythological symbols themselves are expressions of what is most truly real.

In the myth, basic reality proves to be communicative, communicating its very essence, and this essence reveals itself as being the personal concern of the man of faith. Fundamental reality proves to be truth in the most genuine sense of the word truth. Truth is essentially accessible, not hidden, not jealous, but yielding; it is an ever new invitation.

The truth can not be told once and for all. It must be retold, even though it has been told already in a quite adequate manner. If I say that in the believer there is an awareness of the symbolic character of myth, I do not mean to impute to him the notion that the mythological expressions are inadequate to convey the truth. On the contrary, the believer will assure us that the symbols of faith are adequate. But, if his faith is genuine, he will also tell us that these symbols are inexhaustible in their meaning, or that they do not exhaust the reality they proclaim. Quite logically, he calls this reality by the name of mystery.

By the same logic, I said that the truth, the fundamental truth about our existence, demands to be retold in ever new and always genuine terms. To be sure, if I put the matter this way, the believer may feel impelled to dissent and to assert that the terms of his myth are quite sufficient and in no need of translation and retranslation. In fact, he may tell me that his terms are the only adequate ones. But this disagreement between him and me is verbal rather than material. Materially we agree that no set of terms exhausts the truth. For him, this inexhaustibility is conveyed in the efficacy which the very wording of his myth retains in repetition. For him, reiteration is not repetitious but refreshing. So it is for me. Only I am aware of the fact that the old words, when they are repeated by the really faithful, express ever new meanings. More precisely speaking, the old meanings assume ever deeper significance. And this is an instance of translation and retranslation, though the words remain the same.

As a philosopher, I cannot but state this fact explicitly, whereas for the believer the time-pervading efficacy of meanings appears as a power implicit in the specific and unique myth. For him, the myth fills all time, making him sense the majesty of the revealed God. He lives in the fulness of time. My calling is to stand between the times.

But then, so will he say that he stands between the times, that is, between time and eternity, between the historical time in which God deigns to reveal himself, and the anticipated and really timeless bliss of finding home, the blissful return into God. And just as the believer can truthfully confess that he too always stands between the times so, with all due humility, we can experience the fulness of time in our very awareness of the awesome fact that the epoch created by a myth bears the marks of mortality.

This philosophical awareness does locate us between the times. Philosophy is no *Ersatzreligion*; philosophical insight is not the same thing as religious faith. The faithful are quite right when they feel that the explicitness of the philosophical concept does not further their cause whose innermost meaning, for them, remains implicit.

Nevertheless, the explicit concept, though no substitute for the implicit Word of the myth, is as necessary for the health of spiritual life as is faith itself. Without conceptual clarification faith would turn into stifling superstition. The terms of revelation, terms conditioned by the historical circumstances, would take the appearance of timeless impersonal formulae. Magical spells have the same character, and their impersonality makes them a fetter for the man who uses them. They are entirely conditional, hence they enslave.

The revelations of faith bring spiritual health and freedom because they are man's *unconditional concern*. I am borrowing this pregnant and concise phrase from Paul Tillich who, in 1927, defined revelation as that "which concerns me unconditionally" (was mich unbedingt angeht).[9] Most of the affairs of the world concern us only conditionally. If I want to grow grass in my shady front yard, I must get the seed into the soil a month before the trees are in foliage. If I want to be an engineer, I must learn my mathematics. If I am to deliver an address, I must have a topic. I *must* use the proper means, *if* I desire the end. But there is no unconditional obligation to have a lawn, to be an engineer, to make a speech.

No activity in the world is a duty unless it happens to become an articulation of our calling. Any activity, no matter how lowly, can be-

---

9. "Die Idee der Offenbarung." Dresdner Antrittsvorlesung. *Zeitschrift für Theologie und Kirche*. Neue Folge. 8. Jahrgang, 1927, Heft 6.

come such an articulation, yet none can exhaust our calling. This is why the religious feel that our calling is not of this world, that not even the loftiest sacrifice amounts to an exhaustive consummation of the soul. It is a perversion of religion when the Nazi doctrine proclaims a German's soldierly sacrifice of his life as the consummation of his being, as the very meaning of his life. To be sure, the moment may come when we too may be called to quit this business of living in order to make a bit safer that which is more important than living. But we know that not even our most important tasks are identical with the reason for life, with that reason which alone is our unconditional concern.

And what is that reason? There is no answer in general and in the abstract, for the question makes sense only if it is a personal query. In the naïve language of preliminary instruction, the question is put to the catechumen: "Why did God make you?" And he is told to answer: "God made me to know Him, to love Him, and to serve Him in this world, and to be happy with Him forever in heaven." Modern man realizes that this imputed answer bristles with questions. Quite so. But these questions can not be answered at all unless we also realize that catechization concerns persons, not things. We must dare to come forward and ask, not abstractly, "What is the reason for life in general?" but concretely, "What is the reason for my life?" The former question talks about life as a strange thing, an object of argument. But the question about the reason for our own lives posits "a *task* instead of an argument," as Fichte put it concisely.[10] If we ask the question in this adequate manner, we are already in the proper mood to reject as not sufficiently realistic an answer which would permit us to acquiesce in any given goal short of realizing our place in the scheme of things, our relation to the very essence of reality.

Literally, *religio* means the re-establishment of the ligaments which tie man into his origin. But such words may easily obscure the issue rather than clear it up. True religion does not tie and confine man, it liberates him. Man's origin is such that he can realize his essence only in freedom. The myths of the so-called higher religions have proclaimed man's essential freedom. They could not amount to such a proclamation were they not of a symbolic nature. For they speak in terms of things, and things are unfree. But the mythological terms symbolize freedom.

A symbol is no mere allegory. Allegories are only hints; they are con-

10. *Grundlage der gesammten Wissenschaftslehre. Werke*, Vol. I, p. 116.

ventional signs referring to items of an already established agreement among the individuals of the group within which the allegory has significance. This is why allegories have an air of tediousness and outright pedantry. But symbols are fresh, even when they are very old, for they are no mere conventional signs. Their meaning is not conditional upon a conscious understanding among a group of men. It is not a social matter, and its social significance is only derivative and secondary. Primarily and originally, the symbol is meaningful for the individual self who, in the symbol, recognizes the significance of his own reality. The symbol shows him where he stands in the scheme of things. But it cannot do so except by summoning him to come forward without reservations. The symbol is symbolical only in so far as it concerns the individual self unconditionally.

What concerns us unconditionally is nothing extra-mundane. An extra-mundane concern would be conditional, the condition being that we could and would detach ourselves from our worldly existence.

What concerns us unconditionally must concern us as the men we are, men of our age of transition, men of this century who, among other things, cannot ignore their scientific consciences. Fritz Medicus says: "Religious faith appeals to the *whole* man. The desire for wholeness, however, places the intellect within the spiritual currents of the age."[11]

There has been much talk about the conflict between science and so-called religion, and even more talk asserting the nonexistence of such a conflict. The fact is that there must be a clash any time the mythological letter offends the spirit of science, an offense which occurs when the terms of the myth are taken literally.

For instance, scientific conscience demands our recognition of the simple truth that, by definition, spatial limits are boundaries *in* space, and that it is a contradiction in terms to speak of any shape as a limit *of* space. Therefore, if it is legitimate to conceive of physical reality in terms of Euclidian space, it follows that physical space cannot be limited by a sphere, the sphere of the fixed stars. Scientific conscience demanded of Giordano Bruno to deny the alleged nonphysical nature of the space surrounding the sphere of the fixed stars, and consequently to do away with the Platonic and medieval conception of such a limitative sphere. However, in 1600, it looked as if the terms of Christian my-

11. In an unpublished book entitled *Das Mythologische in der Religion,* fourth chapter of the first part. Many of the things I am saying owe their origin to this book. (It was published 1944, Eugen Rentsch Verlag, Zürich.)

thology could not be cleansed of that conception. Consequently, Bruno's assertion of the infinity of physical space had to be counted against him, as one of the eight heretical sentences lined up for his trial.

Bruno's piety made him realize, during the seven years of his imprisonment in Rome, that the unconditional religious concerns of man cannot be considered in separation from his scientific conscience, and that it had been wrong for him to sever the two, at his trial in Venice, in 1592, when he hoped to save himself by appeal to the theory of a twofold truth, according to which scientific and religious truths can go separate ways.

The mythological images of religion can concern us unconditionally only if they do no violence to our scientific conscience. This principle was not only recognized explicitly by Bruno himself who preferred death at the stake to any further violation of the principle; it was also recognized implicitly by the Church which condemned him, thus repeating its previous condemnations of the theory of a twofold truth. The implicit recognition of the principle has since induced the Church to take into the fold the astronomical views it condemned in Bruno.

I chose the example of Bruno in order to underline that significant date of 1600, an historical moment which might be taken to mark the beginning of what we call the modern age. It might be said that the modern age is characterized by the explicit recognition of the truth that nothing can concern us unconditionally which violates our intellectual conscience.

Man does not doff and don historical ages as an occidental changes his clothes. Rather, like the new garment of a cold-bitten Tibetan, the new is worn on top of the old. And the old age is still very much about us. Thus, in this country, there is still a great longing for the comfortable sixteenth century makeshift of a twofold truth. I presume this longing has been enhanced by the actual schism between the churches, and by the apparent schism between science and religion.

As a rule, the theory of the twofold truth is not brought forward in sixteenth century terms. The usual fashion of propounding it today, especially in America, is to declare religion to be an essentially emotional matter which, as such, need not be in conflict with things intellectual. As a consequence of this view, theology is declared to be obsolete, nay incommensurable with the essence of religion, or at the very least inadequate to cope with that essence. Another consequence is the readiness with which so many people accept the pseudo-modern notion that all genuine knowledge is strictly objective or, as the current phrase puts it, scientific.

British empiricism of the seventeenth and eighteenth centuries had the merit of developing the precarious consequences of the notion of objectivism or scientism. The blithe scientism of Hobbes led to the scepticism and solipsism of Hume. Hume woke Kant from his metaphysical slumber—so Kant himself said—but David Hume discontinued his world of perceptions in the very year in which the thirteen colonies seceded from things British. Thus he furnished the latter day homemade scientism on our shores with a kind of a chronological alibi for its Rip van Winkle slumber and unawareness of what had already happened in 1776.

Unfortunately, the matter is too serious to let it go with a facetious remark. Scientism, owing to its very axiom that all thinking is conditional, is utterly unable to cope with the unconditional. And the declaration that the power of religion is merely emotional not only degrades this power to something conditional but it deprives religious thought of logical vitality, turning it into inconsequential superstition.

In truth, religious thought is aware of the unconditional concerns of man, concerns which cannot be apprehended in their unconditionality by mere emotion, which is always a conditional matter. It is the unconditional character of the religious appeal which constitutes the power of religion. Take it away and you destroy religion. Arrest religious thought, and you have truly nothing but superstition, vain assertions about the essentially Unknowable. Once you have gone so far, the next step is inevitable. It becomes imperative that methodical thought abstain from traffic with the fancies of superstition. Putting it in the conciliatory terms of political compromise, it is imperative that the thoughtful pursuits of study, the pursuits of the school, be separated from the mere emotionalism of religion. The separation between science and religion, between thought and faith appears to be complete. This appearance has influenced and, in my opinion, vitiated our educational system. It has made us afraid of fundamental issues.

I am fully aware of the need of these last hundred years to separate the school from the church. Denominationalism made this separation imperative. I am also aware of the need of scientific thought to emancipate itself from the guardianship of prescientific mythological conceptions turned into superstitions. The minimal demand of our intellectual conscience had to be freedom of scientific research.

Scientific conscience quite rightly warns us not to mistake the mythological symbols for objective things. Science is an implicit philosophy. Philosophy would warn us explicitly not to mistake the unconditional for something conditional.[12] Such a mistake is against our intellectual conscience which, notwithstanding the confusion of much of our nineteenth and twentieth century thinking, has yet been sharpened by our scientific and historical endeavors. The greater sensitivity of our intellectual consciences is the positive reason, I believe, why people are willing to accept the erroneous thesis that religion is an emotional matter. More properly speaking, it is a matter beyond the reach of scientific thought, it is not a conditional matter.

It is not any lack of intellectual conscience, it is merely the lack of philosophical clarification of this conscience which has left us in our educational muddle. For we are muddled. We have set up our schools and our churches in a manner which would make it appear as if schools could educate human beings without touching upon their very essence, and as if churches could adequately voice that essence without entering into that public universe of discourse, the realm of philosophy, in which alone there is hope for ascertaining logically anything essential. No wonder common sense objects to ecclesiastical denominationalism. No wonder it looks upon the school as upon an institution merely academic, fondling mere abstractions, and therefore being in need of progressive reform from without, a reform which keeps forcing upon the school the cultivation of the so-called practical pursuits.

The appearances are that the school cultivates thought, but a thought that is abstract and impractical, and that the church promotes the practical attitude of prayer, but a prayer that is superstitious. However, people's sense of reality does not leave them satisfied with these appearances. Common sense counteracts the abstractionism of the schools with a sound feeling for things truly human, and it counteracts ecclesiastic formalism with social work and daily ethics. Nevertheless, owing to its very nature, common sense can fight only a defensive battle. In fact,

---

12. Kant says that, in so far as the concepts of reason, the ideas, "contain the unconditional, they indicate something to which all experience belongs, but which is never itself an object of experience." *Critique of Pure Reason*, p. 367 (pagination of 1787).

many people of common sense have been pushed into the defensive to the extent that they have come to use the language of scientism as if it could ever adequately express their deeply human concerns. And so they are suspicious of mythology.

Common sense is unable to distinguish clearly what is positive in myth. In order to see it distinctly, we must first distinguish between the letter of the myth and its spirit. The letter is objectivistic, the spirit speculative. (I am using the word speculation in the technical sense of the great followers of Kant.) The hard labor of speculation might eventually lead to interdenominational understanding. Instead, there is an easygoing though not insincere desire to dispose of the denominational conflicts by means of compromise. But compromise never solves any difficulties we find in fundamental principles. The craving for compromise dulls the sense of our providential assignment. After all, it is not for nothing that conscientious men stand where they stand. Conscience places some inside the fold, and it puts on others the mark of unbelief.

Now, even if there were no positive ground for the unbeliever to stand on, even if unbelief were identical with evil, the believers of our century could still profitably meditate on a conviction held five hundred years ago, that the Devil himself must serve the ends of God. There used to be a picture in the Old Pinakothek, in Munich, by the Tyrolese mid-fifteenth century painter, Michael Pacher, showing a venomous green devil employed in holding a big open book from which a bishop is reading. Some interpreters say the bishop is St. Wolfgang, others name Nicolas Cusanus. If the latter identification were correct, it would suit to a nicety the purpose I have in mentioning the picture.

Cusanus was the last great thinker before the ecclesiastical schism in which we have all been living for some four hundred years. The thought of Cusanus, though suspect to some of his contemporaries, was never formally condemned as heretical, and until his natural death Nicolas retained his hierarchic dignity of a cardinal. Thus, there was a time when the church still considered as its own a profoundly revolutionary thinker. As long as the ecclesiastic organism keeps such resilience, there is no wonder that a churchman can force even God's antagonist into the service of faith.

Such force, such self-confidence seems to have disappeared from the latter-day churches. And it may be argued, of course, that already in the fifteenth century the tolerance shown Cusanus was a sign of weakness rather than of strength, a sign of senescence. Nevertheless, I suggest that there is profit in meditating on the case of Cusanus, and the picture of Pacher. For, what churchman of today would dare to employ the devil? And what church has the courage to consider the great modern thinkers as genuine churchmen?

What is more, is there any ecclesiastical body steeped deeply enough in conceptual methodology to be able to understand *why* all great thinkers are in truth great churchmen? Perhaps there never was such a church. But there ought to be, if it is true that the church is to be defined as the communion of those who are guided by the Holy Spirit—if it is the very essence of the church to be catholic.

Of course, the invisible church, the communion of the servants of the truth, exists serenely, no matter whether or not there is any church visible resembling it. But there can be no truly all-embracing visible church in our day, unless the institutions of higher education make accessible, for the presumable leaders of tomorrow's public opinion, the conceptual tools forged by the great thinkers, the tools by means of which the basic unity of all thought can be understood. Instead of cultivating the understanding of our substantial unity, our schools still endeavor to be theologically neutral, by the convenient device of being philosophically innocuous. And instead of teaching us how to inquire, properly and hence promisingly, into the meaning of Christian myth, our churches conveniently declare themselves legal heirs to the substance of religion. Owing to such superstitious legalism, the religious substance either is turned into a dead letter, or it is declared to be an ineffable spirit—which is a contradiction in terms.

Our caution and our legalism lead to a facile discrimination between believers and unbelievers. Now, even if the unbelievers were the devil's own, they would still have their function in the economy of the divine plan, and therefore they would still have to be taken seriously. But unbelief is nothing merely negative. Even the *superficial* infidels who seem to lack a conscience are not deficient in the sense for what is expedient. And expediency is something positive, although it is not the highest virtue. The virtue of the *great* unbelievers is their dedication to the truth. From their ranks came the great religious leaders who, therefore, have always shown a subtle appreciation of the outsider's calling. They were never easygoing conformists. Nor were those whom conscience drove into unbelief dissenters for the sake of negative dissent. They saw their duty in understanding more deeply beliefs whose previous formulation had become questionable. Thus, *sub specie aeternitatis*, the dissenters-by-conscience still belong in the fold. Nay, they may belong more genuinely than the conformists-by-indolence.

These are thorny matters, and it is ever so much easier to leave them alone. It is more comfortable to decree, by power of ignorance, that nobody has ever succeeded in thinking out anything with regard to religion. It is safer to declare one's independence from the vain squabbles of the churches. It is more decorous to make one's obeisances when the eye of the sovereign is upon us. It is more political to acknowledge a sovereignty of the vulgar in matters of religion, thus appeasing them, and inducing them to tolerate our sovereignty in matters academic.

But woe unto us when the vulgar find their champion who will rescind the license hitherto granted us. If those who have no personal relation to our cultural past are fit to judge things theological and philosophical, why not also things scientific and pedagogical? If it is proper that the democratic sovereign be left untutored in the matters which—not only allegedly but truly—are man's deepest concern, is it not proper for the same sovereign to disregard tutoring in other matters?

In Europe, the champions of the untutored masses have taken power. To be sure, in taking power they had to depose the democratic sovereign, but their logic is the logic of the untutored. And Hitler's scorn for liberalism is justified. He means the liberalism which gave license not to think, the liberalism whose tolerance was due to the lack of convictions rather than to any profound understanding of human unity. Hitler, himself a member and hence the idol of the spiritually disinherited masses, never knew the true liberalism which is identical with the courageous and assiduous pursuit of education which liberates. Thus, he has nothing to offer to the disinherited but his tedious propaganda. And in order to maintain himself he is under coercion, both personal and political, to eliminate the stewards of the heirloom of occidental culture.

In the war of arms we are waging against his revolt of the masses, the difficulty seems to be the production and transportation of material means. The spiritual war we must wage, not only to prevent a similar revolt in our country—it may be true that it cannot happen here—but in order that our people may prove a wise sovereign at the next peace conference, this spiritual war finds the mere materials already produced and ready on the fighting line. America has built up its schools, and we are not lacking materially, but what use are we making of these weapons, and of the eager will of youth to gain their war of inner liberation?

Some seem to think that Mussolini pointed the right way. They think all we need is a concordat with the Church, or with the churches. This would be very pretty, if there existed an ecclesiastic faith that could be everybody's unconditional concern, and if our churches could furnish sufficient numbers of wise and learned spiritual advisers who could take the pedagogical tiller at the point where the charts of our secularized education give out. What our students want is not a charted course, but charts of the deeps, and a practical knowledge of how to steer by them. No mere revivalism can furnish such orientation. And if pusillanimous academic administrators schedule modicums of mild revivals they demonstrate that they do not know what our students want. They want access to the chart room. They want philosophy.

To be sure, they want more than philosophy, they want faith, or confirmation in their faith. Even those want faith for whom the very word is a stumbling block. They want faith in reality, faith in themselves. They want a calling. They ask: Who are we? For what are we here? What is it all about? A few find satisfactory answers in their church doctrine. Many churchgoing students say these doctrines do not answer their questions. And a perhaps even larger fraction of those outside the fold still more resent the callous indifference of the college which leaves them to their own devices, or which puts them off with the advice to participate in the activities of denominational student clubs. Most students do not even know that it is philosophy they want.

Philosophy is no substitute for religion. But philosophy teaches how to ask our questions properly, translating them into answerable form, instead of mistranslating them into apparent questions about non-existing objects. Faith cannot be had for the asking, nor does philosophy guarantee faith. But philosophy teaches how to distinguish between faith and superstition, between false religion and true. Thus it prepares the way for the latter.

FAITH VERSUS BELIEF

FRITZ MARTI[*]

I SHOULD be at a loss for a word, were I not to use the word "faith" and were I not to use it in distinction from—nay, in opposition to—the word "belief." I know that I have the authority of the dictionary against me, which explicitly lists the word "belief" as the synonym of "faith." The *Merriam-Webster* enumerates several secular usages of the word "faith"; it knows of no religious usage which would not say what "belief" says. True enough, the same dictionary also makes a distinction between the two terms, as follows:

> BELIEF and FAITH, in modern usage, differ chiefly in that *belief*, as a rule, suggests little more than intellectual assent; *faith* implies in addition the element of trust or confidence (cf. "*belief* in God" with "*faith* in God"); as, "One in whom *persuasion* and *belief* had ripened into *faith*" (*Wordsworth*).

This dictionary distinction happens to point in the direction in which I intend to go further, and thus I may let it stand in lieu of an anticipatory definition of terms.

A quibble about words is sterile. As philosophers, it behooves us to point out such distinctions as we may find between realities. The words will fall in line. Realities must rule usage; verbal usage may not overrule reality. Verbal usage, in so far as it seems to be able to hide what is real, marks pools of staleness in the flux of a culture.

I suspect that there is a stale flavor on the tongue of him who, in using the word "faith," is satisfied with the current assumption that to have faith is much the same as to believe in something.

I submit that the word "faith" can point at a reality much deeper than belief—a reality in the face of which any belief, no matter how solidly tested, appears hollow. I also submit that the quest for beliefs is likely to draw us away from the awareness of what is real in faith. The suspicion which the religious often display with regard to intellectuality is not entirely without ground. Belief is only an intellectual matter.

It is my thesis that the reality at which I am pointing with my word "faith" is much more basic than the rationalizations of it in beliefs, creeds, dogmas, words. It is a corollary of my thesis that, in our age and especially in this country, the easygoing identity established, as a rule, between a man of faith and a believer not only ignores the existence of men of faith who are not believers but is detrimental to the profundity and solidity of faith itself. Faith, taken out of its depth and held in the surface fluctuations of beliefs, is likely to lose its flavor.

Those who assume that they are bringing about faith when they promote a belief not only hitch the cart before the horse but endow the horse with the appearance of something made at will,

---

[*] 1945 presidential address read before the Southern Society for Philosophy of Religion.

like a cart. And faith cannot be had at will. Ecclesiastic tradition is quite right when it asserts that faith is a gift of Grace.

Before I raise the question as to the ground and origin of faith, I will endeavor, in three steps, to distinguish between faith and belief.

First, I want to distinguish faith from belief, because faith is not identical with belief but is the ground of a certain kind of belief.

The catechists are fond of quoting the first verse of the eleventh chapter of the Letter to the Hebrews, a verse of rather problematic wording.[1] The meaning to be conveyed seems to be that "faith is the ground for (our belief regarding) things to be hoped for, it (takes the place of) a proof for what has no appearance."

Taking this verse for my cue, I say that, since proof concerns that which has an appearance,[2] there must be another ground for those religious beliefs which regard the nonapparent. In so far as they do not deal with appearances, their ground is faith.

Beliefs regarding appearances concern what is present. Compared with what appears at present, the nonapparent seems to be merely future, "to be hoped for." Thus, religious beliefs seem less certain than secular beliefs. Yet, though they were less certain, there must be a ground for their certainty, whose degree is not zero. In order to designate this ground for the conviction of belief, I borrow the word "faith."

Faith is not the same as belief. It is the ground for those beliefs which do point at things truly to be hoped for even now. There are other beliefs, erroneous beliefs, whose grounds are elsewhere. But no beliefs are without grounds. The ground of belief furnishes belief's conviction. Belief expresses the conviction in terms of some argument. No belief is without its peculiar proof, though the proof be an appeal to authority. Being supported by proof, all beliefs are conditional. In truth, their certainty is conditioned by their grounds; in appearance, by their proofs.

Having taken my first step, and having declared faith to be the ground of belief, I now take the second, saying that, while beliefs are *in solo intellectu*, faith is *in re*.

Beliefs are made of imagery and rationalization. And some beliefs rest on faith. But faith is neither imagination

---

[1] Heb. 11:1: Ἔστιν δὲ πίστις ἐλπιζομένων ὑπόστασις, πραγμάτων ἔλεγχος οὐ βλεπομένων. Vulgate: *Est autem fides sperandarum substantia rerum, argumentum non apparentium.* Jerome's transliteration of ὑπόστασις as *substantia* is followed by the Douay translators and by the King James Version: "Now faith is the substance of things hoped for. . . . ." The American Catholic revision of 1941 gives, more correctly, *things to be hoped for*, but it retains the word "substance," which, in Goodspeed's translation, is replaced by the word "assurance," in line, e.g., with the *Manual Greek Lexicon of the New Testament* by G. Abbott-Smith (New York: Scribner, 1922), which, with regard to our verse, says (p. 463): "here perhaps *title-deed*, as that which gives reality or guarantee." Abbott-Smith renders the single occurrence of ἔλεγχος, in the NT, with *a proof, test*, which is in line with Jerome's *argumentum*. The Douay version says "the *conviction* of things that appear not." The King James text has "the *evidence* of things not seen." Goodspeed corrects "it is our conviction about things that we *cannot see*." The οὐ βλεπομένων of the original may have been meant literally. Jerome's *non apparentium* gives cause for the Scholastic refinement that these things have no appearance; a metaphysically very tenable emendation, worthy of recognition.

[2] Schelling condenses the conclusion at which decisive parts of the *Critique of Pure Reason* had arrived: "As soon as we enter the precinct of proof, we enter into the circle of the conditional and, vice versa, when we step among things which are conditional, we submit to the power of proof" (*Schelling's Works* [Stuttgart: Cotta, 1856], I, 308–9; in the present author's rhetorical but correct translation).

nor rationalization. It is more real than what is merely in the intellect. If we recognize this, we face the question what the word "real" can and must mean in this context.

"More real" than images and reasonings is the soul itself which manifests itself in such acts of consciousness as imagining and reasoning. I prefer the word "soul" to the fashionable term "subconscious." Soul sounds problematic. It is. The subconscious looks final, a fact of human nature, on principle knowable once and for all, not an ever new problem like the individual soul, new on account of the individual's calling and of his responsible freedom. However, if the more current term, "the subconscious," is more likely to convey a meaning to you, let it stand, for the moment, as a very tentative synonym of soul.

Now, if the soul or the subconscious is more real than its imaginative and ratiocinative manifestations, is it itself what is most real, in our context? Is there no ground on which the soul itself rests or from which it springs?

The biologistic trend in contemporary thought would find a rather easy answer, in the body, or in some somatic conditions. Among philosophers, I need not spend many words to stress the strictly conditional character of bodily reality itself and to emphasize that the very organism brings back to our attention the question as to its own ground. Somehow, the organic unity of manifold manifestations, somatic as well as psychic, all of them conditional, manifests in turn an unconditional principle which alone can furnish unity.

Organic unity has a ground, and so has the unity of the soul. The soul can be bent upon this ground—in tune with it, as it were. I do not yet say that the soul can be aware of its ground. Awareness brings with it beliefs. What I am still concerned with is the antecedent of those particular beliefs which have some soundness. This antecedent I call faith. And I said beliefs are only in the intellect, whereas faith is more real. It is a real bent of the soul, an alignment with the reality which is more real than the soul itself. Consequently, faith is a tacit recognition of the fact that the soul is not its own ground, that the soul is nothing ultimate.

Faith therefore has a quality of recklessness; it bestows freedom from too much concern with the individual itself. Faith is the paradox of simultaneous acknowledgment of the unconditional import of our calling, on the one hand, and, on the other, of the ultimate unimportance of the individual who—as we have come to say—is expendable.

Let it be said at once, as an aside, that totalitarianism has taught the expendability of the individual without acknowledging its unconditional importance. Totalitarianism lacks the paradoxical realism of faith. It is nothing new. It is only a decrepit phase in our age of the lack of faith—a lack which does not permit the courageous realization that only in so far as the individual is unimportant can it have unconditional importance. If the individual as such were of ultimate importance, he would be stuck on himself. He would be the slave of the demon of self-concern. He could not dedicate himself to the call of the unconditional—a call which cancels every demonic obsession and which alone can make man free.

The self-obsessed individualist is the unwitting sire of the totalitarian who rightly hates him because of his lack of faith. A good father would clear his son's path of the worst obstructions to the operation of faith. The child has a right to expect this. If the father cannot do his duty, the child feels frustrated. Like his sire, the totalitarian lacks faith and therefore cannot think realistically. He cannot realize the strict logic of the relation of unimportance and importance in the individual. For unrealistic thought, the relation is merely paradoxical. Hence the abstractionist's practical alternative of embracing either the importance (in individualism) or the unimportance (in totalitarianism). Events have shown us how impractical an alternative this is. We had better learn to understand the paradox and its consequences.

I have called faith the *tacit* recognition of the paradox of our life. And I must reassert the tacitness. Faith is an attitude, not a profession; it is an alignment, not an assertion; it is real, not yet rational.

The reality of faith, then, is at least the reality of an attitude, of an alignment. Some may say that that is not much of a reality, and they may argue that, making allowance for the subconscious mind, attitudes and alignments are still merely mental, still *in solo intellectu*. I admit that some are. But I do not admit it of that attitude or alignment which I call faith. For faith is not only a real attitude of the subject, and it is not only an intellectual alignment; it puts us in line with our ground which is unconditional. Being in line with unconditionality, however, means being one's self of unconditional importance, no longer being only subjective, that is, only conditional.

The jargon of the times tempts one to say that faith, though indeed a reality in the subject, is also objectively real. But such jargon is utterly misleading in this context. The objective is as much a matter of conditionality as the subjective. Hence I must not use the inadequate phrase "objective reality," but I must reaffirm the unconditionality with which faith aligns us.

And this affirmation leads to my third step. I said, first, that faith is not belief but the ground of belief and, second, that beliefs are only in the mind, whereas faith is real. Now, third, I say that faith is a gift, not an attitude struck arbitrarily, not an alignment chosen at will.

The word "gift" may lead to misunderstandings. Some theologians are fond of talking about faith as a gift, and often they do not distinguish faith from belief. They use the word "gift" in an entirely ordinary sense. They talk about God as Somebody who makes a gift of faith to somebody else, to man, somewhat after the fashion in which I deliberately endeavor to make you a gift of these thoughts, in the hope that you will find them solid and sustaining. In truth, however, God is not Somebody, and the gifts of God are not temporal transactions. Not without truth did Calvin teach election as having taken place before the beginning of time.

In time, to be sure, faith comes to fruition. Can one speak of faith in a baby? To be sure, what is manifest is the infant's title to life, even his valiant struggle for life, and there is a difference between the soulless struggle for survival and the adherence to a life which is human. Even babies show faith in the human calling; they crave love. Yet, temporal growth alone brings forth what is the call of man, eternally. And in most men there is much temporization before the peace of the eternal alignment quiets the soul.

Just as faith itself is the alignment with the paradox of the utmost importance and the simultaneous unimportance of our lives, so is faith as a *gift* a paradox. It seems certain that only some have the gift, yet none may be said to be surely unfit for receiving it. Though I make bold to distinguish, on principle, between men of faith and men without faith, yet, in practice, I would never dare definitely to classify anyone in the category of the faithless. In practice, we are required to consider all men as men of potential faith. In paradoxical fact, though, the solidity which derives from faith is more manifest in some than in others. And such solidity cannot be had at will. It would be unjust to indict those who lack faith. Justice demands, however, the acknowledgment of the gift wherever it is recognizable. The fact that the recognition can be hampered by an obtuse identification of faith and belief will give me cause for a corollary comment later on.

Beliefs are a matter of imagination and of argument. We can argue at will, and at will we can recognize imagery as mere imagery, which recognition, of course, is a kind of argument. We cannot have faith at will. We cannot even embrace a belief at will. To be sure, there is such a thing designated by the theologians as an *act* of faith. But the name of an act must not induce us to think of an arbitrary act by which we could make ourselves "believe that which we know 'taint so," as the little boy in Sunday school defined an act of faith. Nobody can believe what he *knows* as untrue. To put one's self at variance with truth is an act of faithlessness. Acts of faith must fall in line with the ever specific truth; they must grasp the truth, or prepare us for it.

Some theologians speak of preliminaries of faith; they invite us so to direct our will that our intelligence will recognize certain abstract metaphysical truths fit to be used as base tables for the stilt-legs of the receiving tower of faith. I would call that approach to faith stilted, indeed. The notion of preliminaries furnished by the will of man makes it appear as if the gift of faith could not be bestowed without man's antecedent construction of receiving antennae.

I admit that the reception in consciousness does depend on preliminaries which only a good will can bring about. In fact, my entire argument comes under the heading of such preliminaries.

I do not admit that the gift of faith can be prevented by man's negligence to make straight the way. Such prevention is impossible, in reality, and, in consciousness where it may be attempted, it would remind one of the practice of some aborigines of Borneo who, when they hear the bird of ill omen sing his song on their left, turn the canoe about, thus righting the matter into a message of good luck. Human consciousness indulges in such tricks. But reality cannot be turned about at will.

And faith is a reality. As a gift, it is operative even in the absence of the preliminaries which are required for the true fruition of faith. The gift then operates demonically, producing all kinds of beliefs among different kinds of men and minds, but beliefs which are all alike in this: that they oppress, whereas, in its true aspect, the gift of faith is the ground for human freedom.[3]

My last assertion may sound cryptic. I will not digress into a dissertation on the topic of freedom, which might prove my contention. I will argue only from the opposite of freedom.

The man who is unfree is somehow stuck, stumped, stunted. He may be

[3] It is easy to see that this paragraph is nothing but a crude condensation of Schelling's *Philosophy of Mythology*.

stuck on an apparently insoluble problem, stuck only temporarily. Yet he may be stuck fast. It may be some shortcoming of his, natural or moral, which stumps him or, again, some theory or belief which hampers his freedom. At all events, he is stunted, because whatever is his obsession makes him unfit to take things the way they are, in truth. The oppressive dimensions of things close at hand dwarf things more distant. Things that should have been relegated to the past constitute, for the one who is unfree, a haunting present which befogs the future. He cannot feel at home in reality, because he is caught in a mere corner of reality. He sees only the overwhelming importance of what confronts him, and he is unable to see the other side of the matter, its unimportance.

Nothing is of last importance if we are able to see it in the light of faith. Faith is that light which permits us to see the relative as relative, the conditional as conditional. We cannot see the relative as such except in the light of absoluteness, nor the conditional as such but in the light of unconditionality. That light is the light shed by faith.

Faith aligns our mind with the unconditional. Unconditionality is what faith has in view. Making use once more of the definition in Hebrews, in my wording which takes its cue from Jerome's interpretation, I repeat that "faith takes the place of a proof for that which has no appearance." Proof concerns appearances. Demonstration establishes what is conditional. There is no demonstration of the object of faith, simply because what faith has in view is not an object, not conditional, not apparent. This is why the so-called object of faith necessarily appears as transcendent, if seen by the so-called natural reason, that is, by a reason limited to the conditional. Quite truly, the nonobjective object of faith is beyond the realm of objects. First, it cannot be apprehended as an object, except symbolically. And second, it is beyond in the sense of being above, that is, of *ruling* objectivity, conditionality, the world of appearances.

For those who believe that their reason is naturally limited to the consideration of appearances alone, it is imperative to see in faith a supernatural addition to their intellectual virtue or capacity, a superaddition without which they would indeed be slaves of the world. And so should we be unfree, even as philosophers, had we no realization of unconditionality. Only, by the grace of Providence, *we* happened to come upon teachings which opened our eyes to the fact that unconditionality is not a transcendent objectivity, not a nonobjective object, not a contradiction in terms, but a reality close at hand, so close, in fact, that we cannot attribute to ourselves any merit in seeing it. We are therefore in line with those theologians who, quite realistically, recognize faith as a gift, gratuitously bestowed, and not produced by the scheming of man. Man furnishes such *words* as "absolute," "unconditional," "eternal," "divine," "infallible," "omnipotent," "Providence," "Grace," and the like. And words like these are always connected in some way with beliefs. Belief, therefore, has its human and historical limitations. But man does not produce unconditionality, neither by deliberate invention nor by subconscious motions of the mind. The mind is not the maker of the unconditional. On the contrary, without the unconditional, the mind could not function at all.

Even our errors and perversions borrow whatever persuasive power and whatever compulsion they have from the imperative *form* of unconditionality. But the form, falsely detached from the content, turns into a demonic force.

The content of the unconditional is always freedom and liberation. The form is inexorability and sovereignty. Hence the demonism of all merely formal recognition of the unconditional.

Some call such formal adherence faith. I call it superstitious belief. True faith views the content, though it does not deny the form. To be more precise, I should not use such active verbs as "to view," "to affirm," "to deny," of faith as a *gift;* I should use them only of *acts* of faith, by means of which we give conscious recognition to the gift.

"Now what is an act of faith?" I quote from a recent article by our vice-president, who puts the matter very concisely.[4] "It is an act wherein the intellect assents at the command of the will. Why does it thus assent? It assents because thereby merit is acquired. And why does the will command? It commands because the arguments to which the intellect assents can be only persuasive, not demonstrative; for, were they demonstrative, we should have, not faith, but knowledge, and all merit would evaporate."

Having thus summarized the matter, Dr. Patterson goes on to register his due protest against such interference of the will. And, indeed, as he says, "the 'assent of the intellect at the command of the will' can scarcely appear.... as other than an act of treason against .... mental rectitude, an act which brings with it its own inescapable and appropriate punishment in our consequent inability ever after really to be-

[4] Robert Leet Patterson, " 'Universal Religion' and Special Revelation," *Review of Religion,* IX (May, 1945), 355. The Southern Society for Philosophy of Religion promoted Dr. Patterson to the presidency for 1945-46.

lieve in our own conclusions, since we know that they are not the product of honest thinking, but of thinking whose 'pitch' has been 'queered' at the outset by the arbitrary and unjustified intervention of the will."

The will commanding assent must appear arbitrary and unjustified as long as we share the theologian's belief that there is such a thing as a merely natural reason, restricted to the knowledge of conditional things, among which belongs the deified abstraction of a "God" whose existence is a matter of demonstration. Kant and his successors have long shown that conditional knowledge is impossible without unconditional freedom. Theologically speaking, natural reason could never reach as far as even the mere existence of God, were it not natural in the sense of having its origin in God. Reason, critically understood, is the soul's insight into its foundation in freedom. The uncritical and naturalistic notion of a natural, merely conditional reason needs a corrective supplement, even in the eyes of the theologian. Since his unfree reason, fallen from Grace, lacks the substance of true reason, which is freedom, the correction can be furnished only by that power of the soul which does possess the substance, by the will, whose freedom the orthodox theologian will not deny. I suggest that it is this substance alone which the will can have in view when it commands the assent of the intellect.

A will which would command the intellect to deny freedom and to desist from conscientious thinking would be a truly evil will, and the inability really to believe would, indeed, be its inevitable punishment. Yet, most theologizers who use words similar to those of Dr. Patterson's summary have quite evidently the ability sincerely to believe in the assertions resulting from a thought which has been "queered" by the wilful notion which relegates the frighteningly close God into a safe recess of transcendence. How is such sincere belief possible?

It will not do for us to say that such theologizers mean one thing and say another. Obviously they mean what they say. They do believe that God is the personal ruler of the universe, whose majesty demands that his subjects, by a deliberate act of the will, bring their ever fallible intellects in line with certain doctrines he has deigned to reveal.[5] But do they believe that, without the gift of faith, the will has the power to command the assent of the intellect?

I who am horrified by the blasphemy of likening God to an absolute monarch, no matter how benevolent, am unable to direct my intellect into the paths of monarchistic belief. For me, such paths lead nowhere. Yet I cannot deny that others progress along these paths. Nor is their progress toward wickedness. Therefore, I must ask in what manner faith works in them.

To be sure, I can see no faith in him who would *arbitrarily* command the assent of the intellect. A man who tells me he can at will make his intellect assent to any kind of creed either is a liar, or he must mean abstention from thought when he says assent of the intellect. Intellectual conscience cannot be commandeered arbitrarily. He who says it can displays thereby his lack of faith.[6]

The gift of faith does not pervert, it sharpens intellectual conscience. Faith strengthens the intellect in a degree that permits the subjection of unrealistic quibbles which so often rise in our minds. If the unruly and unrealistic ratiocinations are subdued, and if the conscientious perspicacity of the intellect is restored, then the apparent mystery of the unconditional can be seen in its transparent simplicity. To this purpose, demonstrative arguments, that is, arguments of the pattern "if-then," arguments which apprehend only the conditionality of the conditional, must give way to the persuasive arguments implicit in symbolic imagery. For a mind bent on demonstration, the paradoxical is only persuasive. And symbolic imagery is necessarily paradoxical, since it endeavors to express in terms of the conditional what, in truth, is unconditional. On the level of things, the reality grasped by faith appears "higher," transcendent, a mystery. Yet it is not impenetrably

[5] One cathechist even uses the word "protestation": "We worship and honor God by the virtue of Faith when we make *Acts* of this virtue; i.e. when we make protestations to God that we do actually believe all the truths which he has revealed, and proposes to us as revealed, by his Church, and that we believe them precisely because He, who is Truth itself, has revealed them. This is paying direct homage to God, it is an act of homage to his eternal Truth, it is the submission of our fallible judgment to his infallible word" (Rev. J. Perry, *A Full Course of Instruction in Explanation of the Catechism* [St. Louis: B. Herder Book Co., 1926], p. 359).

[6] Perry (*op. cit.*, pp. 306–7) says: "Doubts concerning any Article of Faith, when they are voluntary or wilfully consented to, are .... grievously sinful. Whenever they arise in the mind they should be rejected immediately as suggestions of the devil, without our stopping to reason them away; ...." If the last sentence of this catechist had no concluding clause, I should call it a piece of advice which nobody can follow except by taking a sleeping powder of instantaneous action. However, Perry concludes: "they should be opposed by *Acts of Faith* and by *Prayer*." I submit that these remedies are precisely what must be called "stopping to reason the doubts away," if to reason means to stick to one's topic. For a shallow mind, the topic may be the mere letter of an article of belief. For a truly pious person, the topic is the ground of belief into whose depth those quibbling arguments cannot reach which Perry calls reasoning. Acts of faith acknowledge the inadequacy of that kind of reason. In true prayer, man reasons adequately, with regard to the ground of faith. Of course, I am left with the question: Will the time ever come when churchmen sacrifice their arbitrary definition of reason, which plays such havoc with their thinking?

mysterious; it does not lack immanence; it is manifest in lowliness. The unconditional rules and, by ruling, redeems the conditional. Its very manifestation is always in the conditional. Hence the proclamation of the most striking religious image: God can be seen, even on the Cross.

Faith bestows the power to see through and beyond the records of images and theories, to see imagery and theorizing no longer as veils of the truth but as its vehicles. He whom we call a man of simple faith simply has not made the historical discovery that there is no exclusive vehicle. Yet the very realism of his faith prevents him from flatly mistaking his own beliefs for exhaustive knowledge. Beyond his belief there is the mystery. Were it not there, belief would assume the tyrannical character of a fixed idea. The argumentative side of belief is less revealing than the side of religious imagination, which more adequately shows forth the ever new essence of freedom. A realistic will detaches the intellect from deadening demonstration and directs the attention to persuasive images.

To be sure, the adventure of faith always pushes beyond imagery. No image is exclusive, though, under specific historical circumstances, the religious imagination brings forth imagery which, in some degree, is indispensable. Thus, the temporal has eternal significance, but it does not have the power to confine the eternal in the boundary of any one belief. The eternal is the liberating and hence ever new call, and faith aligns us with this forceless power of unconditionality.

The alignment cannot be made at will, but its recognition depends on that realistic will which always commands the intellect not to prefer fancy to fact, theory to reality, beliefs to religiosity, demons to God.

Faith affords courage, daring, perseverance. If faith lags, we get into the doldrums. Faith has always brought about the revolutions of belief necessary to redeem belief from stagnation. Faith disrupts the complacency of the smug believers who, therefore, have always hated those whom faith moved conspicuously. Alive religiosity takes its stand with faith and, if necessary, against belief. "Faith versus Belief" is the motto of religious history.

Yet, faith cannot do without belief simply because faith demands conscious recognition. Thus, in the order of time, we have images, and then arguments. And the result is belief, even the belief of the unbeliever.

As an unbeliever I must still bear witness to the truth, and I cannot do so without words and images, assertions and parables, concepts and symbols. There is one advantage in unbelief, the unbeliever is free, under conscience, to borrow the terms of any truly pious believer. Conscience demands that the borrowing amount not to twisting. If the borrower is conscientious in the use he makes of the believer's terms, the latter, if he has the freedom of faith, can recognize in the borrower's usage an interpretation compatible with what is real in his own belief.

This fact that the unbeliever is free to borrow, and the believer free to acknowledge the interest that accrues, makes possible a sound and truly religious discussion between believer and unbeliever. Our age is overripe for such discussions, yet most people are loath even to admit the possibility.

The possibility not only exists. In my opinion it constitutes the very call of our generation. Thus, my distinction between faith and belief can serve a thoroughly practical end, and, in the hope of doing my thinker's part in contribution to fruitful practice—for true theoretic insight always helps wholesome practical life—I will wind up by enumerating a few explicit corollaries to my thesis.

To begin with, it may be proper to restate the thesis, and to do so by means of two formulations which, in words, are at odds with each other.

Belief springs from imagination and argument, which are naturally bent upon the conditional. Faith, however, puts us in tune with the unconditional. In so far as imagination and argument can be said to be natural, in man, faith can be called a *supernatural* gift.

Wording the matter the other way around, however, it can also be said that faith is the most *natural* trait of man, since it is of the very essence of human freedom, whereas belief, which is only in the intellect, only a matter of imagery and ratiocination, is always somehow artificial.

Everybody will point at the artificiality of the philosopher's private crutches. The artificiality of the public conveyance of current belief, however, is equally evident from the fact that such formulations of belief as creeds and dogmas attain the status of legal documents fit to serve as a basis for the juridical determination of who is a believer and who is not. Heresy trials are only a possible consequence. The important thing is the very possibility of legislation in matters of belief.

To be sure, such legislation usually occurs under the impulse of the religious quest, and the purely political motives of power are often quite secondary. The primary desire is to capture religious truth and to inclose it in legally exploitable language. The fact that the letter can then be put before the spirit is not of primary importance. The first thing that counts is the authoritative dignity attributed to certain especially significant linguistic formulations.

Such formulas are usually called articles of faith, and their sum, a confession of faith. I should call such expressions misnomers. Strictly speaking, what can be thus formulated are articles of belief. And the ecclesiastic confessions are formulations of belief.

Faith is free to change belief. This is my first corollary, which I hold to be of eminent practical significance.

In the second place, I would stress that faith is free even under belief. A believer can be a man of faith. It is obvious to anyone with open eyes that there are men of sound and solid faith even among those believers whose tenets are indeed questionable, when weighed by the intellectual evidence which history has made available.

Belief cannot prevent the gift of faith. Depending on the circumstances, belief can only help or hinder the adequate *recognition* of the gift. At its worst, belief can pervert the gift into a demonic power. At its best, it can confirm a man in his faith.

The observation of many spiritual aspects of our century makes me wonder whether or not the modern inflexibility of belief is the cause of much inward unhappiness and outward unrest. In retort, I shall probably be told that, on the contrary, modern belief is most flexible. For instance, church people do not seem to give much weight to the orthodoxy of belief, and they would rather willingly sacrifice the formulas of belief to the fruition of social work. This fact, in *my* opinion, marks one extreme degree of inflexibility. Minds have lost all theological agility, nay, nearly all theological seriousness, and they are therefore rigidly and almost obsessively moving in the one direction of outward performance. If some courage of faith were left to such minds, they would dare to confess their *un*belief, an unbelief not, like ours, due to the incompatibility of most current beliefs with conscientious culture, nor due, like our unbelief, to religious conscience, but due to the apparent absence of such conscience and to the inability to believe which necessarily grows in him who would treat all things pragmatically. Success seems to succeed very especially in making the religious quest appear unnecessary and obsolete. Such is the case even with ecclesiastic success.

My third corollary, therefore, repeats that faith is fact, belief only interpretation, and that the very freedom of faith demands the radical questioning of beliefs. But questioning is not quibbling. Our generation seems to be so much afraid of the kind of quibbling which the twenties cherished that we desist from teaching the young how to question. Of course, they could learn it from truly religious writers, from such men as Augustine and Thomas down to our humble students of the history and philology of religious texts. Still, our schools should not abdicate before the majesty of books. Teaching should still promote the recognition of faith, by giving instruction in the preliminaries of adequate questioning.

Questions prove their adequacy in making us more fit to recognize faith wherever it has been bestowed. My fourth corollary says that there is faith among unbelievers and that *religious* duty demands its recognition. Even the unbeliever himself ought to recognize that he has faith, if that is his gift. And surely the truly faithful should make such emendations in their beliefs as would enable them to see that wider fellowship of faith which reaches beyond the church and beyond "religion."

In history, the faith of unbelievers has usually acted as a leaven. Ecclesiastic beliefs would never have attained their depth or their firmness had not the faith of the heretics challenged thought.

In our century, apostasy may prove to have an even more important function than heresy. Can we really hope to steer clear of trouble, by following the course of the centuries of conquest, in treating non-Christians as poor deluded heathen? On the horizon of twentieth-century Christian statesmanship such entities have appeared as China, Russia, and the Moslem world. Is it certain a priori that whatever gift of faith operates among those peoples can operate only in the perverted form of demonism? The apostate, at least, would say it is not a priori certain.

"Apostasy" is a harsh word, and it is not fit to designate the man whom, perhaps, we had better call a post-Christian, the man, that is, who has not turned his back at Christianity for the sake of another religion or for the sake of none, but who, in the very pursuit of the call of faith, finds that Christianity is of the past. It is of the past, but of his own past, not an impersonal piece of somebody else's history. When he comes upon the clause of the verse from the forty-third Psalm which the introit of the Catholic Mass translates with the words *ad Deum qui laetificat juventutem meam*, he can find himself in agreement even with the present tense of the verb, because the youth of his mind is not something lost and done with; it is a reality which becomes younger as he turns older. Our past becomes younger because it becomes more transparent and less bewildering. If the gift of faith is strong in us, we may even come to understand *why* we harbored the beliefs of our youth. And if, thus, the buried beliefs of my earlier years attain a transfigured life in the peace of understanding, I can feel, as the psalmist, that "I shall yet praise him who is the health of my countenance"; and even the phrase "my God" can be silently pronounced, notwithstanding the quiet fact that I must not live again in the land of theism.

Thus it becomes permissible that I give voice to my last corollary in entirely traditional words. It is not we who bring about faith. Its birth and its growth we must quietly leave in the still care of God, whose ways are not our ways. What we must not do is to set limits to God's freedom; we must not make bold to say that any given belief, no matter how profound and refined, can contain the sphere of faith. The universe itself seems too small for the doings of faith. What we can do is to still our inner unrest, so that we become fit to see and to hear. We do that when we pursue the prime task of the scholar, when we persevere in the courageous critique of belief.

Abutments and Piers for Bridges of Cultural Understanding

THERE IS NO cultural understanding between people who, lacking culture, can apprehend only what appears oddly different in others. Such people are parasites even within the realm of their home culture which also appears to them as something merely contingent, though, on the part of these very people, turned into stubborn rituals and stupid shibboleths.

There is no culture that lives in its own present alone. Genuine culture has a decided past, and an open future. In order to set the past as irrevocable, and to posit the future as an obligation, human consciousness requires one of two things, or both. Either it needs a vision which, not being an arbitrary invention of man, has mythological dignity and, therefore, has the power to establish man in a living relation between past, present, and future; or else, the philosophical historian's insight into the realistic nature of that relation, above all as it relates the past, present, and future of the historian's own circle of culture; or, in the third place, the man who is still at home in the myth that circumscribed his cultural circle, may also have acquired an explicit historical interest in and understanding of his own position, and of the cultural position of others.

There are great myths, like the Judaic and the Christian, which furnish visions that are fit to master the past and to open the future and, thus, to redeem the present from the sterile status of a tedious sequence of apparent novelties. Such myths are required as the solid ground on which the firm abutments must be erected which can stand the strain of cultural bridges.

The abutments themselves are built of blocks of mythological stuff reshaped in view of the spans which reach beyond the circumference of the home culture. If the two home cultures to be connected have their origin in myths too different to permit the construction of a single span, then, indeed, the explicit understanding of historians who, themselves, are no longer under the jurisdiction of either myth, must furnish the intervening piers, if there is to be a bridge of cultural understanding.

Bridges for cultural understanding cannot be permanently suspended from the balloons of sheer good will. They need firm supports. Nor is the academic man the lonely Atlas who can hold aloft their emotional weight as if it were but ethereal. What the academic man can do is to throw across the abysses of misunderstanding the tough cables of historical intelligence. He can use the lines of historical understanding as safe catwalks and become at home almost equally, on both shores. But when we speak of cultural bridges to serve the purposes of world peace and of true humanity, we imply something more than the catwalks of the historians of various aspects of culture. We seem to harbor a hope for a mutual understanding among the multitudes.

Cultural understanding is the historian's calling, be he a student of art or of religion, of language or of law, of economics or of politics. The historian, however, has a peculiar frame of mind, which is not everybody's. As yet, the multitudes are not historically minded. Nor can we hope to make them so, within a generation or two. And the construction of bridges of cultural understanding cannot wait until schools have changed their ways and have made historical-mindedness their prime criterion of judgment, and their definite goal. We must build with the material at hand, that is, we must look for the places which will support our abutments. Not every kind of mind will stand the strain. An inner stress is produced in any mind subject to the contact with a foreign culture. Some minds show a natural allergy to such contacts as too disturbing. At the very least, the foreign contact disturbs the smug complacency of the provincial whose conformity with the local pattern has reduced him to the point where he believes his own pattern of behavior is the only sound one.

Ingrown provincialism and cultural understanding are incompatible.

But there are other obstacles to cultural understanding than provincial minds. Some frames of mind, not at all atrophied, need no understanding that reaches beyond the confines of their own environment. Thus, for instance, the mind of the child younger than four or five. Thus, also, the mind of the quite healthy individual who has found a way of life richly rounded in the localized pursuit of happiness. To such a mind, the foreign is simply the strange, tolerable in its remote place of a curiosity, yet not needed to round out his own sphere of life. Such a mind, in fact, will feel less unfinished than the rest of us who cannot live without what we loftily call cultural understanding. It behooves us not to identify rashly such a happy and healthy frame of mind with provincialism. The former needs no foreign contacts, the latter rejects them because they would make too patent the provincial poverty. Provincialism is not compatible with cultural understanding; it is positively inimical to the promotion of such understanding. Simple happiness is not inimical to our undertaking, but neither does it promote it.

If our enterprise is sound, it cannot but aim at a healthy happiness. We are not at odds with the lucky ones who even now are happy. Nor are we unhappy. But there is a difference of ages between them and us.

Saturn's golden age of simple happiness is not simply an earlier stage of human development. Although, in ancient lore, the pristine peace is broken into by the events of a subsequent age, we must not take mythological distinctions too literally. To a "golden age" mind, our concern with history must appear quite a bit freakish and our blueprints of cultural bridges, artificial.

In truth, many of our constructions have been artifices of no lasting worth, just because, having too easily mistaken healthy happiness for pinched provincialism, we have built bridges which connected not cultures but the international intelligentsia. The depth and historical resonance of a culture is due to the happiness it holds. Being aware of this fact, men have tried, at times, to safeguard their culture and their happiness by building great walls around them. Behind such walls, however, a culture is in danger of becoming stale. Intellectualism is often a by-product of such staleness. The intellectual finds his happiness in historical knowledge. Too easily does he forget that, without the happy mind, a culture will not last.

Compared with the bedrock of primitivism, and with the volcanic pillars of religious innovations, Saturn's happiness may appear soft and alluvial. If alluvial, it is fertile, and if soft, we must still calculate with it, in our bridge building.

Our question is precisely how to rest our bridges on such abutments as will allow us to connect the fertile lands of various cultures. For the moment, I will only say that our abutments are furnished by the relative solidity of a culture's mythological structure.[1] I assert that cultural understanding is impossible among those who are aware only of a present without a past. Cultural understanding can be established either when the mythological structure opens a culture's past into its future, or when the intellectually matured freedom of the spirit demands explicit historical insight. The latter condition must furnish the piers for our bridges if they cannot span without piers the distance between the abutments furnished by the respective mythological structures. So far my cryptic thesis.

I begin the explanation at the point where controversy is least likely. Those who have no genuine past and, therefore, are limited to the awareness of a mere present, are people not used to the effort demanded by cultural understanding. They have never made the effort with regard to their own past, and, with regard to contemporary cultures which they cannot simply ignore, they are restricted to unintelligent judgments based on a mere factual comparison of the foreign culture with their own ways. It is natural that their judgments usually should be derogatory. Examples abound. Omar's alleged judgment about the value of the library in Alexandria is well known. Among the Spanish conquerors of Mexico and Peru there were but few who found in their own Christianity a challenge for cultural understanding. It was much easier, as "Christians," to despise the "ways of the heathen." Nor are Moslems and Christians alone given to judgments without understanding of things foreign. It is a common human trait. How common it is can be gathered from the reading of a few pages of the Old Testament, or even of Herodotus who, among the haughty Greeks, at least took an interest in the doings of the barbarians. Nor is the trait extinct. The frame of mind of a Herodotus is very much the same as that of modern tourists who are interested in the "quaint" things which make travel so entertaining. Entertainment is one thing, cultural understanding is another.

[1] I had perhaps better inform the reader that I am giving no derogatory sense to such expressions as myth, and mythological structure. What I mean by the latter phrase, I must explain anon. However, I will make use of the phrase in stating my thesis.

He who has no *decided past*[2] has difficulty in finding a way to understand a foreign culture in its own contexts, although he is at ease in finding entertainment in many foreign facts. That facts are not final entities he seldom discovers. He is the perennial child, who, owing to his lack of understanding, is bound to label unheard of things with names which imply that they are not quite human. He may lack the utter naïveté of a child displayed by a playmate of my father's who told me that, when he was a country lad, in the late 1860's, peasants from the Guggisberg mountains of his own canton of Bern, would come to the lowland in order to trade cattle. The little lowland boy asked his father: "Are the Guggisbergers also people?" The father wanted to know the reason for the question, and the boy said: "Why, their shirts have no collars!" No mere effort of good will can bring us to the point where we recognize that foreigners too "are people." What we need, in order to be able to make the recognition, is to grow up, that is, to learn to recognize that even we, in our oddly different child ways and ways of adolescence, were people. And a similar recognition of one's past, both as one's own and as now past, must take place in a nation, in order that it emerge from the everlasting round of merely present facts and acquire what is properly called a culture. In short, culture is a prerequisite for cultural understanding.

Culture, however, is something fundamentally religious. Genuine religiosity combats and overcomes the hard-hearted childishness of stubborn home ritualism and of unintelligent judgment about things foreign, or past, or things to come. Genuine religiosity brings forth great myths fit to put the present in its proper place, profoundly obliged to the past which must be understood anew over and over again, and obliged to the future whose demands become apprehensible in the light of the past redeemed in understanding. In short, religion is essentially the sober discovery of the interrelation of what was, is, and shall be.[a]

[2] Schelling's concept *einer entschiedenen Vergangenheit*. See especially *"Die Weltalter,"* works, vol. VIII, p. 259, or, in Bolman's translation, p. 147, Columbia University Press, NY., 1942. (See above, pages 2-6, especially 5.)

[a] This allows for little distinction between religion, history, and philosophy of history. Perhaps the author intends none. But surely, in the West at least, religion has been understood to be essentially the recognition of the relationship between man and his Creator, with all that flows from that fundamental act of worship. It is putting the cart before the horse to say that, "Genuine religiosity brings forth great myths," unless the vague term "myth" means something quite different from what we understand by great religious truths; it is the truths that have produced the religiosity, not the other way around. Otherwise, the

49

And, among the timeless ones who childishly judge everything from the angle that happens to be theirs, religion fosters a more truly human mentality, by its myths. Even the naïve mind can discover the place in the mythological structure to which he, specifically, is called. If he follows his calling and fills that place, he attains truly human dignity; history itself counts on him. He is no longer the nobody he was in the realm of mere physical birth, growth, and death. He is reborn in the realm of the spirit. In this very sense, culture is spiritual, not merely natural. It is essentially historical, not merely a geographic phenomenon.

When I speak of mythological structure, I do not deny that the term mythology covers both, (a) the fetishistic, ritualistic, moralistic, or narrowly theistic ways and notions which mark minds and societies without historical understanding and religious depth and (b) the genuinely religious myths to which I referred above. This is why, in the statement of my thesis, I qualified the phrase, speaking of a mythological structure which opens the past into the future and thus establishes a true culture.

Such a mythological structure of thought and action is historical in essence, yet it need not be historical in the explicit sense in which we moderns speak of historiography and of historical intelligence. If, for instance, "it is written" that in the economy of the fullness of the times all things are to be summed up in Christ (Ephesians I, 10), the writer is thinking as a mythographer and not as an historiographer. In other words, St. Paul is not explicitly aware of the involved development, "From Jesus to Paul," as a Joseph Klausner would unfold it (Macmillan, 1943). The development is implicit in the very calling of St. Paul, but he is aware only of the call he has received and, for him, historiography

whole religious field is reduced to myth in the definitely derogatory sense of purely human manufacture, fiction, fable, or open falsehood. (Walter Farrell, O.P.)

I do not intend to do away with the distinction between religion, history, and philosophy of history, but I do lack any understanding of what, in our West, is meant by the phrase "man's Creator," if it is not to mean what Michelangelo painted on the Sistine ceiling and what the writer of the first chapters of Genesis naïvely describes.

When I wrote that "genuine religiosity brings forth great myths," I was thinking of the fact that consciousness must give articulation to the power that rules it and of which it is but dimly aware as long as it would remain inarticulate. I did not mean to deny that, without that power, there would be nothing to articulate. Nor do I deny the steering part of the power in producing the articulation. I do deny that the articulate myth as such has an antecedent existence, like a Platonic idea, and that consciousness merely copies what is already there. If man's mind were a *tabula rasa* on which the gods inscribe their names, history would be an insipid pastime unworthy of the gods, and man would lack the dignity of being made in God's image. (Fritz Marti) itself is among the things which come to a head only in Christ. The myth absorbs everything, and the mythological structure has a place for everything.

That is, this kind of mythological structure has a place for everything. Other mythological structures may have no room for the mystery of historical reality, or they may reduce it to some such popular metabiologism as the sequence of rulers among Greek gods. Notwithstanding its form of a timetable story, Greek mythology is essentially unhistorical. No wonder that Greek historiography, when it appears in a Thucydides, lacks every relation to mythology which, even without the intention of the historiographer, assumes the face of superstition. And superstition it is, as soon as human consciousness has reached the point of asking a strictly historical question. At that point, the Greek gods take on the air of poetic timelessness. Yet, in the very light of the question of strict history, a mythology like the Christian shows its inherent historical nature.

The Christian myth knows of a time which is no mere sequence of indifferent strokes of the clock, but which is a time of crisis and therefore of fulfilment (*kairós*). Within the flux of clock time, the crises may fill only moments, here and there, yet these very moments gather up the entirety of time, in the time-overruling significance of the mythological insight.

If a myth affords an insight into historical reality, of whose essence is the subjection of the temporal to the eternal, then it is the kind of myth whose structure is fit to carry the weight of one end of a cultural bridge. It is this kind of myth which we need for our abutments. And we cannot reasonably hope, as an Alfred Rosenberg hoped unreasonably, to fashion such myths as we need them. We can only seek them, in an already existent reality, and then fashion our bridges in such a way that they start from such firm abutments, instead of starting from nowhere and, consequently, leading nowhere.

I am too ignorant to say whether or not, at the other ends of the bridges we should like to plan, similarly solid ground can be found for strong abutments. To find them would seem to be the task of our historians, ethnographers, and students of foreign cultures, but it is more truly the task of those foreign men of good will who, at their end of the bridge to be, co-operate with us in surveying the ground for the placement of **abutments.**

Bridges of cultural understanding can rarely be built without the previous construction of appropriate abutments. One of the rare instances of almost immediate understanding is found in the Japanese history of these past hundred years. The pragmatic pattern of Japanese feudalism and emperor worship made it possible, with a little persuading on our part, for the Japanese to understand without much ado the pragmatic side of technology, and Occidental scientism. To be sure, the latter is only one phase or, perhaps, an aberration of Occidental culture, the core of which has left the Japanese quite untouched, it would seem. In all probability, the distance between the culture of Japan and that of the Occident is so great that it cannot be bridged by one span.

At all events, what is necessary as a rule, is the building of abutments. What I mean is perhaps best illustrated by what occurred between early Christianity and the Greek world into which it spread. When the early Fathers discovered the possibility of a merger with Hellenistic Platonism, it struck them that Providence must have prepared the way for their new religion, in Greece, long before its temporal appearance in Palestine. This notion of a providential plan beyond the confines of Jewish history was neither against the tenets of Judaism nor against the implications of incipient Christianity, although neither of these two mythological structures had had a specific place for such extra-Judaic happenings as Platonism. The assignment of such a providential place amounted to the building of an abutment on the Christian shore, an abutment entirely compatible with the Christian ground on which it was erected. And, on the other side, there was no incompatibility between the Hellenistic trend toward illumination and revelation, and its fulfilment discovered in the Christian Logos and Savior, although no such Palestinian conceptions had had a place in the pantheon of Greek thought. Thus, the Greek ground likewise could carry an abutment fit for bridging the gap between the two cultures.

In short, what I mean by the construction of abutments is the rethinking of one's own foundations. If the foundations are sufficiently realistic, that is, if their mythological structure permits the opening of the past into the future, then it is not necessary to uproot the myth for the sake of being able to come to a durable understanding with people of different myths.

What the foreign people are to do is mainly a question for them. What we can do, and ought to do, is clear enough. Ours is the Christian culture even when, individually, we cannot truthfully call ourselves Christians any longer. Large numbers, possibly a majority, are still Christians. Their duty, and ours, is plain. We must rethink this Christianity. We cannot cart away its massive historical strata. Nobody can annihilate past history. But, on its solid ground, we can erect abutments for the bridges that must carry the traffic of the future with non-Christians. We, too, must discover, and we shall discover if we will but rethink our premises, that Providence does not confine its works within ecclesiastic fences.

It becomes more and more necessary for Christian churches to take the cross, as a spiritual charge, even unto the death of this "body of Christ" which is the Church, in order that the redeeming spirit may make its pentecostal entrance. Our abutment requires a deep cut into the gravel and sand and trampled clay of the easygoing assumptions which for centuries, we piled on top of the mythological strata: that all that is necessary is to bring the heathen and the apostates into the Christian fold and, perhaps, to make the Christians adhere a little more consistently to the moral tenets they profess to hold. In the first place, spreading the jurisdiction of the church does not mean spreading Christianity. If there is anything lasting in Christianity, it is its historical explosiveness, its nonconformity. The nonconformists of Reformation times were rather keenly aware of the relativity of all ecclesiastic organization. But the consolidation of Trent was quickly matched by most of the Protestant churches.

This does not mean that truly Christian preaching cannot go on *in* the churches. But, in order to make room for the abutments which we need for intercultural bridge building, we must dig into the loose ecclesiastic material which lies on top of the solid Christian myth, and Christianity must be preached *to* the churches. If properly preached, their repentance for what they are will be the contracting force which can furnish the firmness of an abutment needed to meet the counterthrust of other cultures.

It must be a radical repentance, not a merely moral one. It is not enough for the churches merely to be sorry for not having been more Christian. What they must repent is having been churches. This is entirely in line with the recently renewed impact of what has come to be called existential thinking. Much of it is objectionable, philosophically and religiously. But at its core, the question would seem to be a very

Christian question, whether or not man as man needs to repent, for being what he is, saint and sinner alike. If Jesus declined the title Good Master, is the church wiser with ready answers to the ever-new question what to do? The conception of an *ecclesia docens* is not meaningless, but the church can teach only because there are conscientious thinkers in the church who reject ready-made answers, and who know that the old answers are true only if rethought. If a man desirous to dodge his personal duty of thinking would turn to a representative of the church with the question, "What shall I do?"—looking for an order, which does not require more than literal obedience, and believing that whatever the ecclesiastic tells him is good—does such a man deserve any other answer than, "Why do you call me good? No one is good but God" (Luke 18, 19). And does his human dignity deserve anything less than a challenge to reconsider tradition? The challenge to consider oneself poor is especially saddening to one who is rich. And the Church is very rich, in tradition. Merely to forget tradition is not to sacrifice it. The acceptable sacrifice occurs in rethinking.

No one *is* good. Nor are there any "good" churches among a multitude of not-so-good ones. Organizations are necessary and, if treated merely as necessities, they can be used wholesomely. But the identification of an organization with the sacred purpose for which it is organized is always an evil. The recognition of this evil is by no means beyond the visions involved in the mythological structure of Christianity. In fact, there may not be on earth another myth beside the Christian which so strikingly calls in question all organizing, and every organization. New Testament passages which are of the earliest put a question mark beside the notion of the importance and everlastingness of the Temple. Jesus does not want to save his own life. Is the life of the church any more sacred? Is it not time that every church have an introit to its services, with an emphatic *sum indignus?* And should not the height of the service be a prayer that, if it is His Will, the Lord take the life of the church, for the sake of life more abundant?

Such a prayer would not mean the abolition of the church, performed by its own parishioners. It would mean, however, the abolition of ecclesiastic complacency. It would mean the opening of church doors, not in order to "pack them in," but in order to let men out—fortified, one would presume, by the sacrificial spirit prevailing within. And the true sacrifice is not social work, nor medical missions, necessary though they be, it is the sacrifice of the easy assumption that "having Christ" amounts to an indefinite moratorium laid upon thought and to a definite severing out of the sheep from the goats, domestic as well as foreign.

The goats are creatures of Providence too. And they will prove most necessary in these times we are entering. For it is precisely those who are not in the fold who are fit, in their make-up, to furnish the piers which are necessary when a single span cannot reach from one abutment to the other. In case the distance is so large, intermediary points are wanted from which both shores can be reached. Nor can they be hypothetical points. They must be real. And, in reality, it is the very ones who are outside the fold, yet solid because serious, who can see both sides with equal justice and understanding.

For instance, when it comes to establishing an understanding between us and Russia, it will be very nearly impossible for those in the Christian fold not to see anything but evil in Russian "atheism." Likewise, it will be impossible for the rationalistic Marxist to see anything but opium for the people in the Christianity which still holds sway in the western countries. To be sure, there is that enigma of the Russian Church which forms an island in the midst of the communistic sea. But a church which can come to terms with Leninism is almost as far from western ecclesiastic understanding as the Marxist religion itself. He who stands outside of both religions can more easily recognize and acknowledge their respective religiosity. The pier of such solid understanding is necessary if we are to have more than merely diplomatic relations with Russia, and if there is to be understanding between the peoples.

It is part of my thesis that the halfway piers can be provided by minds intellectually mature and explicitly aware of the freedom of the spirit, and of its demands. I do not mean to imply that such minds necessarily stand outside all mythological realms. To be sure, intellectual maturity will give the mythological structure in which a mind has been nurtured its due dignity of a decided past. But on that very account, it is difficult to imagine any profound maturity without such a mythological past. Nor is every mythological structure of an immature nature. The truly great myths are fit to hold in their folds mature minds as well as mentalities of a more childlike frame.

In summing up, I want to underline the importance of the mutual understanding of each culture's religiosity. I am not speaking of the academic understanding of what foreign *religions* teach and claim to believe. I am speaking of the living *religiosity* of every genuine culture, of the faith in which we can recognize the kindred features of our own faith, even when the beliefs differ irreconcilably.

There are no Cultural Bridges in Religions, as the title of our session would have it. Owing to the religious imagination, religions like pictures are not interconnected by bridges, nor do they need such connections. What establishes the connection is religiosity. Religiosity, however, is not an international religion, nor a natural religion—except in the sense in which religiosity is at the core of every religion. But in that very sense, each religion stands under the natural temptation to believe that it alone has genuine religiosity. Hence the apparently unbridgeable abysses between the religions. It is our practical task to find the religious people, among believers and unbelievers alike, who are fit to put their own solidity under the abutments and piers of our cultural bridges.

This paper was read at the Sixth Meeting of the Conference on Science, Philosophy and Religion in Their Relation to the Democratic Way of Life, held August 23-27, 1945, at Columbia University. It appeared in the volume Approaches to Group Understanding, published by the Conference in 1947 and distributed by Harper and Brothers in New York.

GÖTTERMACHT UND GOTTESFREIHEIT

Von *Fritz Marti*

ὥσπερ εἰσὶν θεοὶ πολλοὶ καὶ κύριοι
πολλοί   (1. Korinther 8, 5)

Für den Aufgeklärten gab es keine Götter mehr und kaum ein Bewußtsein von den Mächten, die seine und seiner Zeit Herren waren. Durch den Auftrieb des Verstandes war es ihm gelungen, sich auf der Oberfläche der Seele zu halten, die ihm keine Zeitstürme tief aufwühlten, und so blieb er leicht im Gleichgewicht. Er war ein bescheidentlich glücklicher Mensch. Auch bleibt das verständige Glück der Aufklärung noch vielen beschieden.

Manchmal kommt es mir vor, es sei das eigentliche Glück Amerikas. Doch weiß ich wohl, daß der Anschein eines einzigen Eigentlichen keinem Lande und keinem Volk gerecht wird. Zur eigentlichsten Geschichte Amerikas gehört auch die Fülle des Segens, welchen die Einwanderer und Ansiedler empfingen von ihrem Gotte, der ihnen menschliche Wege wies in der Wildnis. Mochte auch das Gottesbild abergläubische Züge aufweisen und der verständigeren Strenge der Aufklärer Anstoß geben, so suchte doch stets die tiefere Frömmigkeit in dem Bilde nicht einen der Götter, sondern Gott. Darum hat auch das Bild bis in unsere Zeit seine Kraft bewahrt. Erst neuerdings ist die biblische Berufung des auserwählten Volkes Gottes ihrer religiösen Weite hie und da beraubt worden und verengt auf eine angebliche Bevorzugung der Bevölkerung der Vereinigten Staaten, und ist so schier etwas aufgestiegen wie das Bild eines Gottes der Amerikaner.

Möglich wird ein derartiges lebensverengendes Gebilde nur darum, weil auch heute noch gerade Gott gar gerne verbildlicht wird als der größte und einzig wahre unter den Göttern. Aber dies ist keine den Amerikanern besondere Vorstellung. Der allmächtige, geheimnisvolle Jemand ist kein neuer Gott der neuen Welt. Auch die alte läßt nicht gern von dem großen Gottesbild, das ihr in ihren Wirrnissen segensreich vorschwebte. Gott zu suchen nicht hinter sondern noch vor den Bildern Gottes, ist schwierigste Pflicht.

Von den Göttern zu reden, scheint leicht. Wer glaubt noch an Götter! Ihre Zeit ist vorbei. Einst hatten sie Macht. Der Mensch diente ihnen gern. Sie hatten ihn dem Zwang der Dämonen enthoben. Dankbar pries er sie. Aber im Preis seiner Rede wurde ihre Gestalt poetisch. Auf daß sie nicht entschwebten in die Überwelt der Poesie, suchte der Theolog ihren bestimmten Begriff. Begreifen wollte sie der verehrende Mensch als die der Welt Mächtigen. Doch als Begriffene sind sie Vergangene. Der Begreifende bestimmt sie als mächtig in ihrem Zeitalter allein. So entspringt dem erst scheuen Gedanken die Götterdämmerung. Und es scheint nun leicht, zu erzählen von den göttlichen Gestalten der Vergangenheit.

In Wahrheit haben die Götter das, was unbedingt scheint an ihrer Macht, von Gott, auch wenn es der Mensch noch nicht weiß. Mancher kann es nicht wissen, weil er glaubt, Gott sei der große Machthaber, der Allgewaltige aus bloßer Übermacht. So stellt sich wohl ein Mensch vor, Gottes Macht sei die Gewalt, verwirklichen zu können, was ihm immer einfalle. Doch daß keine Gewalt unbedingt ist, ersah schon das kluge Schülerlein in der Frage, ob Gott eine Felsmasse so schwer schaffen könne, daß es über seine eigene Kraft gehe, sie hochzuheben. Gewalt ist stets etwas Bedingtes. Gott aber ist gewaltlos. Nur darum kann ihm nichts widerstehen. Ahnt dies der Mensch, so spürt er auch, daß die Unbedingtheit Gottes wesentlichen Anspruch hat auf die menschliche Seele. Nur weil die Seele in allem Drange der Welt Gott erfahren kann als das nie drängende Dringendste, als zwangloseste Unbegrenztheit und deswegen als unweigerliche Heimkehr, nur darum ist die Seele im tiefsten Grunde frei. Gottes unbedingten Anspruch auf sie empfindet das zagende Gemüt als schier drohend, und so vermag etwa das Bewußtsein, Gott sich gegenüber zu stellen als den völlig Andern, im Bilde unwiderstehlicher Macht. Leichter zu tragen ist göttliche Gewalt als die gewaltlose Gegenwart Gottes.

Von Gott zu reden ist schwer, doppelt schwer für uns, die wir an keinen der Götter mehr glauben dürfen, auch nicht an die Vergötterung Gottes. So schwer war es nicht, als unsere Väter noch von Gott redeten als von dem größten, einzigen Gotte. Uns ist das nicht mehr verstattet. Vor uns kamen die Großen, Frömmsten, die nicht leichthin redeten, weil sie nicht lästern wollten. Ihnen mußten wir lauschen. Darum ist es uns die größte Lästerung, Gott zu preisen als den größten der Götter. Groß mag die Lobpreisung sein, lästerlich ist sie doch. Schwer ist es, von Gott zu reden, denn gar zu lange mußte selbst das Wort Gott als Namen dienen für den einen Gott, dem gerade das Zeitalter diente.

Gott ist keiner unter den Göttern. Aber ohne Gott gibt es keine Göttermacht. Ungreifbar zwingen den Gottlosen dämonische Gewalten, die umgehen in seiner Seele. Geängstigt dreht sich der Mensch um sich selbst. Aber er kann sich nicht verstehen und darum nicht feststehen, denn er weiß nicht, was ihn umtreibt. Und kein Zauber vernichtet die unfaßliche Gewalt. Zaubernd möchte sie wohl der Mensch sich geneigt machen. Doch die Gewalten, die sein Inneres zwingen, haben keine Neigung. Neigen kann sich nur, wer Jemand ist. Dem Menschen geneigt ist, wer ihm gebietet. Durch das Gebot kann der Mensch dem Unfaßlichen entgegensetzen ein Ja oder ein Nein. «Du sollst» und «Du sollst nicht», mit solchem Machtspruch erlösen die Götter den Menschen von der dumpfen Besessenheit. So erweisen sich ihm die innern Gewalten als Kundgebung dessen, was der Gott will, oder des andern, was der Gott verbietet. Leichter wird dem Menschen das Leben unter der Macht der Götter, bleibt ihm ihr Wille auch Rätsel.

Einem der Götter sich zu eigen zu geben, ist dem Menschen gedeihlich. Es erhebt ihn, einem Gotte anzuhangen, denn alsdann vermag er, die Vielfältigkeit seiner Natur zu bewerten in

Hinsicht auf den Willen seines Gottes, der ihn der wechselnden Willkür menschlichen Wollens enthebt.

Der Gott offenbart einen eigenen Willen. Vorerst scheint er nur Unterwerfung menschlicher Willkür zu wollen und als Folge zielfeste Beruhigung und Befriedigung der menschlichen Seele. Aber der Mensch ist in die Welt versenkt, nicht nur in seine seelischen Regungen. An der Welt hat er teil, und sie an ihm. Was sie nicht verstattet, ist ihm verwehrt. Was er zu verwirklichen vermag, muß in ihr mindestens möglich sein. Kann er sich nun einordnen in die Ziele seines Gottes, so ist diese Ordnung nichts Widernatürliches. So erscheinen denn dem Gotte unterworfen nicht nur die Maße des Menschen, sondern auch die mannigfaltigen Möglichkeiten der Natur, die den Menschen umfängt. Der Gott erweist sich nicht nur als Herr des Menschen, er beansprucht auch Herrschaft über die Natur.

Das ist nicht absonderlich. Die mannigfaltigen Gegebenheiten menschlicher Umwelt sind ja noch nicht Natur für den Menschen. Dem Primitiven ordnen sie sich nicht als ein einheitliches Natürliches, sondern sie umstellen ihn als vielfach Magisches, an dem er auf mancherlei widerspruchsvolle Weise teilhat. Insofern die primitive, magische Welt das dem Menschen ursprünglich Natürliche ist, so erweist sich der Begriff einer Natur als etwas Künstliches, Spätes. Nicht die anfängliche Erfahrung, erst das spätere Begreifen zeigt dem Menschen seine Umwelt als Natur. «Natur» ist ein begriffliches Gebilde, hat also teil an geistigen Grundrichtungen. Richtet sich nun der Mensch gründlich aus auf seinen Gott, so erweist sich in seinen Begriffen auch die Natur als auf den Gott als innersten Mittelpunkt gerichtet. Das theozentrische Weltbild fügt sich zwanglos wie eine schützende Schale um die Geistigkeit des seinem Gott ergebenen Menschen. Im Geiste dieses Menschen ist allerdings das Verhältnis umgekehrt: Erst weil der Gott Grund und Mitte der Natur ist, hat er auch unbedingten Anspruch auf die Unterordnung des Menschen.

Oder ist der Anspruch eines Gottes nicht unbedingt? «Sintemal es sind viel Götter und viel Herrn.» Was wissen wir von ihren Rechten?

Wißbar ist das Wesentliche von den Göttern, und sagbar das, was uns not tut, von ihnen zu wissen. Sagen darf man es wohl, und es konnte auch fast zu jeder Zeit gehört werden. Das Gehörte bedachtsam zu wollen, ist das Wagnis. Denn das Wißbare wollen heißt, die herrschende Macht der Götter innerlichst brechen.

Zuinnerst spüren wir schon früh, welcher Segen uns überkommt, wenn wir vorbehaltlos unter der Herrschaft eines Gottes stehen können. Später, wenn die Vorbehalte den Gott schon der Vergangenheit anheimgegeben haben, kommt uns auch mählich das Wissen, wie segenspendend er gewesen. Es hat den Anschein eines traurigen Wissens, da das Wissen um den Gott die Wiederkunft seiner Herrschaft verwehrt. Insgeheim mögen wir dem Gotte nachtrauern, ob wir's auch nicht bewußt wahrhaben wollen.

Unsäglich ist die Trauer nicht. Sagen sollen wir uns, was in uns bereits antönte, als wir die ersten Vorbehalte wagten, zur Zeit, da wir die Herrschaft unseres Gottes zu verstehen begehrten in ihrer Rechtmäßigkeit. Damals geschah unser Abfall, denn keiner der Götter hält stand vor der Frage der Rechtmäßigkeit.

Segen spenden kann ein Gott nur, solange er fraglos herrscht. Darum sucht mancher willentlich seiner Seele Sicherheit darin, bohrender Fragen bar zu bleiben. Aber der Wille hat keine solche Macht. Einige scheint die gnädige Macht der Götter zu bewahren vor fragendem Abfall. Andere scheint ein übler Eigenwille zu treiben, oder schlimme Neugier scheint sie heranzuschieben an das leichtzu lüftende Geheimnis der Götter. Diesen wird gottlos die Welt. Unwahr scheint ihnen nun alles, was heilig hieß, heillos die Wirklichkeit selbst. Aber die Heillosigkeit selber ist Schein.

Wohl weicht jeder Gott der unwiderstehlichen Frage nach seiner Rechtmäßigkeit. Wohl bringt uns die Frage um den Segen der Götter. Ausweichen dürfen wir ihr nicht. Denn die

Frage selber ist rechtmäßig. Es ist nicht unrecht, sie zu stellen. Unrecht täten wir, wollten wir ihr uns entziehen, wenn sie erst einmal in uns anzuklingen beginnt als wie ein ferner Stundenschlag unseres Schicksals. Geschick ist es für uns, die Herrschaft unseres Gottes in Frage ziehen zu müssen. Aber im ersten Anklingen der Frage ist schon Verheißung.

Was antönt, ist herrlicher als die segensreiche Herrschaft des Gottes. Müssen wir auch des sichernden Segens entbehren, so ist viel gewisser die Sicherheit, daß wir keinem vorbehaltlos anhangen dürfen, der nicht letztlich rechtmäßig gebieten kann. Diese Gewißheit ist der tiefste Grund wahrer Frömmigkeit. Und die Frage nach der Rechtmäßigkeit der Götter ist eine fromme Frage. Die Antwort ist keine Neuigkeit. Fast allen Zeiten wurde verkündigt, die Herrschaft eines jeden Gottes habe ihr Ende, und oft wurde auch in Worten gesagt, was der eigentliche Sinn solcher Verkündigung sei: nicht Schadenfreude über die Götterdämmerung, sondern – wie frühmorgendliche Schauer kommenden Lichts hinter dem darum dunkleren Gebirg – die aufdämmernde Freude Gottes.

Nur ist allzu oft Gott wiederum bildlich geschaut worden als der größte unter den Göttern. Solches Schauen ist uns nicht mehr verstattet. Wir sollen tiefer und stiller sehen. Gott ist nicht Jemand. Wer einen Jemand zu sehen vermeint, der hat nur die Anschauung eines der vielen Götter und Herren. Ist er fromm, so gibt er sich zu, daß das Bild mehr verhüllt als offenbart. Wer weiß, daß den endlichen Gestalten der Götter keine bedingungslose Ehre gebührt, der kann ihnen die frömmste, letzte Ehre erweisen; er kann sie ihrer Vergangenheit anheimgeben.

Tiefe Trauer umschattet das Begräbnis einer Gottesgestalt. Und doch erfüllen die begrabenden Hände eine heilige Pflicht. Was sie tun, muß getan werden, aber der Tuende ist nicht der Gebende. In Rembrandts Radierung (B83) fällt auf die dem Haupte des tot vom Kreuze Genommenen sich stützend entgegenstreckende Hand das Licht, das sie als die im Grunde

Empfangende ersichtlich macht. Gegenständlich ist es nur das Licht einer Fackel. Das Übersinnliche bedarf keines unglaubwürdigen Wunderlichts, um sichtbar zu werden. Es vergewaltigt nicht. Es läßt frei. In dem unbedingten Freilassen alles Natürlichen wird das Göttliche sogar im Unlebendigen sichtbar, so wie uns Hodler die Berge sehen gelehrt («Grand Muveran»; Chicago Art Institute. Und andere Bergbilder Hodlers.). Wird das Lebendige wahres Bild Gottes, so erwahrt es sich erst recht im Bilde des Todes. Gott ist über Leben und Tod.

«Gott ist nicht Jemand.» So ganz einfach kann es Medicus unserer Zeit sagen. Und das ist vielleicht das Neue, das Einfache, das der Vergötterung nicht mehr bedarf.

Schelling nannte Gott «das allerfreieste Wesen» (Werke 1861, VIII, 308). Die Götter aber sind nicht im Grunde frei. Darum ist es in unserer Zeit endlich ein Unrecht geworden, von Gott zu reden als von einem Gott. Darin wurde die Zeit reif. Es ist nicht ein neues Zeitalter, das angebrochen oder im Anbrechen ist. Einander ablösende Epochen gehören der bloßen Vorstellung an. Wir können uns keinen Anfang und kein Ende der Zeit mehr vorstellen, und darum keine anfängliche, mittlere und Endepoche wie etwa ein Joachim von Floris, auch keine fünffache Epochenfolge, wie sie sich selbst noch Fichte zeitlich vorzustellen schien. Es gibt zwar Epochen, aber ohne begrenzte Zahl, und ohne endgültige Ablösung. Die Zeiten überdecken sich, und der Götter und Herren sind viele.

Ein Gott, der nicht mehr Herr ist, bleibt auch noch als poetische Gestalt einer der Götter. Aber das Herr-Sein ist das religiös bedeutsame. So war zum Beispiel die frühchristliche Formel entscheidend, daß Christus der Herr sei. Die Anerkennung einer Gestalt als Herr ist das Zeichen der Epoche, die darum vergeht, wenn die Herrschaft vorüber ist. Nur verliert der Herr der vergangenen Epoche nicht immer alle Macht. Obwohl nicht mehr anerkannt als Herr, mag er untergründig den Menschen weiterhin beherrschen, gleichgültig ob er einen neuen Namen erhalte als Irrgeist oder Teufel, oder ob er namenlos

Göttermacht und Gottesfreiheit

wirke in der darum ihrer selbst ungewissen Seele. Deswegen gebührt es auch dem Menschen, nicht aus Willkür unberufen die Macht der Götter anzutasten. Nur Gott kann sie so überwinden, daß nichts Gespenstisches zurückbleibt.

Nur sofern unsere Berufung für Gott ist, sind wir berufen, gegen die Götter aufzutreten, das heißt, die Götter recht genau als das zu erkennen und zu nehmen, was sie sind. Jedes Einstehen für Gott ist geistigster Kampf und damit allerdings Kämpfen für die Herrschaft des Geistes. Wohl sah der Abt von San Giovanni in Fiore, daß diese Herrschaft kommen muß, aber so wenig wie sie kam zu Beginn des dreizehnten Jahrhunderts, so wenig kommt sie heute oder zu irgend einer einmaligen Zeit. Das Reich des Geistes ist keine äußerliche Endepoche, sondern seine Stille ist ganz innerlich und nicht einmal eine ganz gewiß reifende Frucht getreulichen Dienens. Die Wirklichkeit hat ihres stillen Grundes nie entbehrt, und doch soll die Stille immer erst noch werden. Auch der leiseste, frömmste Diener ist gar zu zudringlich.

Es ist, als entzöge sich Gott der ihm lästerlichen und lästig werdenden Vergötterung und redete nur noch, wo der Mensch nicht hindringt, ganz im Geheimen, aus selbstlosester Ferne gleichsam, obzwar in forderndster Nähe.

Die nahe Freiheit Gottes offenbart, was zwangsmäßig ist an der Göttermacht. Als bestimmte Gestalten müssen die Götter das ihre fordern und können das nicht Übereinstimmende nicht dulden. Das gilt auch noch von dem vergötterten Gott derer, sie sich allzukühn Christen nennen. Nicht schwächlicher Weise unduldsam sind die Götter. Ihre Ausschließlichkeit ist ihre Stärke. Aber gerade in dieser Stärke ihrer Natur sind sie unfrei, eifersüchtige Götter, gezwungene Zwingherren. Eine andere Macht ist ihnen nicht gewährt. Wohl ist ihre Macht nicht physisch sondern geistig, und geistiger Anspruch ist stets Anspruch an Freie. Der Mensch verliert im Dienste der Götter nie völlig seine Freiheit aus Gott. Die Götter selber aber sind unfreie Mächte.

Fritz Marti

Der Macht entledigt entschweben die Götter in den Äther der Poesie, durch die sie die Seelen immer noch erheben, doch nicht mehr beherrschen können. Der von ihnen nicht mehr beherrschte Geist des Menschen nennt erinnernd die Göttergestalten mythisch, erkennend, daß sie ursprünglich nicht poetische Seligkeit waren, sondern herrliche Macht.

Ist nun in unserem Jahrhundert gar vielen der Christus nicht mehr Herr, so ist für sie seine Macht nur die mythische der Vergangenheit. Darum nennt die christgläubige Kirche solche Zeitgenossen gottlos, muß sie doch verneinen, daß der christliche Mythus wie jeder andere einmal eine entschiedene Vergangenheit werden könnte. Dies Nein entspringt tiefgründigem Glauben, und wir wollen es nicht leichthin beiseite schieben. Aber der Andersgläubige und der Ungläubige sieht darin eine schier leichtfertige Verneinung der Freiheit. Gott ist das allerfreieste Wesen. Doch eben um Gottes willen müssen die gläubig Getreuen anscheinend unheilbare Schnitte machen zwischen sich und den Mitmenschen. Der Gesalbte sagt: «Ich bin nicht gekommen, Frieden zu bringen, sondern ein Opfermesser.» Vielleicht denkt er an die Opferung Isaaks, denn er sagt weiterhin, «wer Sohn oder Tochter mehr liebt denn mich, der ist mein nicht wert». (Matth. 10, 34 und 37.)

Wahrscheinlich gab es nie eine Zeit der Glaubenseinigkeit. Gerade die größten Mythen haben nicht nur geeint, sondern auch getrennt. Sollten wir auf einen welteinenden nachchristlichen Mythus harren? Wird ein neuer Gott weltweite Herrschaft gewinnen, der den Christen ebenso Lästerung und Schreckbild sein wird, wie es einst der christliche Gott den Juden war? Oder sollten wir, statt zu warten auf einen neuen Mythus, uns wieder einmal eine Vernunftreligion ausdenken mit so bescheidenen Ansprüchen, daß niemand sich die Mühe machen würde, ihnen zu widersprechen?

Ist eine Vernunftreligion von aller Offenbarungsreligion gründlich verschieden? Sind sie nicht beide allzu menschlichen Ursprungs, und ist es nicht beiden wesentlich, für alle Welt letzte Geltung zu beanspruchen?

Was aber hat es auf sich mit aller Letztgültigkeit? Warum kann der Mensch solch verpflichtenden Ansprüchen nicht ausweichen und sich zufrieden geben mit einem Bilde der Wirklichkeit, das anspruchslos bloß Bild bleibt?

Der Mensch weiß um die Welt. Teil der Welt ist auch er. So wird er seiner selbst gewahr, einmal als weltlich bedingt, ein andermal als wissend um die Bedingungen der Welt. Als wissendes Wesen wird er sich selber ein Rätsel. Wissen heißt, sich auseinandersetzen mit dem Gewußten, heißt sich den gegenständlichen Dingen gegenübersetzen, heißt nicht mehr völlig daheim sein unter den Dingen. Wo bin ich eigentlich daheim als eben Dieser und als Ich? Die dinglichen Zusammenhänge halten mich nicht. Ich brauche Halt noch diesseits der Welt, in einer vorweltlichen Wirklichkeit. Das bloße Gehaltensein als Ding unter Dingen genügt mir nicht. Ein Ich wird erst durch das gehalten, woran es sich halten kann. Vertrauen kann der Mensch nur dem, zu dem er treulich zu stehen vermag. Halt findet er, wo er Treue schuldet. Aber getreu ist er nicht als Irgendeiner, sondern als eben Dieser. Als Dieser sucht er die ihm eigenste Haltung. Was ihm Halt gibt, mag einen anderen nicht halten. Was einem anderen aufgegeben ist, ist nicht auf die gleiche Weise meine Aufgabe. Ich muß mich halten an mein Eigenstes. Dies aber liegt noch vor mir. Was ich war, und was ich bin, ist noch nicht mein Eigentlichstes. Das Gewesene und das Seiende werden mir eigen nur in dem, das mir eigentlich obliegt. In einer Welt ohne Pflichten kann ich mich nicht finden als ein Ich. Als Dieser finde ich Halt an dem, wozu ich da bin. Ich soll handeln, wie ich allein handeln kann. Das Bild der Welt, die mir wahrlich eigen ist, muß mir meine Stelle weisen, auf die eben ich berufen bin. Das eigentlich menschliche Weltbild bindet den besonderen Menschen, nicht als gezwungenes Ding sondern als treu Handelnden. Seine Welt ist eine Welt von Handlungen. Ihr Bild ist nicht dinglich wissenschaftlich, es ist mythisch.

Das Mythische bindet, aber es löst auch. Der Mythus spricht den Menschen an als Handelnden und weist ihm seinen Platz, seinen Dienst, und – so möchte es scheinen – seine Rolle. Von seinem Platz soll er nicht weichen, seinen Dienst soll er getreulich tun, seine Rolle scheint ihm vorgeschrieben. Er scheint nun völlig gebunden. Wäre das Sein wie dieser Schein, so wäre der mythengebundene Mensch wieder unfrei. Aber so ist es nicht. Der Mythus redet nicht wie ein Bühnenbuch, er schreibt nicht vor, er fordert auf. Forderung ist er, der Mensch solle handeln, suchend nach der rechten Handlung. Diese deutet der Mythus nur an. Das mythische Bild bedarf immer der Deutung. Die muß der Mensch wagen. Das Wagnis allein führt auf Letztes.

Hätten Handlungen keine Beziehung auf Letztes, und wäre ihr Sinn bestenfalls immer eine vorletzte Wahrheit, so würden gerade solch pragmatische Wahrheiten den Handelnden einschränken auf die naturbestimmten Bewegungsmöglichkeiten eines unfreien Wesens.

Letztgültigkeit des Weltbildes allein ist einem freien Wesen gemäß. Aber kein bloß für alle erdachtes Weltbild hat einen letztgültigen Platz für mich. Statt bloß beweisbarer Allgemeingültigkeit brauche ich einen Erweis von Einzelgültigkeit. Es soll sich erweisen, daß auf mich Einzelnen gezählt ist in der Wirklichkeit. Bliebe aber solches Zählen stehen bei dem einzelnen Einen, so erhöbe es ihn nicht in die Freiheit Gottes sondern erniedrigte ihn zu einem vergötterten Menschen. Die Eins des Einzelnen muß also auch wiederum als Nichts erachtet werden können. Wäre er nicht auch nichtig, so hätte der Einzelne Einzigartiges an sich nur als Spielart der Natur. In seiner Nichtigkeit aber kann sich offenbaren sein Daheimsein in der Freiheit Gottes. Herkömmliche Rede könnte es knapp und klar sagen: Gott braucht mich unbedingt, und er kann meines Dienstes auch gar wohl entbehren. So ist es offenbar.

Offenbarung nennt der Mensch die ihm angemessene Schau der Wirklichkeit. Er behauptet nicht, es sei ihm darin alles klar. Er ist es ja nicht, der letztlich weiß, was Rechtes er tun soll. Sein Tun ist nichts gewißlich Berechnetes, sondern gewissenhaft Gewagtes. Er handelt. Aber er weiß auch, daß er ein un-

Göttermacht und Gottesfreiheit

nützer Diener ist. Er weiß es, denn der Mythus berichtet bereits über das noch zu Geschehende. So ist der Mensch auch schon über die Mühen der Gegenwart hinaus. Aus göttlicher Freiheit kann er zurücksehen auf das Jetzt und Hier. Frei blicken kann er auf seinen Dienst, als wäre er bereits daraus entlassen. Ernsthaftestes Dienen ist von ihm gefordert, und doch zählt es letztlich nicht eben mehr als Nichts. So nur bezieht sich sein Tun auf Letztes.

Für Gott ist das Zeitliche bereits vorüber, denn Gott ist nicht gebunden in die Zeit. Darum ist in der Offenbarung Gott immer bereits vorüber. So ist es Moses nicht verstattet, die Herrlichkeit des Herrn zu sehen, bevor sie vorübergegangen. Der sich offenbarende Gott will seine Hand halten über den in einer Felskluft stehenden Moses. «Und wenn ich meine Hand von dir tue, wirst du mir hintennach sehen; aber mein Angesicht kann man nicht sehen.» (2. Mose 33, 23.) Der Offenbarte ist schon vorüber. Gerade in der Offenbarung setzt er sich als Vergangenen. Diesen können die Schriftgelehrten hinterher auslegen. Und mit seiner Vergangenheit verbindet den Menschen die ihm vormals so und nicht anders vorgeschriebene rituelle Handlung.

Nur wendet sich der Ritus auch ans Künftige, an den Gott, der frei ist von der Vergangenheit, die er sich in der Offenbarung gesetzt. Als erst noch Kommenden ruft ihn der Ritus an, als Richter und Rechtfertiger.

Vergangen und künftig und immerdar gegenwärtig, so beschreibt mythische Rede Gott. Das versteht der Verstand der Aufklärung nur als Widerspruch und als dunkles Rätsel. Aber auch dem Offenbarungsbegierigen muß Gott erscheinen als im Dunkel verhüllt. Nicht zu nahe tritt darum das Volk dem Schein eines mutmaßlich zaubermächtigen Jemand. «Also trat das Volk von ferne; aber Mose machte sich hinzu ins Dunkel, da Gott innen war.» (2. Mose 20, 21.)

Durchsichtig werden die Bilder des Mythus, so man mählich begreift, es sei angemessen, Gott das allerfreieste Wesen zu nennen. Klar wird es dann, daß wesentliche Freiheit nicht darin besteht, bloß seiner Natur gemäß zu handeln, sondern zumindest darin, seine Natur als entschiedene Vergangenheit hinter sich zu bringen. So ist Gottes Natur allererst gesetzt als eine Vergangenheit. Vergegenwärtigen soll sich der Fromme das Vergangene. Es aber der Vergangenheit entheben soll und kann er nicht.

Christlicher Lehre ist schon bei Paulus die geschehene Offenbarung entschiedene Vergangenheit. Nur ein ungläubiger Thomas will Erfahrungshände legen auf das, was bereits entschieden ist. Was bloß Natur ist an Gott, mußte begraben werden. Und der Ritus verlangt, es sei zu verzehren. Auslegen dürfte man vielleicht, dies sei immerdar das vor Gott allein angenehme Opfer, daß Gottes Natur nichts Letztes ist, sondern immer Sterbendes um des lebendigen Geistes willen. Darum ist das Himmelreich in der Zukunft, solange uns das Ewige in die Zeit versenkt erscheint.

Aber der Theolog wird wohl unberufener Auslegung wehren wollen. Und wir wollen nichts hineinlegen in das längst allen Dargelegte. Philosophische Aufgabe ist es nur, zu erinnern, daß auch dem Mythus und der Kirchenlehre der Gedanke der Offenbarung als eines Vergangenen nicht fremd ist, und zu warnen vor einer Gleichsetzung Gottes mit dem bereits Vorübergegangenen der Offenbarung. Es könnte wohl mit Schärfe gesagt werden, daß für Gott das Nichtmehrsein Bedingung ist des Seins als Allerfreiestes.

An dieser Wahrheit hat auch die Aufklärung ihren geringen Teil, für die die Götter entschieden nicht mehr sind. Der gewichtigere Anteil gehört aber als tägliche Bitte dem gläubigen Gemüt, auf daß es nicht Gott vergöttere; und er gehört als stetiger Richtungszeiger dem Gott suchenden Geist, sei er auch unfähig zu gläubigem Bekenntnis, auf daß er nie glaube, Gott sei unter den Göttern zu finden. Das allerfreieste Wesen findet sich nicht unter den Machthabern.

This paper appeared in the volume of essays <u>Natur und Geist</u> presented to Fritz Medicus on his seventieth birthday, April 23, 1946, and published by Eugen Rentsch in Erlenbach near Zürich. The English translation came out in summer 1953 in Volume 6, Part 3, of FAITH AND FREEDOM, Liverpool, England.

The power of the gods and the freedom of God

I Cor 8:5: for there are many gods and many Lords.

FOR the man of the Enlightenment the gods were no longer real, and he retained almost no awareness of the powers which, nevertheless, were his lords and the lords of his time. Rationalization had given him a buoyancy which allowed him to float on the surface of the soul. The depths of his soul remained undisturbed by any tempests of his time. He could maintain an easy equilibrium. He was a modestly happy man. Even now, the rational happiness of enlightenment is a gift enjoyed by many.

Sometimes I think this is the specific happiness of Americans. But of course I know that it is unfair to speak of a single trait which distinguishes a country or a people. Though America shared and still shares the happiness of enlightenment, another part of American history is the plenitude of blessings which the immigrants and settlers received from their God, who showed them human paths in the wilderness. Though their image of God had superstitious traits, traits objectionable to the more rational severity of men of enlightenment, yet the more profound piety would always seek God, in the image, rather than one of the gods. Thus, up to the present, the image has not lost its strength. Only very recently insidious weaknesses have appeared. The biblical calling of a chosen people has been robbed of its religious broadness by those who would narrow it down to an alleged preferment of the inhabitants of the United States and, in this manner, something has been fashioned which looks very much like the image of a god of Americans.

Such an image makes life pinched and poor. The image itself can be conceived at all only because to this day there is a widespread desire to depict God as the greatest among the gods, perhaps as the one among them who alone is true. Still, this kind of picture is not the peculiar property of Americans. The all-powerful mysterious Somebody is not a new god of the New World. The Old World too is loath to take leave of the great image of God which hovered over the vicissitudes of the world and which bestowed so many blessings. It is a most difficult duty to seek God, not there, not beyond the images of God, but here.

It seems easy to recognize images as images, easy to talk about the gods. Who would still believe in gods! Their time is past. Once upon a time they had power, Man gladly served them. They had lifted him up from among those who stood under the coercion of ineffable demons. In gratitude, man praised the gods. But while he bestowed praise upon them, his very words also endowed them with poetic properties. In order to prevent their departure into the super-world of poetry, the theologian would endeavour to portray the gods appropriately. Worshipping man wanted to comprehend the gods as the ones who quite properly have power over the world. Comprehension, however, locates the gods in the past. Whosoever really comprehends them understands why they had their power during their age. Thus, comprehending thought, though starting with worshipful reticence, eventually issues in the dusk of the day of the gods. And when things have gone that far, it seems easy to tell the tale of the definite deities of the past.

In truth, that which seems to be unconditional in the proper power of the gods is appropriated from the forceless unconditionality of God, even though man does not yet know it. Many a man cannot know it because he believes that God is a great potentate, almighty because of sheer preponderance. Such a man will imagine the might of God as a power to bring about anything which, perchance, should strike God's fancy. But there is no unconditional power. Power is something strictly conditional. This was understood even by the clever little boy in Sunday school who inquired whether it would be possible for God to create a mass of rock so big that it would be beyond the power of God to lift it up. Power in the sense of force is conditional. God however is forceless. On that account alone, nothing can resist God. As soon as this truth dawns in the mind of man, man becomes aware, somehow, that the unconditionality of God makes essential claims upon the soul of man. The soul is free in its deepest ground, only because, in the midst of every urgency of the world, man can experience God as that which is most urgent but which never urges, as that which never coerces and which, therefore, is truly boundless and, finally, on account of its very boundlessness and forcelessness, that which is the irresistible call for man's freest homecoming. The soul is free, but the fearsome mind senses God's unconditional claim as something very nearly threatening, and the result is that, in consciousness, man is capable of setting up God over against himself, as One who is altogether Other, and whose image is the picture of overpowering forces. Man finds it easier to bear up under divine force, rather than to endure the forceless presence of God.

It is difficult to speak of God, doubly difficult for us who no longer dare believe in one of the gods, nor in the deification of God. It was never so difficult in the time of our fathers who still spoke of God as of the greatest god, the only god. For us, such speech is no longer permissible, because there have been those great souls whose profoundest piety forbade them to speak rashly, lest they should blaspheme. We had to listen to them. Having listened, we have understood that, for us, it would be the greatest blasphemy to praise God as the greatest among the gods. Such praise can be great, it is nevertheless blasphemous. It is difficult to speak of God, since, for too long a time, the very word God had to serve as a name for the particular god whom the age happened to serve.

God is not one among the gods. But without God, the gods have no power. The power which the gods wield brings a degree of liberation, and the gods appear as liberators. Their appearance reflects something of the freedom of God.

A godless man is in the clutches of demonic powers which he cannot apprehend, nor comprehend, but which haunt him nevertheless. Frightened, he is made to revolve about his own haunted self. He cannot understand himself and therefore he can find no firm footing, no fixed stand, for he cannot know what haunts him and makes him revolve. He is in the power of something ineffable, and there is no magic which could annihilate the ineffable. Still man would try magic in order, at least, to make these powers favourably inclined. They, however, coerce him inwardly without being able to have an inclination. Impersonal powers have no inclinations. To be inclined toward this or that means to be personal, to be Somebody. And to have an inclination toward man means to make a claim upon man, since man is fit to acknowledge a claim, and since this fitness is peculiarly human. Man experiences such a claim as a commandment.

It is the commandment which enables man to defend himself against the ineffable, with a definite Yes, or an outspoken No. "Thou shalt" and "thou shalt not," these are the peremptory words by which the gods liberate man from his numb possessedness. Now he can grasp the haunting powers as manifestations of what the god either wants or forbids. Though the will of the god remain a riddle, man finds life easier under the commanding power of the gods.

It proves wholesome for man to dedicate himself to a god. In adhering to a god, man finds himself elevated, for he finds himself able to evaluate the manifoldness of his own nature, in respect of the will of his god who, thus, lifts him above the changing whims of the human will.

The god reveals a will of his own. It might seem at first that he demands nothing but the submission of human arbitrariness and, as a consequence of such submission, the peace of the human soul would seem to be the god's concern. The soul has peace if it becomes calm through the firmness of its goal. Yet man is submerged not only in the billows of his soul but in the depths of the world. He partakes of the world, and the world has a part in him. Whatever is impossible, in the world, man cannot do. What he is able to do must be possible in nature. If he is able to make use of himself in the pursuit of the goals of his god, this subordination implies an order which is not counter to nature. Thus, it appears that not only the measures of man are subject to the god, but even the manifold possibilities of nature which surrounds and supports man. The god shows himself not only as the master of man, he also claims mastery over nature.

Such a claim is nothing strange, for the mere manifoldness of data which make up the environment of man does not yet amount in the mind of man to a notion of nature. For primitive man, the multiple and different data do not fall in line, as a uniform nature, they surround him as manifold magical entities in which he must have part in many contradictory ways. Insofar as this primitive magical world is what man originally experiences as natural, the notion of a nature of uniform order is something artificial and late. It is not early experience but late reflexion which makes man's environment appear as orderly nature. " Nature " is a conceptual structure which, therefore, is aligned with some fundamental trend or other of the spirit of man. If a man fundamentally align himself with his god then, in his conceptions, nature likewise must show a trend toward the god, who is its innermost centre. Not strangely, indeed, but like a sheltering shell, the theocentric world view envelopes and puts at ease the spirit of a man who is dedicated to his god. To be sure, in the mind of such a man, the relation stands in reverse: only because the god is the ground and centre of nature can he make an unconditional claim upon the allegiance of man.

Or are we to assume that the claim of a god is not unconditional? " For indeed there are many gods and many lords." What do we know as to their rights and titles.

We are able to know what is essential with regard to the gods, and what we need to know of them can be told. It is proper to tell it, and it has been told ever so often. There seldom was a time at which it could not be heard. But, having heard it, thoughtfully to align one's will with it, that is the daring adventure. For to will what is known of the gods means, at the innermost, to break their ruling power.

Inwardly we feel at an early time what bliss comes upon us when, without reservations, we can stand under the rule of a god. Later, when our reservations have already turned the god over to the turnkey, time, who must lock him up in his due abode in the past, we come to know, by and by, how much bliss the god has bestowed upon us during his rule. It seems to be a sad knowledge, since a return of the god's rule is barred by the very truth about him which we have come to know. In our secret heart we may mourn over the god although, in our conscious mind, we may be unwilling to admit it.

However, such mourning is not unspeakable. We ought to speak of it, in the inwardness of our mind, and we ought to give voice to what softly began to sound in our heart at the time at which we dared to make our first reservations, when we were desirous to understand the rule of our god in its legitimacy. That desire was our secret desertion. At that time we had already lost our god, for none of the gods can withstand the question of legitimacy.

A god can bestow bliss only as long as he rules without question. This is why many a man endeavours to remain deliberately void of probing questions. The endeavour is vain, because deliberate will has no such power. To be sure, some are saved from the inquisitive fall; it would seem they are saved by the gracious power of the gods. Others seem to be driven by an evil self-will to air the esasily lifted secret of the gods. For these latter men the world becomes godless. They come to deem everything untrue which, before, was called holy; to deem reality itself unholy. But the unholiness of reality is a deceptive appearance.

To be sure, every god gives way to the irresistible question as to his legitimacy. To be sure, that question deprives us of the blessing of the gods. Still, we dare not dodge the question. The question itself is legitimate. It is not wrong to ask it. We should be doing wrong had we a mind to withdraw from the quest, after the question has struck. It strikes like the yet far and faint stroke of the hour of our fate. It is fate if we must question the rule of our god. Yet, in the first faint sound of the question there is already Promise.

What rings in the question is the reverberation of something much more glorious than the blissful rule of the god. Though we are bound to miss the feeling of being secure in his blessings, there comes upon us an incomparably greater security, in the certainty that we dare not adhere, without question, to anyone who has no ultimate right to rule. This certainty is the deepest ground of true piety. And the question regarding the legitimacy of the gods is a pious question. The answer is nothing novel. Almost all times have heard the annunciation that the rule of every god must come to its end, and many a time it has been said, in addition and in explicit words, that the true sense of the annunciation is not any gloating over the impending dusk of the gods but the very Joy of God in the making, like early morning shivers of light dawning behind crags all the more dark.

We must remember, however, that too often God has been visualized in the image of the greatest one among the gods. For us, such visualization is no longer permissible. We are to see into greater depths, to see in calmer serenity. God is not Somebody. He who imagines that he is seeing Somebody is beholding only the image of one of the many gods and lords. If he is pious he will admit, in his heart, that the image veils more than it reveals. He who knows that the finite forms we call gods deserve no unconditional veneration can venerate them in the most pious way, resting their case before the supreme court of history which vindicates their legitimacy, as a matter of the past, in which they are buried.

The shadows of profoundest mourning hang about the burial of a god. Nevertheless the burying hands fulfil a sacred duty. What they do must be done. But the one who does it is not the one who bestows anything. In the etching of Rembrandt (B 83) a man's hand reaches up from the dark, in order to support the head of him who has been taken from the Cross, dead. A beam of light falls upon the hand and reveals it as receiving a great gift rather than bestowing a service. Objectively it is only the light of a torch. The supersensuous reality requires no unbelievable miraculous light in order to become visible. The supersensuous does no violence to anything. It leaves everything free. That which is of God leaves everything natural, free, unconditional, and thus it becomes visible even in things which lack life. In that way, Ferdinand Holder has taught us to see mountains.[1] What is living can become a true image of God. All the more does Life Eternal find verification in the image of death. God is over life and death.

"God is not Somebody." In such utterly simple words, Medicus[2] can tell the truth to our age. And that, perhaps, is the novel, the plain, which no longer needs the devices of deification.

Schelling called God "the utterly free being." The gods however are not fundamentally free. This is why, for our age, it is no longer right to speak of God as of a god. In this, our times have come of age. Ours is not a new era, come upon us, or in the making. Epochs which relieve each other like military guards belong to sheer imagination. We can no longer imagine a beginning and an end of time. Consequently we can no longer imagine an initial epoch, a middle age, and a final period, as a Joachim of Floris imagined it, nor a fivefold sequence of epochs as Fichte seems to have imagined. To be sure there are epochs, but without finite number, and without final relief. The epochs overlap, and there are many gods and many lords.

A god who is no longer lord still remains one of the gods, as an entity of poetic significance. But what is religiously significant is his being lord. Thus, for instance, the earliest Christian formula was decisive that Christ was the lord (kyrios). The recognition of a being as lord is the sign of the epoch of that lord, and the epoch passes with the recognized rule of its lord. Still, the lord of a passing or past epoch need not lose all his power. Though no longer acknowledged as lord he may yet continue to rule men, underground as it were, and regardless of either being recognized and named as a deceiving spirit or a devil, or being namelessly at work in the soul which, on account of his lacking recognition and name, is uncertain of itself. Since it is possible for gods to transfer their power underground, it behoves man not to touch the power of the gods out of sheer whim and without calling. God alone can undo the gods in such manner that nothing haunting remains.

Only insofar as we are called to seek our place in the cause of God do we have any calling to touch the gods, that is, to recognize them very accurately as the beings they are, and to treat them accordingly. Every true fight for the cause of God is a struggle for the clearest insight. It can be named variously, as a struggle for vision, an effort toward intelligence, a stand for the rule of

---

[1] "Le Grand Muveran", in the Chicago Art Institute. And other canvasses by Holder. (I had in mind "Le Grand Muveran" in the museum at Bern.)

[2] Fritz Medicus, my teacher, at seventy, in the fall of 1946, retired from the chair of philosophy at the Swiss Federal Institute of Technology where he taught for three decades and a half.

reason, a quest for the realm of the spirit. The spirit must come of age, and the age of the spirit must come. This was already clear to the abbot of San Giovanni in Fiore. But he expected the advent of the spiritual age at a definite date, and the realm of the spirit does not come at any one time. It did not come at the beginning of the thirteenth century, and it does not come today. The realm of the spirit is no outward age, no terminal epoch. Its peace is entirely inward, and it is not even a necessarily ripening fruit of faithful service. Reality was never without its innermost peace, without its still ground. Yet peace is always still in the making. And even the most reticent and pious servant is all too obtrusive and obstreperous.

It is as if God were withdrawing from an obnoxious and even blasphemous deification, as if God were speaking only where man does not penetrate, quite secretly, from a selfless distance, yet in the most challenging proximity.

The nearby freedom of God reveals what is coercive in the power of the gods. Being of definite shape and character, the gods must claim what is due them, and they cannot tolerate what does not agree with them. This is true even of the god of those who too boldly call themselves Christians and who make a god unto themselves, by means of deifying God.

The gods are intolerant in no weakly way. Their exclusiveness is their strength. But owing to this very strength of their nature they are unfree, they are jealous gods, tyrants tyrannized by their own essence. They have no other strength. To be sure, their power is not physical but mental. And every appeal to the mind, in the last analysis, is an appeal to responsible freedom. Even in the service of the gods, man cannot completely lose his freedom from God. But the gods themselves are unfree powers. Their very power marks them as unfree.

Relieved of their depressing power, the gods ascend into the ether of poetry. As poetic entities they can still elevate the mind of man but they can no longer rule his soul. In retrospect, and rid of their rule, man will call the gods mythological entities. By the word myth he signifies that, originally, these entities were more than matters of poetic bliss; they were lordly powers.

In our own century, many no longer see in Christ their Lord. For them his power is that of a myth of the past. This is why they are godless in the eyes of the Church, which believes in Christ and which, consequently, must deny that, like every other myth, the Christian myth could ever become something decidedly past. Such a denial of the ordinary historical process springs from a faith whose roots often reach into the very depth of human existence, and we do not want to make light of the denial. Still, one who believes differently, or one who is an unbeliever, cannot but see in the negation of any possible end of Christianity a slighting and almost frivolous denial of freedom. God's is the utmost freedom. Yet on the very account of God, faithful believers must make seemingly incurable incisions between themselves and their infidel contemporaries. The anointed one says: "I have not come to bring peace but a sacrificial dirk." Perhaps he is thinking of the sacrifice of Isaac, for he shortly continues, "no one who loves son or daughter more than he loves me is worthy of me."

Probably there never was a time of uniform belief. The very greatest among the myths not only brought unity but also division. Should we wait for a post-Christian myth which would unify mankind? Is the rule of a new god in the making, of a god who, in Christian eyes, will be as terrifying and blasphemous an image as was the Christian god in Jewish eyes? Or, instead of waiting for a new myth, should we again resort, for a change, to some religion of reason, to a minimal religion so modest of claims that nobody will take the trouble even to contradict it?

Is a religion of reason fundamentally different from a religion of revelation: Is not the origin of both all too human? And is it not essential for both to claim an ultimate validity, in all minds?

But what about ultimate validity? Why can man dodge such claims? Can he not acquiesce in a view of reality which, without making claims, remains but an image?

Man does view the world. And he views it as real. Furthermore, he himself is part of the world. Thus, he cannot but have a double view of himself, the first of a being conditioned by his environment, past and present, and the second of a knower of the conditions in the world. As a knower he becomes a riddle unto himself. To know means to stand off from the known, to take distance from things which become strange. To know means no longer to be quite at home among things. Where can I be at home, as this very one, and as a self? As myself, the objective context of things cannot contain me. The world of things has no hold upon me. What alone can hold me must lie hither of the world of things, not thither. My reality is on this side of the objective world, not in it, nor beyond it. My place as a mere thing among things cannot satisfy me. Things hold each other conditionally. I want more. That alone can hold me which I can hold firmly. And nothing conditional is firm enough. It affords no unconditional faith. I can have faith only in reality by which I can stand faithfully. Man finds a firm hold where he owes faith, where faithlessness would be treason unto himself. But man cannot be faithful as just anybody. If I am to be faithful it is as I, as this specific self, not as "someone." As myself I seek my specific and peculiar position, my own spiritual posture. What holds my allegiance may not at all hold another's. The task which commands the allegiance of another is not my task, strictly speaking. In order to become my task also, it requires transformation and translation. I must hold unto my own task. My task is what is most peculiarly my own. As my task it is of my future. What I was and what I am is not yet my very own. The past and the present become mine only insofar as my concern with them is also my concern with my distinguishing duty. In a world without duties I could not find myself as a self. It is my duty to do what I alone can do. As the particular self I am, I find a firm hold only upon my calling. The only view of the world which, in truth, I can call *my* world view is a view that clearly shows the place of my calling. The peculiarly human view of the world binds man, the one man in question. He is bound, but he is not coerced. He is not a thing tied among things by coercive forces. He is bound in faith; he desires faithfully to do his duty. His world is a world of cheerful quest. The image of his world cannot be objective, detached, scientific; it has to be mythical.

Myth binds but it also liberates. The language of myth addresses man as one who is to act, and it assigns him his place of action, his service, nay—so it would seem—his rôle and his character. He is not to relinquish his post, he is to serve faithfully, his very rôle seems to be prescribed. He seems to be totally bound. If this outward appearance of the mythical view were also its inner meaning, man would be irredeemably bound indeed. Bound by myth, by the letter of mythical language, man would be utterly unfree. But that is only an appearance. In truth, the myth is no scenario, no stage manager's book of lines and directions. Myth puts before us not orders but challenges. The myth itself is a challenge. Man is to act, and to seek the right action. Which action is right, the myth does not tell. The stories it tells amount to hints only. The mythological story is always in need of interpretation. Man must dare to interpret. Such daring alone can lead to the ultimately valid.

If human actions had no reference to anything ultimate, and if their meaning, at best, were a penultimate truth, such pragmatic truths would have the very effect of restricting the agent to the possibilities of movement implied in his unfree nature.

If a world view is adequately to fit a free being, it must involve ultimate validity. And ultimate validity is never the same thing for all, nor the same, once and for all time, for any one individual. No mere view made to fit all men can present a picture in which I can see my ultimately valid place. Nor could I take a place, as a responsible being, where I should be unable henceforth to seek my place anew. What I need are not logically demonstrable commonplaces, nor psychological straightjackets, but freedom for my soul and, therefore, the simple demonstration, that is, the pointing out of the place on which I can take my valid and valiant stand now, in the expectation that I shall find an equally dignified place on which to stand tomorrow. What is to be shown is that, in this world, I am not only accounted for but counted upon. However, if such counting should stop at any one contingent aspect of one of these singular units called men, it could not lift man into the freedom of God. It would degrade him to a deified entity. For a free being, deification is a degradation, for the gods can never be freed of their own nature. This chance unit of the individual, therefore, must also be counted as naught, in turn. If he were not also nothing, individual man would have uniqueness only as a matter of natural mutation. In his nothingness, however, the revelation can be made of his ultimate abode in the freedom of God. In the language of tradition, we could say it clearly and concisely: God calls me unconditionally, and he can also very well dispense with my services. Thus our true status is revealed unto ourselves.

Men call their adequate view of reality revelation. They do not usually claim that, in such a view, everything is entirely clear. After all, man as an individual is not the one who will know without fail what is the right thing he is to do. His action is not something accurately calculated, but something conscientiously ventured. He acts. But he also knows that he is a useless servant. He knows it because, in the imagery of the myth, he sees beyond the present. The myth does not predict temporal events; mystical images reduce time itself to its relative place. In this manner, man is already lifted beyond the struggles and pains of the present. Out of a divine freedom he can look back upon what is now and here. In freedom he can look upon his servitude, as if he were already discharged. The most serious service is demanded of him and yet, ultimately, it counts for nought. Thus alone can his actions refer to the ultimate.

For God, the temporal is already past. God is not tied into time. This is why, in revelations, God is always already past. Thus, Moses is not permitted to see the glory of God before it is past. The Lord who reveals himself will hold his hand over Moses who stands in a cleft of the rock. " I will cover you with my hand until I pass by; then I will take away my hand, so that you may see my back, while my face shall not be seen." (*Exodus xxiii*, 22-23). The revealed one is already past. He posits himself as past, precisely in his revelation. Afterwards, the scribes can interpret and expound this past one. And it is with God's past that man is connected by the ritual. Tradition tells him the ritual must be performed the way it was performed of yore, and in no other way.

True, the ritual faces the future too. It appeals to the God who is free from his past which he posited in revelation. The ritual invokes him as the one still to come, the Judge and the Redeemer.

Past, and future, and ever present, thus mythical speech describes God. This appears contradictory to the ratiocination of enlightenment, for which it remains a dark riddle. Even for those who avidly seek a revelation, God must appear as veiled in darkness. Not too closely, therefore, will they approach the appearance of a Somebody who seems to possess the power of magic and miracles. " The people stood off at a distance, while Moses approached the dense darkness where God was." (*Exodus xx*, 21).

The mythical images become transparent only as, by and by, we learn to see that it is more adequate to call God the utterly free being. Then it becomes clear that essential freedom is not a matter of merely acting according to one's own nature but, rather, to put one's nature into the place where it belongs, that is, to get it behind one, as one's decided past. Genuine freedom consists at least in such acts by which we posit our past. Similarly, the nature of God is a nothingness if it is not posited as a past. To be sure it is the duty of the pious man to put before him, to have present in mind, to re-present the past, the nature of God. But it is not his duty to remove the past, nor could he do it.

In Christian doctrine, the revelation that has come is a decided past, already decided at as early a time as the days when Paul wrote. Only an unbelieving Thomas will want to put the hands of experience upon that which is already decided. What is only nature of God had to be buried. And the ritual demands that it be consumed. Perhaps we may make bold to interpret that, forever, the only sacrifice acceptable before God (*oblatio acceptabilis*) is the fact that the nature of God is nothing ultimate but always something dying for the sake of the living spirit. Therefore, as long as, in our eyes, the eternal appears plunged into time, the kingdom of heaven must be of the future.

The theologian will want to put a restraint upon unauthorized interpretations. Nor is it our intention, in interpreting, to read anything novel into the old words which have long been read for all to hear. The philosophical task is only to remind ourselves that, even for the myth and for church doctrine, it is nothing strange and unheard of to say that revelation is always something past, and to caution ourselves against any identification of God with the things of revelation, which are already past. To put it sharply: for God, being past, being no longer, is the condition of being the very freest.

Of this truth, enlightenment too partakes, in a small measure, since for enlightenment the gods are decidedly no more. But the larger measure belongs to the pious heart, as its daily prayer, lest man in his heart deify God. And an important measure of the same truth belongs to the God-seeking spirit, though that spirit—in many —be unable in conscience to join in the profession of current beliefs. The God-seeking spirit is in need of our simple truth, in order that it never be tempted to believe that God can be found among the gods. The most free being is not found among wielders of power.

Schelling on God and Man

THE core question of the *Critique of Pure Reason* was: How is objective scientific knowledge possible? Kant found that the objects of science are phenomena. God is not a phenomenon. It is not possible to conceive of God as an objective entity. Theology as objective science is impossible.

The theme of the *Critique of Practical Reason* is: How is moral obligation possible? Heteronomous commands cannot possibly be obligatory, in conscience. Only a free being can be responsible. The fact of our moral responsibility makes it impossible to consider God as a heteronomous lawgiver. Moral theology is impossible as a study of allegedly binding heteronomous commandments.

How then is theology possible at all? This question is a central one in the minds of Kant's successors. Kant himself had opened the discussion.

The theological parts of the *Critique of Pure Reason* deal with "the transcendental ideal (prototypon transscendentale)."[1] "The intention of reason with its ideal is total determinateness [of reality][2] in line with rules a priori" (599). "In everything which exists one necessarily finds a universal determinateness, and what lies at its ground is a *transcendental ideal* which constitutes the highest and complete material condition of the possibility of whatever exists. The thinking of any object whatsoever is led back in content to that highest condition" (604). "Not as a *sum* [Inbegriff] but as a *ground* [Grund] does the highest reality form the basis of the possibility of all things" (607). "Now if we hypostatize this idea we will, in so doing, try to define it with all its predicates, and call it one, simple, self-sufficient, eternal, etc. The notion of such a being is the concept of God, and in this way the ideal of pure reason becomes the object of a transcendent theology. However such a use of the ... idea would go beyond the character and purpose of the idea. For reason grasped this idea as the very

---

1. Page references in the text are to the second edition (of 1787) of the *Critique of Pure Reason*.
2. The insertions in square brackets are mine.

ground of every concept of reality, but did not demand that the idea be a thing in turn, nor be given objectively. Such a thing is a fiction [Erdichtung] by means of which we sum up what we know of the idea, as if it were a separate being. We have no right to do so, nay we may not even assume the possibility of such a being, by way of an hypothesis" (608). If, illegitimately, we still do it then: "The ideal, though it now turn into a fiction, is first *realized* [realisiert], i.e., turned into an object, then *hypostatized*, and finally, through a quite natural process[3] of reason, even *personified*" (611). In so doing we follow ratiocination [Verstand] which argues "that it would seem that only in an *intelligence* could things be tied into order" (611). In short: God is not a thing, not a separate objective entity, but the idea of God is the ground of the very possibility of strictly conceiving an objective universe.

It may not be superfluous to stress the difference between ground and cause. The category of causation is a constituent of objectivity. But to seek a cause of the objective world as such is meaningless. *In the world of objects, the series of causes is endless*, and Kant might say with Thomas Aquinas "si procedatur in infinitum in causis efficientibus, non erit prima causa efficiens," but he would reject the inference: "Ergo est necesse ponere aliquam causam efficientem primam."[4] Kant would admit, of course, that a first efficient cause is what most if not all men call God. The *Critique*, however, teaches: One cannot speak of a cause of the causal order. Neither can one ignore the question concerning the ground of causation. Obviously it is that which St. Thomas means when he says: "necesse est ponere aliquid quod sit per se necessarium, non habens causam necessitatis aliunde, sed quod est causa necessitatis aliis."[5]

To operate with the concept of cause, beyond the world of objects, means to transcend the legitimate domain of ratiocination. If God were an objective entity, a thing among other things, then it might be possible to infer the existence of God from the existence of things or events immediately dependent on such a God, e.g., from miracles.

---

3. In his *Philosophy of Mythology*, Schelling investigates this natural process.
4. *Summa Theologica*, Q. 2, Art. 3, Resp.
5. *Summa Theologica*, Q. 2, Art. 3, Resp. While A. C. Pegis in 1945 still translates "est *causa* necessitatis aliis" by "*causing* in others their necessity," in 1933 the Benedictines and Dominicans of Austria and Germany had in their translation already used the word "Grund" instead of "cause."

It is such inferences for which people usually look when they ask for proof. As early as 1795, at the age of twenty, Schelling had warned: "As soon as we enter the realm of proof we step into the territory of the conditional" (I, 308).[6] And in his long footnote we read: "The proposition: God is, is the most unproven, unprovable, *groundless* proposition, as groundless as the first principle of criticism: I am!— Yet still more unbearable for a thinking head is the jabber about a plurality of *proofs* for the existence of God. As if one could make *probable* a being which is intelligible only through itself, through its absolute *oneness*; as if it were a *manysided*—historical—proposition. ... One can read such advertisements as: *Essay of a new proof for the existence of God*. As if one could make essays or trials of God, and at any moment discover something new about God! The reason for such most unphilosophical essays, like the reason for every unphilosophical procedure, lies in the inability to abstract (from the merely empirical) and, in this case, in the inability to perform the highest abstraction. Incapable thinkers would fain imagine the being of God, not as *absolute* being, but as an *existence* [Dasein] which is not absolute *by itself*, but allegedly absolute merely because one does not happen to know of anything higher. This is the empirical concept which a man will form of God, if he is incapable of abstraction. ... It is remarkable that even our language distinguishes between *real* (which is present in sensation, what acts upon me, to what I react), *existent* (what is *at all*, in space and time), and *being* (what *is*, by itself —simply independent of all conditions of time). Having completely mixed these three concepts, how could one expect to have even the slightest notion of what a Descartes or a Spinoza meant? While they spoke of absolute being, we substitute our crude notions of real, or at best the pure concept of *existence*, which is valid only in the phenomenal world, but is utterly meaningless outside."

A few years later, in 1799, Fichte wrote: "For me, God is a being entirely free of everything of sense and of every sensuous attribute, and I cannot even attribute to God the concept of existence which I can understand only as relating to the world of sense."[7]

---

6. Quotations from Schelling are cited by volume and page of the *Sämmtliche Werke* (Stuttgart and Augsburg, 1856–1861). I to X indicate the ten volumes of the Erste Abteilung, XI to XIV the four volumes of the Zweite Abteilung. The translations are mine.

7. Fichte is quoted from *Sämmtliche Werke* (Leipzig, 1844f.). The translation is mine.

Schelling in later years says: "There is no proof of the existence of God as such, because *there is no existence of God as such* [keine Existenz Gottes überhaupt]. The existence of God is instantly and immediately definite; from an indefinite being of God one cannot get anywhere. This is why neither Descartes nor his followers could obtain any *knowledge* [Wissenschaft]" (XI, 274).

Schelling means positive knowledge of the really actual God, not the merely conceptual knowledge of the essence of God, a knowledge which stops short of the existence. Schelling calls the mere knowledge of the concept or of the essence negative because it does have the merit of negating attributes—sensuous attributes for instance—which do not pertain to the divine essence. Such negative philosophy, or negative theology, has long been available, and Schelling stressed that fact as early as 1809, in his crucial book *On Human Freedom*:[8] "Since nothing is before God or outside of God, God must have in himself the ground of his existence. This is what all philosophers say; but they speak of this ground as of a mere concept, without making it real and actual. This ground of his own existence, which God has in himself, is not God absolutely considered, that is, not insofar as he exists. For it is only the ground of his existence, it is the *nature* of God in God. Though inseparable from God, it is yet a being distinguishable from God. . . . God has in himself an inner ground of his existence, and in that respect the ground precedes God as existent; yet in turn God is also the *prius* of the ground, because the ground could not be, as such, unless God existed *actu*" (VII, 357 f.).

This passage formulates the motive of Schelling's later quest for what he calls positive philosophy. His terminology requires comment, and a few historical comparisons may not be amiss. The term "negative" had systematic significance for Nicolas of Cusa, who warned us that the statements of positive theology turn easily into superstition unless corrected by negative theology. The latter points out the inadequacies and the onesidedness of positive statements. Similarly, negative philosophy is a necessary prerequisite for Schelling's positive philosophy. The first volume (XI) of his *Philosophy of Mythology* has two parts, the first an "Historical-critical Introduction" (XI, 1) and the second a "Philosophical Introduction into the Philosophy of Mythology, or Presentation of Purely Rational Phi-

---

8. Translated by James Gutmann (Chicago, 1936). I have translated this passage.

losophy" (XI, 253). This presentation is a critical survey of the main results of occidental philosophy, results which Schelling by no means rejects. They are negative in much the same critical sense in which the negative theology of Cusanus is indispensable. They also constitute the body of negative philosophy in a derogatory sense: they are bent upon essences but cannot thereby grasp existence. Gaunilo's perfect island is an essence but does not necessarily exist. Gaunilo, Thomas, Kant, and Schelling reject the ontological argument which would cull existence from essence. Schelling holds that the start must be made from existence—from the "I am who am" (Exodus 3:14; compare Schelling XIII, 270²)—and that the concept of divine essence is an inference a posteriori. The start, of course, must be nonfinite existence, nonconditional existence; in short, God as act. In that act there is nothing of a concept, that is, no dichotomy between an object or essence known, and a knower. And since reason is necessarily bent upon its object, sheer existence as yet nonobjective is beyond the reach of reason, beyond the knower. However, reason can acknowledge what sheerly is, what "is altogether" ('ἁπλῶς Ὄν) or "what only is." But as acknowledged it is no longer sheer existence, it is no longer *as* act. Nor can act be known before it occurs. It is known a posteriori. What is known a priori is the necessary. Free act can not be known as necessary. But the very freest can be recognized as what it is, as God. In 1811, Schelling wrote, in his book on *The Ages of the World*:[9] "God in his highest self *is* not revealed, he reveals himself; he *is* not real, he becomes real, precisely in order to be manifest as the most utterly free being [das allerfreieste Wesen]" (VIII, 308). The utter freedom of God is outside and above reason. Yet it is neither irrational nor forbidden to reason. Schelling seems to stand very close to Augustine's *credo ut intelligam*. God being the very ground of our freedom, and our reasoning—as Kant stressed—being possible only as responsible act, that is, through freedom, we can recognize the act of God, though never as an object of reason, yet as the immanent ground of reason itself. What is *absolutely* immanent in reason is what makes reason itself possible, as reason. Our reasoning would be nothing but a flight of obsessive ideas, were it not for the fact that our reasoning is a response to the perpetual invitation extended to us to become free. And indeed when, by means of reason,

9. Translated by Frederick Bolman (New York, 1942). I have translated this passage.

we master a problem, we experience the freedom of that mastery, nay, we find in this experience a sample case of the free life for which we are meant. This meaning of our life, this freedom always yet to be attained, this human vocation which we can joyfully acknowledge and embrace, is nothing we ourselves have picked, in the way in which, for instance, we pick our profession. It was picked for us, even before we were born. And if you would ask who picked it—a question of mythologizing trend—the answer is: God.

In recapitulation then of an already quoted word of Schelling, we can say: "There is no existence of God as such" (XI, 274). There are only acts of God. And, as far as we are concerned, these acts amount to a perpetual summons or, in other words, they are the ever-repeated invitation to us, in ever-new circumstances, to become free, by means of making ourselves responsible. If you tell me this is, at bottom, Kantian ethics, I agree. But it goes beyond Kant. Kant would not admit the possibility or, as Schelling more justly says, Kant did not see the possibility of recognizing a posteriori that every summons to responsibility, every invitation to freedom which we receive, is of God. For, if it were not, if it were not the unconditional call it is, then it would be an obsession, a happenstance psychological fact which would keep us captive in sheer conditionality and would make freedom impossible.

What Schelling calls negative philosophy or purely rational philosophy does negate the would-be philosophy of objectivism, which would turn the *I* into an *It*, and which is no philosophy at all. In Schelling's view, the two great exponents of negative philosophy were Fichte and Hegel, and its initiator—in more recent times and long after a Plato, an Aristotle, a Plotinus, and an Augustine—was Kant. Kant and Fichte and Hegel had made quite clear that the core of reason is responsibility, and that responsibility is free act. Also that God is the very spirit of freedom. But, so Schelling tells us, those three had not clearly seen that the sheer freedom of God is beyond reason, and beyond concepts. To recognize it would mean to go beyond, to go back of concepts, and to come upon acts, calls, invitations which—a posteriori—can be recognized as being of God.

In Schelling's own words, the entire argument runs thus: "Kant forbids transcendence in metaphysics. Yet he forbids it only for dogmatizing reason, that is, for a reason which would start from *itself* and, by means of inferences, would reach what exists. But he does not forbid another way, of which he did not think, because that possibility had not occurred to him. This reverse way starts from what *sheerly* exists, from the nonfinitely *existent*, in order to reach the concept of the highest *being* [Wesens], as posterius. Reason can acknowledge what *sheerly* is [jenes bloss Seiende, ἁπλῶς 'Όν] absolutely *outside* of reason, just because there is nothing of a concept in that being. That being is the opposite of every concept. Yet, while so positing it, reason still intends to make what is outside and above reason, in turn, into a content of reason. It becomes the content of reason if recognized as God, a posteriori. Reason posits the conceptless being, in order to reach the concept. It posits what transcends reason in order to transform it into the absolutely immanent, and in order to have this *absolutely* immanent at the same time as existent, which is possible only in this way. For even negative philosophy already had this absolutely immanent, but not as actually existent. . . . What is a priori incomprehensible because it is not mediated by any antecedent concept, becomes comprehensible in God, that is, it attains its concept in the concept of God. What exists non-finitely [that is in utter freedom] or what reason can not contain, becomes immanent for reason, as God. . . . God is not, as so many imagine, what is transcendent. God is what transcends reason and is made immanent, i.e. is made the content of reason. That this has been overlooked constitutes the great misunderstanding of our time." (XIII, 170)

A dozen pages earlier, Schelling states clearly in what manner positive philosophy proceeds in a way opposite to negative: "In positive philosophy I do not start from the concept of God, as previous metaphysics had endeavored, and as the ontological argument had started from. On the contrary, I must drop this very concept, the concept of *God*, in order to start from the sheerly existing, in which nothing can be conceived except the existing presence,—and in order to see whether from here there is a way to the godhead. . . . If now the godhead is the *what*, the essence . . . then I do not go from it to the being but, on the contrary, from the being to the essence. Here the being is *prius*, the essence *posterius*." (XIII, 158)

Schelling's later terminology, "negative" and "positive" philosophy, does not mean a break with his earlier position. Two or three decades earlier, in 1806, he had already voiced what we might call[*] his "empiricism," had not the customary use of the word "empiricism" endowed it with a very un-Schellinglike meaning. Schelling

---

[*] See Schelling's Darstellung des philosophischen Empirismus, X, 225.

said: "We know nothing but what is experience, says *Kant*. Quite correct; but that which alone is in experience is precisely the living, the eternal, or God.—The existence of God is an empirical truth, nay it is the ground of all experience.—He who has grasped this and has intimately understood it, has acquired a sense for Naturphilosophie. —This philosophy is not a theory. It is the real life of the spirit in and with nature." (VII, 245)

Theories are fashioned as reasonable guesses of what might be the case. Theories deal with the probable. But the godhead is no mere probability. Even the "being" of Parmenides was an anticipation of the later theological insight of a Plato, an Aristotle, and of the medievals, that the *essence* of God is what cannot not be. At twenty-three, Schelling had already said: "that to speak of God as a probability is a true blasphemy." (I, 486)

The later Schelling calls it an insight of positive philosophy, to know that the being of God is *prius* and the essence *posterius*. What he calls negative philosophy is the knowledge of essence. The proposition "God is Being, does not actually affirm that God *is*. It is not an existential but merely an attributive proposition. However, this to-be-Being is also a being, only not the being of God *as God*. Descartes thought he had proven the latter, by means of the ontological argument, but he had only proven the essence, posited in thought. This we can also call the pure being-in-reason, or the being of God enclosed in the *idea*. Being, quite universally speaking, is not *an* idea, but *the idea itself*. Insofar as God is only the Being, he is only in the idea, eternal to be sure, but only in the sense in which we call truths eternal which are posited in pure thought." (XI, 273) "The concept developed so far is only the concept of divine being a priori, that is, the concept we have of this being *before* its actual being." (XII, 58)

"Only what is Being itself *can* be God. But, on that account, it is not already God." (XII, 25) "The proposition, God is Being itself, means that God, considered in his pure essence, is merely that which *will be*." (XII, 32) "This expresses a free relation of God to his being. ... In *this* sense, God is outside of being, above being ... utter freedom to be or not to be." (XII, 33) "In this respect, God is only the power to exist ... the immediate potentia existendi. But if he were *nothing* but *that*, it would amount to pantheism, i.e. a system of blind being. ... A pure potentia existendi not merely *can* turn into actus, lift itself into being; it is its very *nature* to take this turn." (XII, 35 f.)

"Thus, God would be blind being, i.e. non-spirit (and therefore non-God). But by negating such a non-spirit he posits himself *as* spirit." (XII, 40) "The true *concept* of God (not yet his reality) is: God is the being which, by the negation of the opposite, posits itself . . . *as* spirit." (XII, 42)

I would comment that God, as the object of belief and doctrine, is an inert entity, dead as it were. Yet, believer and unbeliever alike can make the discovery of this deadness and, *in* this sad discovery, they can experience the life of God who summons them to reject what is dead and, at the very least, to long for the living God, if they do not already realize his alive presence in their very discovery. In traditional words: the spirit denies that God is dead. This alive denial is the superrational but not irrational presence.

"Precisely by *not* being what he would be only by nature (merâ naturâ) he is God, i.e. the super-natural. . . . But he can not posit himself as *not* being mere essence without positing himself, in another, as purely being, i.e. as being, without turning *a potentia ad actum*." (XII, 44) This amounts to what has already been quoted above: "There is no existence of God as such. The existence of God is instantly and immediately definite." (XI, 274)

I should say, God always exists—for us—in the form of a problem, a task, a call, a summons, an invitation. Thus he is always "in another." In short, Schelling says: "God as such *is* not in existence [Gott an sich nicht seiend] but is utter freedom to be or not to be; he is the *super*-being [der *Über*seiende], as older thinkers already called him." (XII, 58)*

As such he is always pure self-revealing act. And Schelling rightly stresses: "What is sheer act withholds itself from the concept." (XI, 316) The concept is hindsight. Or, to put it in the grandiose image of myth: "I will put you in a cleft of the rock, and cover you with my hand until I pass by; then I will take away my hand, so that you may see my back, while my face shall not be seen." (Exodus 33:23) Like the visions of myth, the concept comes after the event. Yet it is the task of the concept to establish the essence, to find the ground.

"God is the groundlessly existent [das grundlos Existierende]. Kant[10] calls this the abyss [Abgrund] for human reason." (XIII, 164)

---

10. Schelling is referring to Kant's sentence: "The unconditional necessity which we indispensably need as the ultimate carrier of all things is the true abyss for human reason." (*Critique of Pure Reason*, 641)

* E.g. Nicolas Cusanus: De docta ignorantia I,vi: quod est supra omne esse nominabile.

"Indeed this existence is incomprehensible if, by incomprehensible, one would understand what is not comprehensible a priori. Negative philosophy deals with what is comprehensible a priori, positive with the a priori incomprehensible, but only in order to turn it into the comprehensible, a posteriori. What is a priori incomprehensible becomes comprehensible in God." (XIII, 165)

"It is the *I* which says: I want God outside the idea. . . . To say: I want God outside the idea is to say: I want what is above being." (XI, 570) The comment seems evident: If God were contained in the idea then there would be no other way to God except through the idea, and philosophically untutored men would be out of touch with God. But Schelling reminds us that "it is conscience—the potential God—which draws man away from selfish will. As he takes this step from active into contemplative life, however, he *steps over onto the side of God*." (XI, 556) God is free to reveal himself to any man, that is, to become a reality for man. However, "the real God is not also immediately the true God. . . . The true God, God as such, *can* be only in knowledge. . . . God not *known* would not be God. . . . And this relation of man to God can be only a free relation, whereas man's relation to God outside of God's truth, as it occurs in polytheism and in mythology, can be nothing but an unfree relationship." (XI, 176) Still we must remember "that *God* is really at the basis of the gods, that God is the true matter and the *ultimate* content of mythological imagery." (XII, 120[1])

Such imagery is natural in human consciousness. "The question is: How does consciousness come to God? But consciousness does not *come* to God; its very first move is away from the *true* God. In the first real awareness there is only one trait [Moment] of God . . . no longer He Himself. Thus, since consciousness, as soon as it *moves* at all, moves away from God . . . God, as it were, is inflicted on consciousness in its very origin [ihm ursprünglich angetan] or: God is *in* our consciousness, in the same sense in which we say of a man that a virtue is in him, or more often yet a vice, meaning that it is not objective for him, is not something he wants, nor even something he knows." (XI, 186) "Man, as soon as he *is* and has not yet *become* anything, is consciousness of God." (XI, 187)[11] "He does not *have* this consciousness, he *is* it. Precisely in *not* acting, in not moving is he the

---

11. An awkward English phrase. Yet I dare not translate "Bewusstsein Gottes" as "awareness of God," a translation which would make God objective.

one who posits the true God." (xi, 187) Let consciousness stir, and God is posited in man's dim awareness of a *numen*, or in the clear cut image of *a* god, or even—if man can maintain his awe—in verbal assertions which pass for theology. All these situations, however, come about by man's act, the act of attentive awareness, the act of imagining, the act of verbalizing, in short, some act of real consciousness.

But "the ground that consciousness is at all in relationship with God can not lie in the first real consciousness, it lies antecedently beyond. Beyond the first real consciousness, however, nothing can be conceived except man or consciousness *in its pure substance* antecedent to all *real* consciousness. There, man is not conscious of *himself* (for this would be impossible without *becoming* conscious, without an act). Therefore, since he must be conscious of *something*, it can only be consciousness of God,[12] but not with an act, e.g. the act of knowing or willing, hence purely substantial consciousness of God. . . . Man in his *original* being has no other meaning but to be the nature which posits God. Originally he exists only in order to be the God-positing being, therefore not being *for himself*, but being a nature turned toward *God*, as it were enraptured in God." (xi, 185) "Man is created into the center of God." (xi, 206)

Schelling is emphatic in saying: "I do not make humanity start with a *concept* of God. On the contrary, human consciousness is originally ingrown in God, as it were . . . It has God *in* itself, not as an object *before* itself." (xii, 120) "However, man can not remain in this being-outside-himself. He must strive to get out of this submersion in God, transforming it into a *knowledge* of God, and thus into a free relationship. But this he can reach only step by step. When he does away with his original relation to God, he does not terminate the relationship as such, for it is eternal, interminable. Having himself become *real*, he falls into the clutches of the *real* God." (xi, 189) The real God is the power of the gods.

Later he may find the free relationship, the relation to the *true* God. Thus, man's life is a theogonic process. Out of the gods must come God, in truth. Though the gods hold sway over groups of men, over nations and eras, we must not forget the final warning of Schelling: "The species, or mankind, has but an indirect relation to God, through some *law* in which God seems to be contained. Only the in-

---

12. See above, fn. 11.

dividual has a direct relation to God, can *seek* him and, if he reveals himself, accept him." (XI, 556³)

This warning leads, of course, back to the Kantian ethics and to what Fichte had stressed, that God summons us to find for ourselves what is our duty at each turn of the road. However, ethical insight is precisely *not* the last word.

"*All* moral action has its ground in our falling away from God, in our being outside of God, and this makes moral action doubtful. . . . Therefore the *I* now craves God himself. It wants to have *Him*, *Him*, the God who acts, with whom there is providence, who *as himself actual can actually withstand the fall*, in short who is the *LORD* of being (not transmundane, as is the God who is final cause, but supermundane). In this alone the *I* sees the *really* highest good." (XI, 566)

The testimony is around us: "In this life we so easily assume that our friends and companions are *ours*, whereas they are only God's, free beings, serving none but the One." (IX, 18) The "knowledge of the true God is always in the making, because the true God himself is for consciousness always the one who becomes and who, as the ever becoming, is also called the living God." (XI, 177)

ON KANT'S CONTRIBUTION TO METAPHYSICS

FRITZ MARTI[1]

Southern Illinois University at Edwardsville

In the Critique of Practical Reason (1788) from which I take my first half a dozen quotations, I come upon a sentence which, compared with the usual diction of Kant, sounds almost dogmatically metaphysical: "The concept of creation does not pertain to the sense representation of existence and to causality, but can be applied only to noumena."[2]

Creation is a metaphysical concept. Kant uses it. But he uses it in order to correct the misuse by previous metaphysicians. For some of them, creation was the same as the cause of the universe. Kant would remind us that cause and effect occur in the world of sense, and that a man will get involved in antinomies if he talks about a cause of the world itself.

Cause and effect are outside each other. Since, according to Kant, creation is not a species of causation, it is a question whether the creator should be posited outside the creature, and whether Kant ought to say that God "should be known as given *outside of ourselves.*"[3]

Kant does say it. It is in line with his notion of objective knowledge. His pure forms of understanding require something "given" in sensation. What is so given can be apprehended only in the forms of intuition (time and space) and in the conceptual forms of the categories, which thus constitute the objects of our knowledge. Kant often insists that all the knowledge we can have is bent upon objects. This insistence ignores the fact that critique itself is not objective knowledge. It is not an enterprise of psychology which would investigate its *object,* the mind.

Objects are conditional. There can be no objective, that is, conditional knowledge of the unconditional. The latter, Kant assures us, can not be known theoretically or, as he puts it, speculatively.

Nevertheless he speaks of "something unconditional, hence of a causality which entirely determines itself."[4] According to Kant, the only unconditionality *we* know is the moral obliga-

---

Read before the Ohio Philosophy Conference at Kent State University, Spring 1965.

---

[1] *Translations* mostly by Marti. Borrowed translations adjusted to render the original meaning as closely as possible.
Footnote symbols:
pureR—Kant, *Critique of Pure Reason,* pagination of the edition of 1787.
pracR—*Critique of Practical Reason* (ed. Ernst Cassirer; Berlin: Bruno Cassirer, 1914), Vol. V, pp. 1-176.
Prol—*Prolegomena,* Ibid. (1913), Vol. IV, pp. 1-139.
Quotations by volume and page from:
Fichte, *Sämmtliche Werke* (ed. I. H. Fichte; Leipzig: Mayer and Müller, 1834-46).
Schelling, *Sämmtliche Werke. Erste Abteilung* (Stuttgart: Cotta, 1856-61).
[2] pracR, V, 111.
[3] pracR, V, 115
[4] pracR, V, 54f.

tion. This is not knowledge by inference. Inference is conditional. In matters of morality, inference can only say: *If* you would that, *then* do this. Thus an inferred command is heteronomous. Only autonomy can furnish an unconditional obligation.

Of the moral law Kant says it "is given, as it were, as a *fact* of pure reason of which we are aware a priori, and which is apodictically certain."[5] But this certainty, Kant keeps repeating, is merely practical. He stresses this mere practicality in contrast to a non-existent objective knowledge of metaphysical entities which can never appear as objects of experience. Nevertheless, what is merely practically known is still known. Kant says:

"The moral law, though it affords no vista, yet does provide a fact which can not be explained by any data of the world of sense nor by the entire range of the theoretical use of reason. This fact is an intimation of a world of pure understanding, nay it even indicates this world positively and lets us know something of it, namely a law."[6]

In Kant's language, world of understanding (Verstandeswelt) is the same as noumenal world. And, as responsible beings, we know ourselves as noumena or, to use the cruder expression, as things in themselves. This very term of Kant, thing in itself (Ding an sich), shows how much he is stuck on the notion of *objective* knowledge. He is also stuck on the notion of reason as a faculty (Vermögen) which we have.

Schelling says: "Reason is not a faculty, not a tool, and cannot be made use of. Anyhow there is no reason which we could have, but only a reason which has us."[7]

As soon as we understand this, and realize that Kant's notion of reason as a faculty is a leftover of empiricism, or a psychological notion, we can more clearly see what, in contrast to this notion, is Kant's own positive contribution to that "metaphysics which can claim the dignity of a science" as the subtitle of the Prolegomena puts its.— Kant says:

"Perhaps more than any other science metaphysics, in its basic traits, has been put into us by nature itself, and it can not be regarded at all as the product of an arbitrary choice, nor as an accidental extension occurring during the progress of our experience (from which it is radically apart)."[8] Thus Kant does not condemn metaphysics as such but only the inadequate and hence untenable kind of metaphysics which the empiricists and especially Hume had already questioned. Kant points out its basic flaw, saying: "Since all illusion consists in holding the subjective ground of our judgments to be objective, a self knowledge of pure reason in its transscendent (exagerated) use is the sole preservative from the aberrations into which reason falls when it mistakes its mission, and refers that to the object transscendently, which only concerns its own subject and its guidance in all immanent use."[9]

Kant teaches that the immanent use of the categories constitutes objective experience. The attempt to transscend experience and to reach objects by means of the categories alone, or again by means of turning ideas into objects is what Kant calls "dogmatism" which he defines as "the dogmatic procedure of reason without antecedent critique of its own power."[10] Kant says he does not "speak in favor of scepticism which makes short shrift of metaphysics. Instead, critique is the necessary prelimi-

---

[5] pracR, V, 53.
[6] pracR, V, 49.
[7] VII, 148, 46. (1805–06).
[8] Prol.§57, V, 108 (124).
[9] Prol.§40, V, 81 (93).
[10] pureR, xxxv.

nary enterprise to further a thorough metaphysics as science . . . which must be strictly systematic and therefore professional, not popular." [11]

We must understand why and how popular dogmatism comes about. In 1796, at twenty-one, Schelling wrote: "Every bold expression in philosophy borders on dogmatism, because it would represent something which can in no way be an *object* of the imagination. The expression *symbolizes* what it cannot present in *sensuous* form. If the symbol is taken for an object, a philosophy results which is more fantastic than the religion of the ancient Egyptians or the mythology of the Hindus." [12] The empiricists were quite right in saying that there are no such objects, except in fancy. Kant points out that "scepticism originated in a metaphysics which did not police its dialectics." [13] In 1802, Schelling wrote: "Complete scepticism has as its true opponent only dogmatism, that is, the kind of philosophizing which tries to determine by the forms of mere reflexion, for instance by the law of cause and effect, what is in itself (das An-sich)." [14]

Kant's critique limited the application of the forms of reflexion, the categories, to the realm of objects, and Kant distinguished the categories from the ideas, which latter do not constitute objects as do categories but are regulative, that is, are the way reason rules ratiocination. Ratiocination deals with the given, with the objects of experience. But we must be clear about the rule of reason if we want a true metaphysics. Kant says.

"The distinction of ideas, that is of pure concepts of reason, from categories, or pure concepts of the understanding, as cognitions of a quite distinct species, origin and use, is so important a point . . . that without this distinction metaphysics is absolutely impossible," or else sets up a mere "house of cards". [15]

It is impossible for metaphysics to set up, alongside the natural world, an equally objective supernatural realm, and to dovetail the two. Kant says: "But if we entirely quit nature . . . and delve into the realm of mere ideas, we cannot then say that the topic is incomprehensible . . . For we are not then concerned with nature nor at all with given objects but with concepts, which have their origin merely in our reason," and "reason can and must give a full account of its own procedure." [16]

We might quibble about words and say Kant should restrict the term concept to the categories and not speak of pure *concepts* of reason when he means ideas. Nor should he speak of our reason as if it were a psychological property. But we have no time for such quibbles.

Nor will I take time to touch upon the ideas of universe (Weltganzes) and of immortality. But I will turn to the two main ideas, of self, and of God.

I start with a long quotation: "The moral law is to provide the world of sense or *sensuous nature* (with regard to rational beings) with the form of a world of reason i.e. of a *supersensuous nature,* yet without prejudice to the mechanism of the world of sense. Nature, in the widest meaning of the word, is the existence of things under laws. The sensuous nature of rational beings as such is their existence under empirically conditioned laws; hence, for reason, it is *heteronomy*. The supersenuous nature of these very same beings however is their existence accord-

---

[11] pureR, xxxvi.
[12] I, 405.
[13] Prol.§57, V, 105 (121).
[14] V, 189.
[15] Prol.§41, V, 81 (93).
[16] Prol. §56, V, 103 (118).

ing to laws which are indepedent of every empirical condition, laws therefore which belong to the *autonomy* of pure reason. . . . Thus, supersenuous nature, as far as we can conceive it at all, is nothing but *a nature under the autonomy of pure practical reason*. One could call it *primal* nature (natura archetypa), and since its ideas furnish the motive for the will and its possible effect in sensuous nature, the latter could be called copied nature (natura ectypa)".[17]

Such passages in Kant make it plain why Fichte could write to Reinhold: "I believe I have understood Kant's writings. To me it looks more and more probable that Kant drew his inferences from my principles although he does not set them forth plainly but often has wordings which seem to contradict the meaning of the principles."[18] In the long quotation I just read, Kant's wording is plain; he does say that the "supersensous nature is a nature under autonomy" and he does call this nature "primal," and sensous nature "copied". This does indeed sound like Fichte who said that things really are what we ought to make of them, or who says more formally: "In the critical system, the thing is what is posited in the I; in the dogmatic system, the I is posited in the thing."[19]

Kant *is* an idealist, if it is idealism to recognize and acknowledge the reality of moral obligation, of autonomy, of freedom. This reality is truly noumenal. To be sure, many a passage in Kant makes it seem that the term noumenon designates the kind of thing in itself which has its origin in empiricism. Empirical knowledge gives us the appearance of things, never the things in themselves. Things in themselves would have to be known, if at all, by some kind of revelation. Short of that, any metaphysics is impossible which claims to know the transcendent kind of thing in itself.

It is not only an impossibility in fact, but in form. According to Kant, objective knowledge comes about when the *given* of sensation is being apprehended in the pure forms of cognition. The impossible kind of metaphysics would use these forms of cognition, but it could have nothing *given*, no data of intuition. At least none of sensuous intuition. And, according to the letter of Kant, there is no intellectual intuition. Nevertheless, we do have knowledge of the supersensuous, in the moral law.

"Critique . . . investigates whether and how pure reason can be practical, i.e. can determine the will . . . In this business it can start without blame from pure practical laws and from their reality. Instead of an intuition as their basis, reason uses the concept of its existence in the intelligible world, to wit: freedom. The concept of freedom signifies nothing else . . ."[20]

I underline that reason exists in the intelligible world. Or—Kant's German allows this other translation — the reality of pure practical laws has its existence in the intelligible world. At all events, we do know that the intelligible world is the world of freedom and responsibility. It is not a world of objects. Making free with Kant's words, we might say: Noumena are not *things* in themselves. Fichte will say, explicitly, they are selves. Kant says (in his second edition of the Critique of Pure Reason):

". . . in the consciousness of myself, in sheer thought, I am the essence (Wesen) *itself* . . ." To be sure, under the compulsion of his object-thinking, he ends his sentence with the remark:

---

[17] pracR, V, 49.
[18] Brfw. II, 210 (3/1/1794).
[19] I, 120.
[20] pracR, V, 52.
[21] pureR, 429.

"Of which essence however, nothing is yet given me for thought."[21]

I speak of a compulsion, and compulsions have historical reasons. In a review of Charles Villers' book, "Philosophie de Kant" (Metz 1801), Schelling raised the question "whether the Kantian philosophy is not, after all, a provincialism or at least a Germanism. . . . in order to philosophize with Kant, one must talk like Kant . . ."[22] And Schelling goes on to say: "It can be proven historically that Kant had never studied philosophy in its great and universal forms as such, that he had come to know Plato, Spinoza, Leibniz only through the medium of a certain metaphysics of the schools which, some fifty years ago, was current in German universities, as a second or third hand derivation from Wolff."[23]

If Kant says "I am the essence itself"[24] he sounds like an existentialist. But I would rather try to set such positive statements by Kant into the historical context to which they belong in philosophical fact though not in Kant's own historical knowledge. And, looking for this context, I find a much closer tie between the self and God than indicated by Kant.

It is my thesis that, if God is posited outside the self, the self remains empty, and God remains a mere postulate, as Kant tells us. I would fall back upon Augustine who said God is closer to me than I myself.* Or again: "The soul is not its own life, but God is the life of the soul."[25] Or I would go forward to Fichte, or to Hegel, or especially to Schelling. Schelling says: "Reason does not *have* the idea of God, it *is* this idea, and nothing else. . . . As, in the case of light, one cannot ask whence its clearness comes, since light is clearness, thus one cannot ask whence the idea of God *comes* to reason, since reason itself is this idea."[26] Again: "In no kind of insight or knowledge can God be in the condition of what is known, what is the object; as an objectified known entity he ceases to be *God*. We are never outside of God so that we could set him before us as an object."[27]

Schelling warns, however: "As soon as, in the fullness of reason, the idea of God is born, ratiocination comes forward in order to partake of this good, . . . to fashion a reality outside of the idea, out of that which is real only *in* the idea."[28]

Kant himself had criticized this kind of objectification. He said: "The ideal of the most real being . . . is first *reified*, i.e. turned into an object, then *hypostatized*, and finally . . . even *personified*."[29]

Since God is not an object, a thinker bent upon objects and unable to make out anything about the God-object, is likely to deplore the weakness of his human reason. He should listen to Schelling who says: *"Weak* is not that reason which *cannot* know an objective God, but the reason which *wants* to know an objective God . . . that is, such a toy of reason . . ."[30]

Kant has not toyed with a God-object. He has pointed out that there is no such *thing*, but that the idea of God is indispensable in the system of reason. Knowing his objectivistic compulsion, we may find it amazing how

---

[21] V, 185.
[22] V, 186.
[23] pureR, 429.
[24] Augustinus, sermo 156 6;6. See E. Przywara, *An Augustine Synthesis* (New York: Sheed and Ward, 1945) 22.
[25] VII, 149, 47.
[26] VII, 150, 52.
[27] VII, 151, 55.
[28] pureR, 611.
[29] I, 290f.

* Tu autem eras interior intimo meo et superior summo meo. Confessiones III,vi,11.

far he has gone in the direction in which his successors would go farther. I shall quote only a few salient fragments, not even whole sentences.

"Insofar as the proposition 'I think' means 'I exist thinking' it is not merely logical, but it determines the subject (which is then simultaneously object) with regard to its very existence . . ."[31] In the very words of Kant, then, we have the origin of the post-Kantian expression subject-object. Kant speaks about the "I not only referring to itself as object-in-itself but even determining the kind of its existence, that is, recognizing itself as noumenon."[32] To be sure he immediately adds that this is not possible because inner intuition is sensuous. We can question this and ask what is the insight we have of moral obligation if it is not intuition. But that may be a quibble about words. As I have already quoted, Kant himself calls our awareness of the moral law a fact of reason. And he goes on to say: "The moral law proves its reality by giving unto reason . . . for the first time an objective though merely practical reality, and by thus turning the *transscendent* use of reason into an immanent use (through ideas to be itself an actual cause in the field of experience)."[33] We should mark that here Kant calls the practical *objective*, thus locating metaphysical objectivity definitely in the practical, in which reason is immanently at home.

Again Kant says: " . . . our own self, on the one hand, through the moral law determines itself as an intelligible being (owing to freedom) and, on the other hand, recognizes itself as active in the world of sense, owing to that very determination . . . The one concept of freedom makes it possible that we need not go outside ourselves in order to find the unconditional and intelligible . . . in addition to the conditional and sensuous."[34]

In this connection we should remember that Kant has said: "Pure reason is a sphere so separate and self-contained, that we cannot touch a part without touching upon all the rest. . . . In the sphere of this faculty one can determine either everything or nothing."[35]

If then "we need not go outside ourselves in order to find the unconditional and intelligible"[36] it follows that the unconditionality of God is not outside either. (I do not mean to deny that the theologians are touching upon something very real when they speak of the transscendence of God. I do mean that this transscendence must be conceived in such a way that it does not negate the Kantian and post-Kantian immanence.)

Of course, problems pile upon problems. One example only, to wind up with: "The existence *in time* is a merely sensuous manner of representing thinking beings in the world, and therefore it does not concern them as things in themselves; the creation of these beings, however, is a creation of the things in themselves, because the concept of creation does not belong to the sensuous representation of existence and to causality, but can refer only to noumena. Therefore, if I say of beings in the world of sense: they are created, I am regarding them in that respect as noumena. As it would be a contradiction to say God is a creator of appearances, so it is also a contradiction to say that, as creator, he is the cause of actions in the world of sense, . . . although he *is* the cause of

---
[31] pureR, 429.
[32] pureR, 430.
[33] pracR, V, 53f.
[34] pracR, V, 115.
[35] Prol. V, 11 (10).
[36] pracR, V, 115.
[37] pracR, V, 111f.

the existence of the active beings (as noumena)."[37]

A final quibble would rule out the word cause and substitute ground. There is no cause of freedom, since what is caused is conditional. A caused freedom would be heteronomous, unfreedom. And so, as Windelband said, we must indeed go beyond Kant if we want to understand Kant. Or Fichte says: "In my opinion, not to have understood *Kant* is indeed no discredit. I will say as loudly as desired that I hold his writings for *absolutely unintelligible* for him *who does not already know what CAN be found in them.* This does not impair Kant's merits as a *thinker* . . ."[38]

---

[38] Fichte, *Leben und literarischer Briefwechsel* (ed. I. H. Fichte; Sulzbach, 1831), Vol. II, 261.

FRITZ MEDICUS*
(1876—1956)

Versuch einer Würdigung des Werkes

Fritz Marti, *Southern Illinois University, Edwardsville*

> *Utquid ergo ei praeceptum est ut se ipsam cognoscat? Credo, ut se ipsam cogitet, et secundum naturam suam vivat, id est, ut secundum naturam suam ordinari appetat, sub eo scilicet cui subdenda est, supra ea quibus praeponenda est; sub illo a quo regi debet, supra ea quae regere debet.*
> Augustinus: de Trinitate X, v, 7.

Fritz Medicus, geboren am 23. April 1876 in Stadtlauringen in Bayern, ist am 13. Januar 1956 in Zürich gestorben, wo er fünfunddreißig Jahre lang, von 1911 bis 1946, an der Eidgenössischen Technischen Hochschule Philosophie dozierte. Die hinreißende Beredsamkeit des Dozenten hatte ihren Grund in der unermüdlichen Arbeit des Gelehrten, der wohl wußte, daß philosophische Gelehrsamkeit nur fruchtbar sein kann, wenn sie, der Tradition tiefst verpflichtet, das Wißbare und Gewußte immer neu begreift. Der Titel des letzten Buches von Medicus sagt genau, was die hohe Aufgabe des Lehrers der Philosophie ist: er soll künden „Vom Überzeitlichen in der Zeit."

Medicus promovierte im Juni 1898 zu Jena mit einer Dissertation über „Kants transscendentale Ästhetik und die nichteuklidische Geometrie". Gleich der erste Satz stellt die Frage nach der richtigen Beurteilung eines Philosophen, und Medicus glaubt, „daß die Geschichte der Philosophie dazu zwingt, über jene pragmatische Auffassung hinauszugehen", die alles nach

---
* Beitrag zur Sektion „Philosophiegeschichtliche Forschung". Vgl. Akten Bd. V (1970), S. 401—652.

* Eine bis 1946 nachgeführte Bibliographie von 164 Titeln findet sich in der Fritz Medicus zum 70. Geburtstag überreichten Festschrift „Natur und Geist", Eugen Rentsch Verlag, Erlenbach-Zürich 1946. Hier werden nur vier Bücher zitiert, unter folgenden Sigla:
F „J. G. Fichte. Dreizehn Vorlesungen." Reuther und Reichard, Berlin 1905.
W „Vom Wahren, Guten und Schönen. Kulturphilosophische Abhandlungen." Eugen Rentsch Verlag. Zürich 1943.
M „Menschlichkeit. Die Wahrheit als Erlebnis und Verwirklichung." Artemis-Verlag, Zürich und Stuttgart 1951. English edition: *On Being Human* (Frederick Ungar, New York 1971).
U „Vom Überzeitlichen in der Zeit." Artemis Verlag, Zürich 1954.

dem abmißt, was ein Denker etwa erreicht hat. „Kant hat seine eigene Bedeutung viel zu sehr nach den Resultaten seines Forschens gemessen." Medicus hält es für richtig, „daß man die Bedeutung eines Philosophen weniger nach dem beurteilen soll, was den Inhalt seiner Lehre ausmacht, als nach dem Grund seiner individuellen Art der Problemstellung."

So hat Medicus schon ein halbes Dutzend Jahre vor seinen Hallenser Vorlesungen über Fichte (F) das Persönliche betont. Fichtes eigenes Wort ist bekannt: „Was für eine Philosophie man wähle, hängt davon ab, was man für ein Mensch ist: denn ein philosophisches System ist nicht ein toter Hausrat, den man ablegen oder annehmen könnte, wie es uns beliebte, sondern es ist beseelt durch die Seele des Menschen, der es hat" (Werke I, 434). So muß denn auch der Ausdruck „wählen" verstanden werden. Der Anfänger wählt ja wohl irgend ein Buch, schreibt sich ein für eine Vorlesung, und es steht bei den Göttern, ob das Buch oder der Professor ihm ersprießlich sein werde. Über kurz oder lang aber hört er die stille Aufforderung der Vorsehung — *sume, lege* — und kommt zu sich selber in seiner ihm eigenen Art zu lesen und die Probleme zu sehen. Ein begnadeter Lehrer kann ihm da gar förderlich sein, einfach durch klarste Darlegung der Sachlage, wie sie in Wahrheit heute ist. So habe ich den akademischen Lehrer Medicus erfahren dürfen und schulde ihm noch heute Dank dafür, daß er mich in das *Leben* der Philosophie eingeführt. „Die Philosophie ist eine Wissenschaft", aber eben als solche nicht unpersönlich, „nicht wie die andern und neben den andern, sondern über ihnen" (U 254).

In welchem Sinne die Philosophie über den anderen Wissenschaften steht, muß sich erst erweisen. Medicus hat in seinen Vorlesungen oft das Wort „über" als unphilosophisch verurteilt, nämlich so, wie es etwa Wolff gebraucht hat, wenn er sich Gedanken machte *über* irgend ein Thema. Jedermann macht sich so Gedanken. Aber sind sie auch zutreffend? Der Philosoph soll *aus* dem Problem denken, aus dem Wesen der Sache. Statt *über* die Sache zu reden, soll er sich *in* sie vertiefen. Vorerst ist ja jede Sache, auch die philosophische etwas Fremdes.

„Als etwas in der Form des geschichtlichen Daseins Gegebenes kann ein fremder philosophischer Gedanke immer nur endlich und bedingt sein. Aber als *philosophischer* Gedanke beansprucht er, von uns nachgedacht zu werden, d. h. er fordert von uns, daß wir ihn aus seiner historischen Bedingtheit lösen und ihm damit seine ihm ursprünglich eigene Freiheit wiedergeben. Jeden philosophischen Gedanken, der uns von außen begegnet, müssen wir in unsere Sprache übersetzen, ihm seine Gegenständlichkeit, seine Fremdheit nehmen und ihn in Unmittelbarkeit verwandeln, so daß sein Verlangen nach Unendlichkeit in uns widertönt. Soweit uns dies gelingt, erweist sich die Machtlosigkeit der geschichtlichen Bedingungen gegenüber dem systematischen Denken. Aber dieses ist darum nicht zeitlos: jeder systematische Gedanke erhebt sich aus einer bestimmten geschichtlichen Problemlage, und sein wesentlicher Inhalt ist sein Beitrag zu deren Überwindung" (U 34).

„In den großen systematischen Leistungen der Philosophen werden die alten Probleme zwar beantwortet, tauchen aber trotzdem, nach neuer Antwort verlangend, wieder auf: die Antworten, die sie bekommen haben, können der späteren Generation nicht mehr genügen — ja, es ist nicht unwahrscheinlich, daß sie schon dem Philosophen, der sie gegeben hat, nicht ganz genügt haben. Auch vom Leser oder Hörer verlangen philosophische Lehren nicht etwa Glauben, sondern Zweifel. Immer muß die Frage wach sein: ‚Stimmt das wohl auch, was der da sagt?‘ " (U 144).

So sprach zum Beispiel Medicus soeben vom „Verlangen nach Unendlichkeit", das „in uns widertönt". Der wache Leser fragt sich sogleich, was da gemeint sei, etwa das, was Hegel das schlechte Unendliche nannte, d. h. das Endlose, oder nicht eher das Nicht-Endliche, das Nicht-Hypothetische, das Unbedingte. Eben solch waches Fragen begründet echte Gelehrsamkeit. Die ist kein *auswendig* Lernen, sondern innen.

„Die genaue Bestimmtheit der durch die jeweilige Situation gestellten Aufgaben zu suchen, ist der freien Verantwortlichkeit überlassen, die der Mensch für seine Menschlichkeit trägt" (W 38). „Dafür freilich, daß der Gedanke des Historikers auf der reinen Höhe der Zeit ist, gibt es keine Gewähr" (W 42).

„Geschichtliches Wissen ist bloß, was an einem geistig erlebten Horizont seine Stelle und von ihr aus eine bestimmte Beziehung auf sein persönliches Ich hat — eine Beziehung, in der sich die Richtung auswirkt, in der dieses Ich den Sinn seines Lebens, die substantielle Erfüllung der ihm gewordenen und werdenden Zeit sucht. Mit anderen Worten, der Geschichtspositivismus ist eine nicht zu Ende gedachte, willkürlich abgebrochene Philosophie. Und wo er zur Methode wird, droht die Gefahr der geistigen Verödung. Das Suchen nach dem Sinn der Geschichte liegt aller geschichtlichen Erkenntnis zugrunde" (U 52).

„Der Sinn der Geschichte ist nicht ein *Ziel*, zu dem sie geführt würde und dem sie darum entgegentreiben *müßte*... Die Geschichte würde überhaupt keinen Sinn haben, wenn sie die Freiheit unserer Entscheidungen anders als durch die Entscheidungen anderer und durch deren Schicksale einschränkte. Nur weil ihr tatsächlicher Verlauf nicht für ein bestimmtes Ziel prädestiniert ist, umfängt unsere Entscheidungen letztgültiger Ernst unserer Verantwortung" (U 233).

„Nur ein durch eigenes verantwortungsvolles Tun und Leiden in irgend einem Grade zu persönlicher Selbstgestaltung gereiftes Ich ist das Subjekt der geschichtlichen Erkenntnis, und noch im Prozeß des Erkennens wird es weiterreifen" (W 56).

„Verantwortlichkeit ist nur durch Beziehung auf Überzeitliches möglich" (W 79). „Zeitlos ist, was kein Verhältnis zur Zeit hat (wie das Einmaleins); überzeitlich, was zu jeder besonderen Zeit auch sein besonders Verhältnis beansprucht (wie die Kunst oder das Recht oder die Moral)" (W 75).

„Das Wesen der Sittlichkeit ist weder ein Erzeugnis der geschichtlichen Bewegung, noch ist es geschichtslos: es ist *überzeitlich, übergeschichtlich*" (W 91). „Die sittlichen Aufgaben *sind* da, und wir haben sie anzuerkennen. Wir *stellen* sie uns nicht — sie *sind* uns gestellt. Sie stammen nicht aus unserm sittlichen Bewußtsein: sie appellieren an dieses ... Jener Appell aber bedeutet immer das Verlangen nach *Gegenwart* — im ethischen Sinne dieses Wortes: immer gilt es, die *Entscheidung* zu treffen, durch die wir *hinter uns bringen* und damit zur *Vergangenheit,* zu etwas Erledigten für uns machen, was hinter uns sein soll" (W 89). „Das menschliche Leben hat nur dort Höhe, gerät nur dort lebenswert, wo es seine Vergangenheit immer von neuem hinter sich bringt" (U 110).

„Das geistige Leben jeder Zeit weist in seiner Problematik über die Gegenwart hinaus. Die Höhe des Lebens ist dort, wo noch keine Abgeklärtheit, noch keine eindeutige Entscheidung gewonnen ist, sondern wo noch Gegensätze auszutragen sind, wo — mit nach Möglichkeit klarem Bewußtsein vom Wert des in der Vergangenheit Geleisteten — Verantwortung für das Werdende, das noch Ungewisse getragen wird. Eine Geschichtsdarstellung ist auf der Höhe der Zeit, wenn sie an dieser Verantwortung teilhat, also ‚Partei nimmt' " (W 46 f.).

„Die ‚Höhe der Zeit' ist über die ganze Erde hin eine unsichere Angelegenheit, und die ‚Verwirklichung des Wahren' bleibt in dem Buch der Menschheitsgeschichte ‚ein klein Kapitel, fragmentarisch'. Diese letzten Worte sind bei Goethe geborgt: bei ihm beziehen sie sich auf das ‚Buch der Liebe'. Und Liebe, aus letzter Seinstiefe quellende und im Menschen die menschliche Tiefe suchende Liebe allein kann die Gefahr bannen, daß der harmonische Zusammenhang bloße Forderung bleibt" (U 230 f.). „Für einen jeden liegt auf der Stelle, die er einnimmt, Verantwortung dafür, daß seine Zeit die ihr *mögliche Höhe* gewinne, und er nimmt diese Verantwortung nur dann ernst genug, wenn er sich bemüht, die Möglichkeiten recht einzuschätzen, die ihm in seinem Wirkungskreis offenstehen" (M 227).

„In uns allen wirken ungezählte andere Menschen fort: wir hätten nicht die werden können, die wir sind, wenn sie nicht gewesen wären... Von einem jeden fordert das überkommene Erbe, daß er um die Höhe *seiner* Möglichkeiten bemüht sei" (U 233). Jeder hat „Aufgaben, in denen er sich als Charakter gerade dadurch erweist, daß er über das, was er ist, hinauskommt durch Orientierung an den überzeitlichen *Ideen* des Guten, des Wahren, des Gerechten, des Schönen. Die Überzeitlichkeit dieser Ideen besagt, daß sie selbst nicht gegeben sind, sondern immer neu bestimmt werden müssen" (W 82). „Diese Lebensmächte gehen in den Wandel der Zeiten ein; sie sind nicht seine Produkte, sondern seine ideellen Beherrscher. Sie behaupten sich in ihm: in jeder Epoche sind sie mit ihren hohen Forderungen da, von keiner werden sie ausgeschöpft: jede folgende bekommt ihren eigenen Auftrag" (M 38).

„In den übergeschichtlichen (in aller Menschengeschichte bestimmend gegenwärtigen) Wertgegensätzen Wahr—Falsch, Gut—Böse, Schön—Häßlich, Gerecht—Ungerecht erwacht, von wertwidrigen Erlebnissen angestoßen, unser aller Selbstbewußtsein und damit die Verantwortung für Menschlichkeit, die nach dem Maß seiner Möglichkeiten einen jeden betrifft. Sie sind nicht menschliche Erfindungen, diese grundlegenden Wertgegensätze; alles selbstbewußte Wirken, alles Erfinden setzt sie schon voraus. In ihnen dokumentiert sich die transzendentale Ordnung der Vernunft. Nach einem auf Friedrich Heinrich Jacobi zurückgehenden, von Schelling aufgenommenen Wort hat nicht der Mensch die Vernunft, sondern sie hat ihn (Werke VII, 148). Die Vernunft will Menschlichkeit: sie will, daß jedes uns beanspruchende Ergebnis als das genommen werde, was es in Wahrheit ist" (U 240 f.).

„Die Vernunft, die uns hat, übt keinen äußeren Zwang aus; sie gibt Freiheit: ihre Verehrer, ihre Gläubigen leitet sie zur weltüberlegenen Freiheit der wahren Liebe, und ihre Verächter noch speist sie mit der Freiheit der zwar wesenlosen, doch stets zu substantieller Konzentration rufenden Subjektivität" (M 104).

„Unsern Verstand haben *wir*, und jeder hat seinen eigenen. Aber die Vernunft hat *uns*: in ihrer überindividuellen Notwendigkeit sind wir gehalten. Zwischen Wahr und Falsch *müssen* wir unterscheiden, müssen das Wahre als das Wertvolle, das Falsche als das Wertwidrige einschätzen; da hat der Unterschied der Individuen und hat deren Freiheit ein Ende" (M 105).

„Die Freiheit des Menschen ist in einer Ordnung gehalten, die nicht von ihm stammt, zu deren Wirkung er sich unfrei verhält. Aber nur in dieser seiner Willkür entzogenen Ordnung vermag er Herr seiner selbst und damit wahrhaft frei zu sein. Das höhere Ich, das sich ihm als Norm des Geisteslebens kund macht, ist lautere Notwendigkeit, die, indem sie seine Willkür bindet, ihm Sicherheit seiner selbst gibt" (U 101). „Wer aus dem Glauben an die absolute Wahrheit lebt, erfährt deren befreiende Kraft" (U 221).

Ich bitte zu bedenken, daß Medicus vom Glauben an die Wahrheit redet, nicht vom Fürwahrhalten autoritärer Glaubenssätze, welche Sache des immer bedingten Verstandes sind, dessen Gegenstände nicht an das Unbedingte heranreichen.

„Offenbarung des Übergegenständlichen ist Inhalt der *religiösen* Verkündigung. Sie kann auf Kunstformen nicht verzichten. Ihre Symbole appellieren an die innerste Tiefe, die für nüchterne Buchstäblichkeit und Objektivität unerreichbar ist. Wo die Symbole als Prosa aufgefaßt und zu Objekten eines (obendrein unter Androhung ewiger Strafe anbefohlenen) Fürwahrhaltens gemacht werden, geht ihr Inhalt in Aberglauben über. Was in gegenständlicher Bedeutung für wahr zu halten ist, hat nach seinen unpersönlichen Kriterien der *Verstand* zu entscheiden, er ganz allein" (U 249). „Fesselung des Verstandes macht unaufrichtig" (U 250).

Aber übergegenständlich ist „die Frage nach dem Letzten, aus dem alles Geschehen kommt. Worte wie ‚Urnebel' und dergleichen sind keine ‚Begriffe' sondern bloß Versuche, mehr oder minder gut formulierte Rätsel zu benennen. Auch das Wort ‚Gott' ist kein Begriff — wenigstens nicht für den, dem die Verstandesbeweise für sein Dasein nicht genügen, und sie genügen niemandem, dem deutlich geworden ist, daß alles Beweisen sein Gebiet im Objektiven hat, daß aber Gott kein ‚Objekt' ist. Dort wo es Gegenstände zu erkennen gibt und wo darum Begriffe zuständig sind, ist keine abschließende Wahrheitsgewißheit zu gewinnen" (U 239 f.).

„Dies aber ist der ewige Gehalt der in Weltentiefe leitenden Gnade, daß der transzendente Grund allen Wahrheitsverlangens — daß *die* Wahrheit sich im erleuchteten Erlebnis einer Mythologie erschließt und so der Mensch (mit Kant zu reden — Kritik der reinen Vernunft 868) seiner ‚ganzen Bestimmung' entgegengeführt wird. κινεῖ ὡς ἐρώμενον, hat Aristoteles von Gott gesagt: Gott bewegt uns, indem tiefste Notwendigkeit uns treibt, die Wahrheit, und das heißt letztlich *ihn*, zu lieben" (U 251).

„Die ontologische Wahrheit hat mehr als ein Gesicht: sie umfaßt das ganze geistige Leben. In dieser umfassenden Bedeutung ist sie die Wahrheit der Religion und (in notwendiger dialektischer Auseinandersetzung mit ihr) auch die Wahrheit der Philosophie. Ist die symbolische Sprache der Religion Verkündigung der überzeitlichen Wahrheit in Indikativen, so spricht die Philosophie in Sätzen, die zwar fast stets in indikativischer

Form erscheinen, doch (im allerdings nicht immer klaren Bewußtsein ihrer geschichtlichen Bedingtheit) zugleich als Fragen gemeint sind und deshalb nicht geglaubt, sondern mit Kritik aufgefaßt sein wollen" (U 230).

„Bei Schelling ist die dualistische Entgegensetzung gegen Gott lediglich im Bewußtsein des philosophisch unorientierten und darum in seinen weltanschaulichen Vorstellungen von den Verstandestendenzen beherrschten Menschen begründet, der sich von seinem wahren Verhältnis zu Gott keine Rechenschaft gibt: der Verstand, ‚der nur in Gegensätzen sein Wesen hat' (Werke VII, 157), vermag auch Gott nur zu denken, indem er ihn — und mit ihm die unbedingte Wahrheit — sich entgegensetzt! Aber eben damit verfehlt er ihn. Gott ist kein ›Gegenstand‹ und darum dem Verstand überhaupt nicht zugänglich" (M 101 f.).

In den dreißiger Jahren, als mich Medicus auf einem Alpweglein ihm vorangehen ließ, sagte er im Gespräch beiläufig: „Gott ist nicht Jemand". Ich drehte mich um mit dem Ausruf: „*Das* haben Sie noch nie gesagt!" Er aber: „Ich habe es immer gesagt!" Und es ist auch immer zu sagen, zur Berichtigung und Rechtfertigung des besonderen Mißverständnisses des Verstandesmenschen, dem zwar bewußt ist, Gott sei kein toter Gegenstand, und der dann, im dämmernden Bewußtsein, als Ich angerufen zu sein durch die Autorität unbedingter Wahrheit, und im Gegensatz zum autoritätslosen toten Ding, behauptet Gott sei eine Person. Die landläufige Vorstellung einer göttlichen Persönlichkeit bewegte mich auch einmal in meiner Unreife Medicus zu fragen, warum er überhaupt das Wort Gott brauche. Er antwortete: „Es gibt kein besseres!" — Doch hören wir ihn selbst: „Augustinus, der mit dem Gedanken, daß Gott die Wahrheit ist, ernst gemacht hat, hat Gott als die tiefste Innerlichkeit der menschlichen Existenz anerkannt. Jene Epoche seiner eigenen Vergangenheit, in der er ihn im äußeren Dasein gesucht hatte, galt ihm nun als eine Zeit der Selbstentfremdung: Ubi ergo eram, quando te quaerebam? ... a me discesseram nec me inveniebam: quanto minus te! (Conf. V, 2)" (M 120). „Unangemessen bleibt freilich jedes menschliche Wort, das Gott durch eine Eigenschaft bezeichnen möchte" (M 158).

„Naturgottheiten sind launisch: die Götter der Griechen waren nicht *gut*. In den Hochreligionen ist der Gehalt der Mythen das rein Menschliche" (M 317). „Die sogenannten Hochreligionen sind dadurch ausgezeichnet, daß sie das Naturhafte als das Überwundene oder zu Überwindende werten. In ihnen weiß man, daß nicht in der objektiven Welt der Sinn des Daseins zu suchen ist; deren Rätselhaftigkeit bleibt ohne entscheidenden Einfluß auf den *Sinn* der menschlichen Existenz, und *dieser* hat zentrale Bedeutung" (M 316). „Hochreligionen unterscheiden sich darin von primitiver Götter- und Götzenverehrung, daß die Deutung ihrer Glaubenslehren im Wandel der Jahrhunderte an den um die Höhe der Zeit geführten Geisteskämpfen teil gehabt hat und darum in den großen Epochen der Philosophiegeschichte in fruchtbarer Fühlung mit deren Bestrebungen gewesen ist: deren Ertrag ist dann *allen* zugute gekommen, die jene Lehren gläubig angenommen haben, und einiges davon sogar deren Bestreitern" (U 239).

„Jede Gemeinschaft hat Geschichte; ihr jeweiliges Sein ist von überindividuellen Aufgaben bestimmt, durch deren Inangriffnahme sie sich auf dem Grunde neuer Entscheidungen eine neue Gegenwart schafft. Verkennt, vernachlässigt sie aber ihre Aufgaben, so bleibt sie hinter ihrer Zeit zurück, und das Verhältnis ihrer Glieder wird irgendwie leer; die Gemeinschaft verliert an Kraft und an Freudigkeit, sich durchzusetzen" (U 60). „Wo immer der geschichtliche Fortgang Gewaltlösungen seiner Schwierigkeiten sucht (denn um diesen Gegensatz handelt es sich: Menschlichkeit oder auferlegter Zwang), drängen die Probleme *rückwärts* zu Zuständen, die *hinter* der Gegenwart liegen sollten" (U 110).

„Es kann geschehen, daß den nach geistiger Entscheidung verlangenden Auseinandersetzungen die Möglichkeit genommen wird, geistig durchgeführt zu werden. Kulturkatastrophen sind dämonische Verdrängungen der Wahrheit. Für Situationen, die von dämonischen Mächten *beherrscht* sind, gibt es überhaupt keine Höhe ihrer Möglichkeiten mehr. Da ist die *Basis* des Handelns vergiftet" (M 128 f.). „Eine schlechthin ‚gute' Sache kann es, wo dämonische Mächte wirksam sind, überhaupt nicht geben" (M 254). „Dämonische Mächte haben niemals legitimen Herrschaftsanspruch" (M 232).

„ ‚Objektivität' suchen — vielmehr behaupten und damit das Symbolische verkennen, ist das Mißverständnis, das den Orthodoxien immer wieder unterläuft" (U 211). Daher „die Gefahr, daß etwas der Kultur Angehöriges, in ihr, durch sie Bedingtes, für religiös verbindlich ausgegeben wird und darum auf diejenigen, die ‚auch im Kopfe ihr Gewissen haben' (Nietzsche: Zarathustra III, Von den Abtrünnigen 2.), abstoßend wirkt. Die Kultur braucht Freiheit, sie kann keine Fesseln dulden" (U 212).

„In der Beziehung auf religiöses Erleben ist die ganze Aufgabe des Intellekts, dafür zu sorgen, daß die Worte, in denen es (soweit das geschehen kann) mitteilbar gemacht und in denen Rechenschaft von ihm gegeben wird, auf der Höhe der Zeit seien" (M 154). „Dogmatische Lehren einer Religion können viele Jahrhunderte lang unverändert dem Glauben, dem sie zugehören, begriffliche Stütze sein und den geschichtlichen Zusammenhang wahren: aber durch die Kunst dieser selben Jahrhunderte werden bedeutsame Wandlungen erkennbar" (U 248). „Sofern aber die Kunst Unersetzliches für die Menschlichkeit zu bedeuten hat, ist sie Offenbarung ontologischer Wahrheit" (M 320). Kunst kann noch — oder wieder — frei sein, wo etwa verstockte Tradition die mythologischen Symbole tot erscheinen läßt. In hohen Werken der Kunst „wird Wahrheitstiefe offenbar. Diese, an die die logischen Formen nicht reichen, kann dem Menschen nicht anders zuteil werden als in *Symbolen* — Gestaltung des ästhetischen Bewußtseins. Alle Propheten sind Künstler: sie haben etwas zu sagen, das in nüchtern prosaischen Sätzen niemals gesagt werden könnte, etwas, das nicht ohne den Verstand aufgenommen sein will, aber durchaus nicht bloß ihn in Anspruch nimmt. (Auch die Umkehrung gilt: alle Künstler sind Propheten; — freilich nicht alle sind Propheten des Wahren)" (M 45).

„Das vom Unermeßlichen zeugende Kunstwerk erfüllt eine mythologische Funktion; es gibt der Gemeinschaft ein Bewußtsein dessen, was ihre Glieder in der Tiefe ihrer Existenz miteinander verbindet" (U 176). „Die tatsächlichen Feststellungen bleiben der Wissenschaft überlassen; Kunstwerke sind Symbole; sie weisen auf den Sinn des Lebensganzen" (U 93). „Die Kunst ist das Leben selbst, sofern es sich ausspricht. Das Leben ist überzeitlich. In keiner Zeit geht es in deren Gestaltungen und Bewegungen auf; stets ist es voller Spannungen, und mit ihnen drängt es aus jeder Zeit heraus zu einer anderen; aber in jeder ist es da, und in allem künstlerischen Schaffen bringt es sich irgendwie zum Ausdruck" (U 172 f.). „Nur wenn das Kunstwerk Inhalt unseres ästhetischen Erlebens wird, uns also nicht ‚gegenübersteht' (wie dem Chemiker die Substanz, deren Reaktionen er beobachtet), wird das Künstlerische an ihm erfaßt: die Trennung von Subjekt und Objekt ist aufgehoben. Kunstwerke erleben heißt innerliche Bereicherung erfahren, — es heißt vom Wesen der Wirklichkeit so nahe berührt werden, daß sie weniger fremd, und die Fähigkeit, sie zu verstehen, größer wird. Durch ihre Kunstwerke werden uns alte, längst versunkene Kulturen zugänglich; und die Kunst der Zeitgenossen deutet uns etwas von dem Leben, das, immer voll von Geheimnissen, *uns* umfängt" (M 44).

Das systematische Buch, das Medicus mit fünfundsiebzig Jahren veröffentlicht hat, trägt das eine Wort *Menschlichkeit* zum Titel. Mit seiner klaren Einsicht in das Überzeitliche, das uns Aufgabe und Würde gibt, steht Medicus auf der Höhe *unserer* Zeit. 1944 hat er gesagt: „Wenn man mich fragte, welche Gewißheit ich als unzweifelbar und für die geistige Existenz des Menschen grundlegend anerkennen möchte, so würde ich antworten: es ist die Gewißheit der Notwendigkeit, uns um die Gestaltung unseres Daseins anzunehmen" (U 96). Und 1938 schrieb er in der Zeitung:

„Der Mensch kann sich nicht mit dem begnügen, was er ohne eigenes Zutun ist; er ist nicht Mensch, ohne etwas mit sich anzufangen" (U 90).

Vor anderthalb Jahrtausenden hat einer, der auf der Höhe *seiner* Zeit stand, Augustinus, ebenfalls seine Zeitgenossen aufgefordert zu bedenken, an welchem Platz sie einen festen Stand haben könnten. Als Motto habe ich sein Wort denen von Medicus vorausgehen lassen, und ich zitiere es hier zum Schlusse in der Verdeutschung von Erich Przywara (Augustinus. Die Gestalt als Gefüge. Hegner, Leipzig 1934, Seite 73).

„Warum also ergeht an ihn die Weisung, sich zu erkennen? Ich glaube, damit er sich selbst denkend bedenke und nach seiner Natur lebe, das heißt, gemäß seiner Natur geordnet zu werden verlange: unter Ihm nämlich, dem er untertan zu sein hat, über dem, dem er Herrscher sein soll." ‚Ihm' klingt mythologischer als ‚eo'.

The Proceedings (Akten des XIV. Internationalen Kongresses für Philosophie, Wien, September 1968, Vol. VI) printed only a shortened version of this contribution. My English translation of the entire paper follows, 113-123.

FRITZ MEDICUS
(1876-1956)

English version of a paper submitted in German to the Fourteenth International Congress for Philosophy held September 2–9, 1968 at Vienna, Austria

Utquid ergo ei praeceptum est ut se ipsam cognoscat? Credo, ut se ipsam cogitet, et secundum naturam suam vivat, id est, ut secundum naturam suam ordinari appetat, sub eo scilicet cui subdenda est, supra ea quibus praeponenda est; sub illo a quo regi debet, supra ea quae regere debet.—
Augustinus: de Trinitate X, v, 7.

Fritz Medicus, born April 23, 1876, at Stadtlauringen in northern Bavaria, died January 13, 1956, in Zürich where, for thirty-five years he had taught philosophy at the Swiss Federal Institute of Technology. His inspiring eloquence had its roots in the untiring labor of the scholar who well knew that philosophical learning can be fruitful only if all its ties to tradition lead to an ever new rethinking of what is and can be known. The title of the last book by Fritz Medicus amounts to a precise definition of the lofty task of the teacher of philosophy: he ought to tell *About the Supertemporal in Time*.[1]

Medicus made his doctorate in June, 1898, at Jena with a dissertation on 'Kant's transcendental aesthetics and non-euclidian geometry.'[2] The very first proposition raises the question about the correct evaluation of a philosopher. Medicus believes "that the history of philosophy impels us to go beyond the pragmatic notion" which would measure a man's importance by his doctrines. "Kant himself attributed his importance too much to the results of his research." Medicus believes "that a philosopher's importance should be judged not so much by the content of his doctrine as by the reason for the individual manner of his formulation of his problems."

In this way Medicus stressed personality already half a dozen years be-

See note on page 112.

---

[1] In order to simplify my documentation I shall give in ∧ parentheses only the pages of the four books I am quoting and I shall use the following capitals to indicate each book.
A bibliography of 164 titles, down to 1946, is given in the memorial volume of essays presented to Medicus at his seventieth birthday: *Natur und Geist*. Eugen Rentsch Verlag, Erlenbach-Zürich 1946.
    G   *Grundfragen der Aesthetik*. Vorträge und Abhandlungen. Eugen Diederichs, Jena 1917.
   WGS *Vom Wahren, Guten und Schönen*. Kulturphilosophische Abhandlungen. Eugen Rentsch Verlag, Zürich 1943.
    M   *Menschlichkeit*. Die Wahrheit als Erlebnis und Verwirklichung. Artemis-Verlag, Zürich und Stuttgart 1951.
    U   *Vom Ueberzeitlichen in der Zeit*. Artemis-Verlag, Zürich 1954.
[2] *Kants transscendentale Aesthetik und die nichteuklidische Geometrie*. Inaugural-Dissertation. Druck von Ehrhardt Karras, Halle a.S. 1898.

fore he gave the series of lectures on Fichte at the University of Halle, later published as his first book.[3] Fichte's own words are well known: "The choice of one's philosophy depends on the kind of man one is; for, a philosophical system is not a dead chattel one could acquire or dispose of, at will; it is animated by the soul of the man who harbors it."[4] The word "choice" must be properly understood. Of course a beginner will choose a book, or register for a course, and it is in the lap of the gods whether the book or the professor is profitable for him. But—the gods being gracious—sooner or later he will hear the silent summons of providence — 'take, read' — and he will attain his own way of reading and of seeing problems. A blessed teacher can be of great profit to him by merely presenting problems as, in truth, they are at that time. Such was my privilege in finding Medicus, and to this day I owe thanks to him for having introduced me to the *life* of philosophy. "Philosophy is a discipline," yet as such it is not impersonal, "it is unlike the other disciplines and does not stand alongside of them but above them." (U 254)

It remains to be seen in what sense philosophy stands above the other disciplines. (I might borrow Fichte's word Wissenschaftslehre and translate it, badly enough, as 'discipline about discipline.') In his lectures, Medicus often pointed out that the word 'about' is unphilosophical, at least in the sense in which Wolff used it when he conceived some thoughts *about* some random topic. Everybody can conceive such thoughts about random topics. But are they to the point? The philosopher ought to think *from* the problem, from the essence of the matter at hand. Instead of talking *about* the matter he ought to steep himself *in* it. For, at the outset, every subject matter, even the philosophical, is something foreign and strange.

"Having the form of historical existence, a foreign philosophical thought is always finite and conditional. Yet, being a *philosophical* thought, it makes the claim that we, too, should think it, that is, it demands of us that we detach it from its historical conditions and thus restore the freedom it had originally. We must translate every philosophical thought which comes to us from outside, into our own language, and thus release it from its objective form, its strangeness, and transform it into immediacy, so that its claim to non-finiteness can reverberate in us. Insofar as we succeed in doing this, the historical conditions prove to have no power over systematic thinking. Still, on that very account, systematic thinking is not timeless. Every systematic thought arises from a specific historical problem, and its essential content is its contribution to the solution." (U 34)

"In the great systematic accomplishments of the philosophers the old problems do find answers. Nevertheless they reappear, demanding new answers. The earlier answers cannot satisfy a later generation. In fact, it is not improbable that they did not quite satisfy the philosopher who first gave them. In the same way, philosophical doctrines demand from the reader or hearer not belief but doubt. The question: 'Can it be true what this fellow says?'" must always be present. (U 144)

For instance, we hear the words of Medicus already quoted, about the philosophical "claim to non-finiteness reverberating in us." The alert reader or listener immediately asks what is meant. Obviously not that which

---

[3] *J. G. Fichte.* Dreizehn Vorlesungen. Reuther und Reichard, Berlin 1905.
[4] Fichte: *Erste Einleitung in die Wissenschaftslehre.* Sämmtliche Werke. Meyer und Müller, Leipzig. Erster Band, 434. In the six volume edition published by Fritz Eckardt and Felix Meiner, Leipzig 1911–1912 and edited by Medicus, see Volume III, page 18.

Hegel called the bad infinite, that is, the endless, but rather, in contrast, the non-finite, the non-hypothetical, the unconditional. Such alert questioning is the basis of genuine scholarship, which is not a matter of mere memorizing of information which comes *from without.*

Medicus says that, like the claims made on us by philosophical insight, "so also historiography appeals to the personal experience of the reader to whom it can then offer insights which do not come to him from without (for instance, the amplitude of an oscillation or the radius of the earth), but insights which, while bringing him the tale of events of long ago, fill his ego with a more precise awareness of his own concrete existence. . . . This 'participation' does not mean being part of a situation which must be simply accepted (like the part of an organism that is to be understood biologically). 'Participation' must be understood as a spontaneous relating oneself to the contents of historical interest. This spontaneity is a sovereign (though by no means an arbitrary) decision of the subject who, owing to a personal sense of responsibility acknowledges significance in one point and denies it in another." (WGS 34f) "The search for the precise meaning of the intellectual tasks presented by each historical situation is left to the free responsibility which man has for his humanity." (WGS 38) "To be sure, there is no guarantee that the historian's thought will rise to the pure height of his time." (WGS 42)

"Only that is historical knowledge which has its place within a keenly experienced horizon and which, in that place, has a definite relation to the self of the thinker, a relation significant of the direction in which he seeks the meaning of his life and the substantial fulness of the time into which he finds himself placed and which becomes his own time. In other words, every mere positivism in historiography is an arbitrarily truncated philosophy not thought through. And wherever positivism becomes a method there lurks the danger of intellectual stagnation. At the basis of all genuine historical knowledge lies the search for the *meaning* of history." (U 52)

"The meaning of history is not a fixed *goal* set for it, a goal towards which it *has to move.* . . . History would have no meaning at all if it restricted the freedom of our decisions by anything but the decisions of others, and by their fortunes and misfortunes. Only because the actual course of history has no predetermined goal can there be any ultimate seriousness in our responsible decisions." (U 233)

"The only subject capable of having historical knowledge is a self whose own responsible doing and suffering has let it mature to the point of a self-made personal character. And in the very process of knowing history he will mature further." (WGS 56)

"Responsibility is possible only in relation to the supertemporal." (WGS 79) "That which has no relation to time (for instance the multiplication table) is timeless. Whatever, at any given time, requires its own particular relation to time (like art or law or morality), is supertemporal." (WGS 75)

"The nature of morality is neither a product of historical movements, nor is it extra-historical; it is *supertemporal, superhistorical.*" (WGS 91) "The moral tasks exist, and we must acknowledge them. We do not *set them up*—they *are set* for us. They do not originate in our moral consciousness; they appeal to it. . . . But that appeal is always a desire for *presence,* in the moral sense of the world. The challenge is always that we make a *decision* by means of which we get *behind us* and turn into a *past,* into something settled, whatever ought to be behind us." (WGS 89)

"Every past is historically conditioned. And wherever we are entitled to speak of a past, that past must be understood from its conditions. (The reader understands that 'past' does not mean dates.) However, that which, at some future time, will be known as a past, at first appears in consciousness only as the task of intellectually mastering an antecedent event, and as long as that is the case, the understanding of its historical conditions does not yet exist for consciousness. It can occur only at some later time that this nonexistence is recognized as a shortcoming of systematic thought." (U 33f) "Human life attains its proper height and becomes worth living only insofar at is gets its own past behind itself, ever anew." (U 110)

"At all times, the life of the spirit points with its problems beyond the mere present. The height of life is attained already when there is as yet no full clearness, no unambiguous decision, when a decision must still be made between opposites, and when that which is still uncertain is still our responsibility which we shoulder with as clear as possible a knowledge of the insights already gained in the past. Historiography is at the height of its time when it shares this responsibility and, therefore, is partisan." (WGS 46f)

"All over the earth, the 'height of the time' is a very uncertain affair, and in the book of human history the 'realization of the true' remains 'a tiny chapter and fragmentary.' The last words are borrowed from Goethe who uses them with regard to the 'Book of Love.' And love alone, love springing from the last depth of being and seeking the human depth in man, can dispell the danger of harmony's remaining nothing but a task." (U 230f) "On the spot where he stands, *everyone is responsible* for his era's attainment of the *height possible* at the time. He can take this responsibility quite seriously only if he endeavors to evaluate correctly the possibilities open to him in his sphere of influence." (M 227)

"Innumerable other men keep working in all of us. If they had not existed, we could not have become the ones we are. . . . This heritage demands of each one of us the labor of attaining the height of *his own* possibilities." (U23 3) Everyone has "tasks in the fulfillment of which his character proves itself by rising beyond that which he is, through his orientation toward the supertemporal *ideas* of the good, the true, the just, the beautiful. To say these ideas are supertemporal means to point out that they are not given but must be determined ever anew." (WGS 82) "These powers of life enter into the change of the times. They are not its products but its ideal rulers. They maintain themselves in the change; in each epoch they are present with their high demands; no epoch can exhaust them, but every subsequent epoch receives its own charge." (M 38)

"Art, morality and law, even these powers of life have an intellectual touch. However, their peculiar essence is determined by the ideas of the beautiful, the good, the just, ideas which use ratiocination as their servant (though the servant may prove overbearing at times). These ideas do not pretend that their manifestations are rigid orders nor that their demands are the same at every time. The ideas are realized in free creations which try to ennoble the forms of life of the time by letting shine forth from those forms the supertemporal as a documentation of the eternal which is present at the time in a particular form." (M 40)

"The supertemporal value-contrasts true-false, good-evil, beautiful-ugly, just-unjust are present in the entire human history and determine it. Impelled by experiences adverse to those values, our *self-awareness* awakens in terms of those contrasts, and thus there awakens our *responsibility* for the humanity which concerns everyone in the measure of his possibilities. Those fundamental value-contrasts are not human inventions. Every self-certain activity, and every invention already presupposes the contrasts. They document *the transcendental order of reason.* Making use of an expression of Friedrich Heinrich Jacobi, Schelling said that man has no hold on reason, but reason holds man.[5] . . . Reason demands humanity. It demands of us that we take every event which concerns us as that which it is in *truth.*" (U 240f)

"Only meaningless words could dispute the *unconditional* truth of the distinction between the true as a value and the false as averse to value. The distinction is so indispensable to the human spirit that man comes to an awareness of himself, finds *himself* only in that distinction. We can understand ourselves and we can understand others only owing to the unconditionality of this value-contrast. When *we make* the distinction between true and false, we merely confirm for our own person that necessity which is based not in us but in reason, and by means of which we are reasonable creatures. We do not make the distinction arbitrarily, at our pleasure, but because reason lets us make it; the distinction pertains to reason. What is *necessary* in our being is *reason's* necessity. And whatever *the individual* can posit and retain as a necessity which determines the forms of *his personal* life, has its form from reason and remains in the superindividual frame of reason insofar as it has any human value." (M 82f)

"The reason which holds us exerts no outward coercion. It affords freedom. It leads its adherents, its faithful to the supermundane freedom of true love, and it feeds even its scorners and detractors with the freedom of a subjectivity which, though without substance, yet always is a challenge to substantial concentration." (M 104)

"*We* have our ratiocination, and each one has his own. But reason holds *us;* we are held in its superindividual necessity. We *must* distinguish between true and false, we *must* take the true as a value, and realize that the false is adverse to value. In this respect there is no difference between individuals and their freedom." (M 105)

"The freedom of man depends on an order which does not come from him, and he is unfree with regard to the efficacy of that order. But only within that order beyond the range of his arbitrariness can he be master of himself and truly free. The higher self which manifests itself as the norm of the life of the spirit is pure necessity which, by restraining his arbitrariness, gives him assurance of himself." (U 101)

"Reason is one and indivisible. The fourfoldness of the supertemporal values does not mark parts of the realm of reason. All four make legitimate claims upon every spiritual act. To be sure, the form in which a specific certainty of truth unfolds, indicates which one value dominantly attracts the interest. He who reads these lines will read them in critical anticipation of their truth content. Still, the form of expression, too, can be critically evaluated, in an aesthetic judgment. Likewise, the author's use of his time when he wrote this can be subjected to a moral evaluation." (M 202f) "Each one of the supertemporal values which are the goals of unfolding human freedom has its own necessity, its autonomy. What gives them their coherent unity is *the idea of the true.* The true is the ground of all real freedom." (U 244) "The supertemporal ideas of the good, the beautiful, the just are

---

[5] Schelling: *Aphorismen zur Einleitung in die Naturphilosophie.* 1805. Sämmtliche Werke, J. G. Cotta, Stuttgart und Augsburg 1860. Vol. VII, 148f: "46. Reason is not a faculty, not a tool, nor can it be /149/ used. Anyway there is no reason we could have, but only a reason which has and holds us."

forms and realizations of the *unconditionally* true. What becomes accessible in these forms is not some truth *about* something (that kind of truth is always conditional). *The* true radiantly enters into consciousness — radiant and yet in a way which makes us feel that every human accomplishment lags behind that which is unconditionally valid." (M 42)

"The *just,* however, is a value meant to make *possible* the formation of humanity in social life. In its fundamental meaning, the just designates not a positive value of human accomplishments or of men, but the appropriate shape of the *basis* on which alone the positive life values of the true, the beautiful, the good can be realized." (M 203) "The necessary function of the forces which serve the idea of the just is to protect the care of the true, the beautiful, the good from dangers and to deliver it from actual encroachments." (M 209)

"*The unconditionality of which we are certain is the unconditionality of the human task.* — Only through his faith in truth is man *man.* Without it his existence would remain within the happenstance of animality." (M 119) "He who lives in the faith in absolute truth experiences its liberating power." (U 221)

Let me remind you that Medicus speaks of the faith in truth, not of the belief in authoritarian dogmas. The latter are a matter of the always conditional ratiocination whose objects do not approach the unconditional.

"Our ratiocination attains its certainties in mental experiences which are never fully transparent. But the insight into the imperfection of every accomplishment of ratiocination is not disconcerting. For it is precisely this insight which makes ratiocination aware of the fact that the truth which is unconditionally true furnishes a measure which challenges us to go beyond every already attained level of knowledge. We must have *faith* in the absolute truth. The whole life of our intellect is carried by this faith." (U 220)

"The liberty of human knowledge is inescapably restricted. The idea of *the* truth which is *unconditional* can not be realized as any knowledge of an 'object.'" (M 53) "*Objective* truth can be attained by the subject which stands *in opposition* to the objects. But in moral relations the agent does not stand in opposition to a situation. (That seems to be the case only in an intellectualistically stunted view.) The agent himself *belongs* to the moral situation whose very essence is the task he is to resolve." (U 222) (We might remember Fichte's thetical judgements.⁶) Yet not only the moral but the aesthetical consciousness, too, goes beyond the limits set for ratiocination. "The wealth which unfolds in art makes it possible for the life of the spirit to *believe* in the objective truths (the truths valid of objects). Objective truths are contents of *knowledge,* goals of ratiocination. But reality is more comprehensive, more powerful and more engulfing than the sphere structured by ratiocination." (U 226) Objects are conditional and finite. Morality and art desire the unconditional, the non-finite.

"The practice of ratiocination often falls into the error of dealing with the non-finite as if it were finite, an error often criticized yet often repeated even to the point of constructing a scientific

---

⁶ Fichte: *Grundlage der gesamten Wissenschaftslehre.* 1794. Werke I, 116: "A thetical judgment would be one which would not equate one thing with another nor contrast one with another, but which would merely equate the subject with itself. Such a judgment could presuppose neither a ground of relation nor a ground of distinction. Since, owing to its logical form, it would have to presuppose something, this third thing would be a *task* instead of a ground. The originally highest judgment of this kind is 'I am.'"

world-view, especially by means of borrowing terms of natural science." (M 153)

"The content of any *religious* message is the revelation of the superobjective. It cannot be announced in renunciation of the forms of art. The symbols of the announcement appeal to the innermost depth which is beyond the reach of sober literalness and objectivity. Wherever the symbols are taken for prose and turned into objects which must be believed (perhaps under threat of eternal punishment) their content turns into superstition. What is to be accepted as objectively true must be decided by the impersonal criteria of *ratiocination,* by ratiocination alone." (U 249) "Fetters laid on ratiocination make man dishonest." (U 250)

"The question about the ultimate whence all events come" is superobjective. "Words like 'original nebulae' are not 'concepts' but attempts at finding a name for some riddle, more or less formulated. Even the word 'God' is not a concept—at least not for him who is not satisfied with any so-called proof for the existence of God. Such proofs of ratiocination cannot satisfy anyone who has the clear insight that all proofs have their dominion in the territory of objects, and that God is not an 'object.' Wherever the task is to recognize objects and where, therefore, concepts are competent, no final certainty of truth can be gained." (U 239f)

"This, however, is the eternal content of that grace which leads into the depth of the universe, that the transcendent ground of all desire for truth, that is, *the* truth reveals itself in the illuminating experience of a mythology. As Kant says,[7] man is led toward his 'whole calling' (seine ganze Bestimmung). Aristotle said of God that he moves as the beloved. God moves us, as the deepest necessity drives us to love the truth, that is, in the last to love *Him.*" (U 251)

"Ontological truth has more than one face; it comprehends the entire life of the spirit. In this comprehensive sense it is the truth of *religion* and (in the necessary discussion of religion) also the truth of *philosophy*. The symbolic language of religion speaks in terms of *indicatives*. Philosophy speaks in sentences whose form is almost always indicative, but whose content always has the meaning of a *question* and therefore cannot be believed but must be taken critically. (To be sure, the question does not always appear in the light of a clear awareness of its historical conditionality.)" (U 230)

"For Schelling, the dualistic opposition between man and God occurs only in philosophically untutored consciousness, that is, in a mind whose world view consists of imagery ruled by the trends of ratiocination, a mind lacking the insight into its true relation to God. Ratiocination, 'which moves only in terms of opposites,'[8] cannot conceive of God except in opposition to itself! Therefore it finds itself in opposition to unconditional truth. Thus it misses God entirely. God is not an 'object' and, therefore, is beyond the reach of ratiocination." (M 101f)

In the nineteen-thirties when, on a narrow footpath in the Alps, Medicus let me take the lead, while we talked back and forth, he said quite casually: "God is not Somebody." I turned around with the exclamation: "You have never said *that* before!" He retorted: "I have always said it!" — Indeed it must always be said, both, as a correction and as an exculpation of the particular misunderstanding on the part of a man of sheer ratiocination.

---

[7] Kant: *Critique of Pure Reason,* 868: "Essential purposes as such are not the highest. There can be only one highest purpose, and that is none other than the whole calling of man."
[8] *Aphorismen zur Einleitung in die Naturphilosophie,* 78. Werke II, 147.

Such a man is well aware that God is not a dead object. He also has a dim awareness of the authority of unconditional truth which challenges him as a self. And then, in contrast to a dead thing which as such lacks authority, he will say that God is a person. The current image of a divine personality once moved me, in my immaturity, to ask Medicus why he used the word God at all. He replied: "There is no better word!"—But let us return to his writings.

"*Augustine* who took seriously the notion that God is the truth, recognized God as the deepest inwardness of human existence. The epoch of his own past during which he had sought God in outward existence now proved to have been a epoch of alienation. 'Where was *I*, when I searched You? . . . I walked away from myself and could not find even myself; how much less Thee!' (Conf. V, 2)" (M 120) "To be sure, every human word which would designate God by a property remains improper." (M 158)

"Nature deities are capricious. The gods of the Greeks were not *good*. In the higher religions the content of myth is the purely human." (M 317) "The so-called higher religions are distinguished by their evaluation of the natural as that which is overcome or ought to be overcome. In those religions man learns that the meaning of our existence must not be looked for in the *objective world*. Its puzzling nature has no decisive influence on the *meaning of human existence*, but this meaning is of central importance." (M 316) "The higher religions differ from the primitive adoration of gods and idols in this that the interpretation of their own doctrines always participated in the spiritual struggle toward the height of the time, a struggle of centuries. And owing to that participation those religions were in fertile touch with the great epochs of philosophy and their endeavors. The result of this participation benefitted not only those who accepted the religious doctrines in good faith, but even some of those who rejected the doctrines." (U 239)

"Every community has a history. At every time its existence is determined by superindividual tasks. By tackling those tasks, the community creates a new present for itself, in its own decisions. But if it misconstrues or neglects its tasks it lags behind its time, and the relationship between its members turns to be vapid, in some way or other. The community loses the strength and good cheer needed to carry the day." (U 60) "Thus there arises an opposition: humanity versus imposed coercion. And wherever the historical process seeks the solutions of its difficulties in coercion, the very problems of the time lead *backward* into situations which should be *behind* the present." (U 110)

"The disputes on hand ought to find an intellectual solution, but it can happen that the very possibility of a truly intellectual solution vanishes. . . . Cultural catastrophies are a demonic repression of the truth. . . . In situations where demonic powers *rule,* there is no longer any height of possibilities. The very *basis* of action is poisoned." (M 128f) "Where demonic powers are at work there is no absolutely 'good cause' at all." (M 254) "Demonic powers never have any legitimate claim to rule." (M 232)

"In the totalitarian state the notion of 'legal order' attained a position independent of the idea of the just. Once the *unconditional* acknowledgement of that idea was surrendered, the consequences became clear; the very basis of human life lost its *necessary* relationship to humanity. An ostensibly philosophical theory of right blazed the trail by destroying the safe roots of humanity in the ground which alone can carry its unfolding, and thus conjuring up the danger of devastation of that ground." (M 123) "Sociological theories and political ideologies are inadequate if they neglect the inseparable connection between social reality and the idea of the just." (M 213)

It is the same in every totalitarian organization; "the ideas are *manipulated,* they are *tools* for the enforcement of conditional ends, no longer guide posts in the struggle for free humanity." (M 248) The same can happen in the church.

" 'Ecclesia' is a wall,' Paracelsus jots down (Karl Sudhoff: Paracelsus-Handschriften, G. Reimer, Berlin 1899; 338), and he does not mean only the old church but also the churches of the Reformers. The Pope, Zwingli, Luther — 'they condemn each other' (*ibid.,* 411); they are right in their condemnations and therefore they are all wrong. . . . Although Paracelsus praises highly the superiority of the divine spirit over tonsure and chasuble (*ibid.,* 446), he nevertheless knows that fixed orders, binding laws and forms are necessary. Even the wall which is the church comes from God; it is not inevitable that it should restrain the spirit. 'Two temples we need in the blessed life, one for the doctrine, and it is a wall, the other for fulfilling the doctrine, and we ourselves are that temple, in our heart.' (*ibid.,* 259)" (M 99f)

"To seek 'objectivity' — or rather to assert it and therewith to misconstrue the symbolical, this is the misunderstanding which again and again creeps into every orthodoxy." (U 211) Hence "the danger that something which belongs in the domain of culture and is culturally conditioned be twisted into religious validity and therefore offends those who 'have a conscience in their head, too.'*Culture requires freedom; it can tolerate no fetters." (U 212)

"Denominations cannot do without dogmas. Dogmas should be understood as endeavors to give an account of the religious certainty as it is manifest in the historical community, though an account given with the inadequate means of logic. He, however, who believes in *dogmas* thereby narrows the very life which has its home in his denomination; he mistakes its formulations for the life itself." (M 134) "Insofar as dogmatics must make use of ratiocination, its legitimate use can do nothing else but bring about some order in the religious imagery, an order in line with the spiritual life of the time. It cannot bring about any new religious insights. The imagery itself must be understood as *symbolical hints* at the superobjective. . . . With regard to religious experience, the whole task of the intellect is only to see to it that the words in which (as far as at all possible) that experience can be voiced and accounted for, attain the height of the time. —This assignment does not serve the religious insight itself, but only the clarifying order of the words whose true meaning is symbolical. The assignment to the intellect can be fulfilled only where the functions of the spirit are gathered in a personal unity of life which so penetrates ratiocination that the latter cannot even be tempted to assert its independence." (M 154f)

"Wherever life, directed by the superobjective, has freedom of spirit, it will take the mythological shell for what it is, distinguishing it from the content of the faith which the shell protects. However, as long as the sense of objectivity imperiously comes forward in consciousness and does not permit the distinction between shell and content, mythology will set up boundaries between men, even enmities, and it will fetter the minds. But understood *as* mythology it not only gives depth to the life of the spirit but also makes it wide and free. —*Objective imagery* which tries to hold fast superobjective experiences, in short mythology, cannot bring any *unconditional* certainty. (Most of those who would dispute this statement passionately, know 'certainty' only as conditioned by fear or by hope.) Such minds are tied to an outward authority. The tie can remain for a lifetime, and as long as it lasts it will not permit the critical attitude in which every historian accepts the tradition." (M 168)

"A mature freedom of the spirit includes certainty of faith, a certainty no longer bound by mythological shells nor deceived by them. Such freedom leaves to historical critique the *objective* meaning of the sacred (as well as of the secular) tradition. Preventing erroneous conflicts with the timeconditioned presuppositions of the myths, historical critique makes accessible, within the condition of the new times, the supertemporal content of the myths." (M 169)

"A community is in decay if it defames as infidels those who desire the freedom of the spirit. In order to prevent that danger, it is necessary that those whose calling is the care of the intellectually immature do not serve them any thing which would produce in them a conscious opposition to the demands of a serious search for truth." (M 169)

"Dogmatic doctrines of a religion can remain *unchanged* for many centuries and yet furnish conceptual support for the respective confession and thus preserve historical continuity. But significant changes become patent in the art of these same centuries." (U 248) "Art, however, furnishes irreplaceable contributions to the humanity of man and, in this respect, it is revelation of ontological truth." (M 320) "One may speak of 'ontological' truth only where there is a free and alive experience of reality." (M 190) Where an obdurate tradition makes the mythological symbols look as if they were dead, art may still be free or may be free again. In high works of art "the depth of truth becomes manifest. Logical forms do not reach into this depth. It can be revealed only in *symbols,* in creations of aesthetic consciousness. All prophets are artists; what they have to say cannot be told in sober, prosaic sentences; it cannot be accepted without ratiocination, but it does not appeal to ratiocination alone. (The converse also is true. All artists are prophets. Of course, not all are prophets of what is true.)" (M 45)

"A work of art which bears witness to the immeasurable fulfills a *mythological* function. It furnishes the community with an awareness of that which connects its members in the very depth of their existence." (U 176) "Factual evidence must be ascertained by science. Works of art are symbols. They point at the meaning of life as a whole." (U 93)

"Art is *life itself* insofar as it *speaks.* Life is supertemporal. At no time is it exhausted by temporal creations and movements. Life is always full of tensions, and in them it moves beyond every given time toward another. Yet it is present at every time, and it expresses itself, one way or another, in artistic creations." (U 172f) "What is artistic in a work of art can be apprehended only if the work becomes the content of aesthetic experience and, thus, no longer merely 'confronts' us (like substances which confront the chemist who observes their reactions). In aesthetic experience there is no separation between subject and object. To experience works of art means to become inwardly richer. It means to be touched by the *essence* of reality so closely that reality appears less strange and that our ability to understand it increases. Old, long gone cultures become accessible through their works of art. And the art of our contemporaries interprets something of the life which, always full of secrets, embraces us." (M 44)

"Where self-certainty is attained, the form of the ego becomes the bearer of a faith in the substantiality of the *supertemporal ideas,* no matter how that faith is attuned. Among those ideas the ego finds the *content* of the purely human. . . . The faith in the ideas brings the clear and immediate certainty of human freedom." (M 166) But right here we see the precariousness and limitations of our situation. "To speak of an immediate certainty or even to think of it means to objectify it, and to rob it of its immediacy. Wherever immediate certainty becomes the content of knowledge or of communication it is wrapped around with *imagery* which belongs to the *objective* order and therefore is not at all immediate. Without this wrapping we can neither retain the superobjective in our consciousness nor unite a community. Yet the mythologizing wrappings tend to smother the original immediacy, and they can make the contents of faith dubitable, even unbelievable. For, as Kant says, this wrapping 'really turns that which cannot be an object of experience into an appearance'. (*Critique of Pure Reason*, xxx)" (M 167)

In this sense every philosophical doctrine is problematic, and we ought to know it. If we do, the problematic character is no obstacle to our mutual understanding. "He who formulates philosophical doctrines will take care to make it difficult for his readers and hearers to criticize him. His defense against carefully formulated objections requires of him specific lucidity. In such discussion more light is shed on the objectionable proposition, and its truth content becomes clearer. Even if neither of the parties concedes defeat, both have gained owing to their serious evaluation of a foreign point of view. Many a naiveté will be set aside." (U 147)

Philosophy *is* a discipline or science. However, Medicus reminds us, "the last depth of truth is inaccessible to science. Philosophy *knows* about it but does not comprehend it. It acknowledges that depth which embraces in its unity all the spheres of our knowledge and which is the ground of their validity and their limits." (U 268)

The systematic book which Medicus published at seventy-five, bears for its title the one word *Menschlichkeit*, humanity. With his clear insight into the supertemporal which furnishes us with our task and our dignity, Medicus stands on the height of *our* time. In 1944 he said: "If I were asked which certainty I would recognize as indubitable and as basic for the very existence of the spirit of man, I should answer: it is the certainty that we ought to take charge of the shaping of our existence." (U 96) And in 1938 he wrote in the newspaper: "Man cannot be satisfied with that which he is without his own participation. He is not man unless he does something about himself." (U 90)

A millennium and a half ago, a thinker who stood at the height of his time, Augustine, likewise challenged his contemporaries to ponder on the place where they could take a firm stand. For a brief indication of the standpoint of Medicus, I am borrowing a few words from Augustine which I will here translate for a conclusion. Augustine speaks of God without using the word.

"Why is man challenged to know himself? I believe it is in order that he should ponder on himself and live in line with his nature, that is, that he should crave to be in order according to his nature, namely, to be under that under which he ought to be put, and over that over which he ought to stand; under that by which he ought to be ruled, and over that which he ought to rule." (de Trinitate X, v, 7)

121* Nietzsche: Zarathustra, Third Part, Von den Abtrünnigen ?.

Note to page 121*: Medicus is thinking of Nietzsche's expression "wer auch im Kopfe sein Gewissen hat". <u>Zarathustra</u>, Third Part, Von den Abtrünnigen, 2.

AQUINAS AND KANT ON THE IDENTITY OF ESSENCE AND EXISTENCE[*]

There are four and one-half centuries between the death of Thomas and the birth of Kant, a span of time which covers the Renaissance, the Reformation and Counter-Reformation, the development of national sovereignties and colonial powers, modern science, and the Enlightenment. The views of Thomas and Kant seem worlds apart. What do the two thinkers have in common? Surely their concern with morality and, perhaps less obviously, with theology. I propose to look into the latter and its ties with the moral dignity of man.

In his lectures on the *Philosophy of Religion*, Hegel says: "The topic of religion as well as of philosophy is the eternal truth in its own objectivity, God and nothing but God, and the explication of God. Philosophy merely explicates itself when it explicates religion, and when it explicates itself it explicates religion."[1] "The topic of philosophy is God and, properly speaking, God is its only topic. Philosophy is no secular wisdom *(Weltweisheit)* as it has been called, in contrast to faith. It is no worldly wisdom but knowledge of what is not worldly, what is eternal, what is God."[2]

Thomas likewise finds no contrast between faith and philosophy. He says that "the concern of almost all philosophy is with the knowledge of God; on that account, metaphysics whose concern is the divine, is the ultimate part of philosophy to be taught." However, since the administration of temporal affairs leaves little "leisure of contemplation, most men cannot spend the time to reach the height of human inquiry, the knowledge of God." Furthermore, laziness prevents some from undergoing the severe discipline of philosophy. "For, many preliminaries are required for the knowledge of those traits which reason can find in God." On account of such obstacles, "divine mercy provided the injunction that even the insights reason can reach by investigation should be held by faith, so that all could easily partake of the knowledge of the divine, without doubt and error." [3]

Faith as a confirmation of and substitute for philosophical insight is what the Enlightenment will reject. The *Critique of Pure Reason* distinguishes between three steps, from uncertainty to certainty: "The holding of a thing to be true, or the subjective validity of the judgment, in its relation to conviction (which is at the same time objectively valid), has the following three degrees: *opining, believing and knowing. Opining* is such holding of a judgment as is consciously insufficient, not only objectively, but also subjectively. If our holding of the judgment be only subjectively sufficient, and is at the same time taken as being objectively insufficient, we have what is termed *believing.* Lastly, when the holding of a thing to be true is sufficient both subjectively and objectively, it is *knowledge*. The subjective sufficiency is termed *conviction* (for myself), the objective sufficiency is termed *certainty* (for everyone)."[4] It is necessary "to subdue the rashness and presumption of those who so far misconstrue the true vocation of reason as to boast of insight and knowledge just where true insight and knowledge cease, and to represent as furthering speculative interests that which is valid only in relation to practical interests." However "we should not be cut off from employing intellectual *presuppositions* and *beliefs* [Smith translates *Glaube* as faith] on behalf of our practical interest; but they could never be permitted to assume the title and dignity of science and rational insight."[5]

Fichte, Hegel and Schelling have taught us to see that the popular identification of faith and belief is a mistake. Many who cling to a specific set of beliefs and who will surrender none of them, may have no faith at all. Faith does not depend on beliefs. In fact, the strengthening of faith often depends on the surrender of beliefs which prove to be obstacles.[6]

When, in 1787, in the preface to the second edition of the *Critique of Pure Reason* Kant said he had to do away with *knowledge* in order to make room for *faith*, the context and also his second Critique show that he meant the *ostensible* knowledge of transcendent objects, and that his *faith* was the firm conviction of moral obligation and of the autonomy which alone can establish obligation. This is why he speaks of the primacy of pratical reason. In the second Critique he says, "if pure reason of itself can be and really is practical, as the consciousness of the moral law shows it to be, it is only one and the same reason which judges a priori by principles, whether for theoretical or for practical purposes. ...Thus in the combination of pure speculative with pure practical reason in one cognition, the latter has the primacy. ...Nor could we reverse the order and expect practical reason to submit to speculative reason, because every interest is ultimately practical, even that of speculative reason being only conditional and reaching perfection only in practical use."[7] Kant said of "the whole of pure reason" that "this also is presented to reason through its final end in the sphere of the practical."[8]

One must remember Kant's odd doctrine that "theoretical" or "speculative" reason is restricted to the knowledge of objects, and Kant's critical insight that all objects are conditional entities. The categories, for instance substance, or cause and effect, constitute the conditionality of objects but do not apply at all to non-objective entities like the moral law and its obligatory authority. Yet Kant stresses that reason is one, and speculative reason cannot ignore the verdicts of practical. For the sake of reason's oneness, both parties "have to sacrifice proud claims." Practical reason cannot claim to guarantee happiness, and the theoretical cannot claim any *objective* knowledge of what is noumenal. While the *categories* are constitutive conditions of objects, the *ideas* of pure reason are regulative. Kant says, "I accordingly maintain that transcendental ideas never allow of any constitutive employment. When regarded in that mistaken manner, and therefore as supplying concepts of certain objects, they are but pseudo-rational, merely dialectical concepts."[9]

The mistaken employment of the ideas leads to the untenable notion of soul, universe, and God, as three *objective* entities which turn out to be beyond the reach of objective knowledge, mysteries in ecclesiastic language. Yet, says Kant, we cannot, "according to the canon of Epicurus, reject everything as empty sophism which does not certify its objective reality by manifest examples from experience."[10] From the angle of objective reason, entities which are not objective can only be postulated. Kant says: "By a postulate of pure practical reason, I understand a theoretical proposition which is not as such demonstrable, but which is an inseparable corollary of an a priori unconditionally valid practical law."[11] I submit that it is not practical but theoretical reason, not practical *Vernunft* but theoretical *Verstand*, which postulates such objectified entities as soul and God. Theoretical understanding tries to explain why an event happens. But "in practical philosophy it is not a question of assuming grounds for what happens but of assuming laws of what ought to happen even though it may never happen."[12] "Practical philosophy *generaliter* has objective rules of the free mode of acting *(des freien Verhaltens)*. Every [practical] objective rule says what ought to happen, even if it never happens. Among the wicked, too, there are rules according to which they act."[13] I should say the wicked are less free and more tied to rules than the virtuous who are freeer to see that the rule may not do justice to the case at hand. By means of rules the past endeavors to govern the present. Lest injustice be done, moral autonomy ought to overrule such heteronomous intrusions. Such ethical considerations bring into clearer light the dignity of the autonomous self and the danger of mistaking Kant's postulates for objective entities. With regard to the third postulate, God, Kant himself warns against the objectification of the "ideal of the *ens realissimum*" which is first "made into an object" and finally "personified".[14]

As for the soul, insofar as the word designates our irreplaceable selfhood rather than some putative substance, there is no real difficulty. Already the first *Critique* said: "In the consciousness of myself in mere thought I am the being itself (*das Wesen selbst*)....The proposition, 'I think', in so far as it amounts to the assertion, 'I exist thinking', is no mere logical function, but determines the subject (which is then at the same time object) in respect of existence."[15]

In passing, let us note that here Kant himself is on the verge of using the hyphenated phrase subject-object which his followers, Fichte, Hegel and Schelling liked to use. The phrase does not matter. What counts is that, with regard to the self, there is identity of essence (objective content) and existence (subjective form). The 'I think' (i.e. my awareness of myself as a self) determines both aspects, existential and essential.

Following the clue given by Kant, Fichte pointed out that the self "*posits* itself by merely existing and *exists* by merely being posited. I am absolutely *because* I am; and am absolutely *what* I am; both for myself" alone. [16] It is this certainty that I am I which, if put in Kant's words, "amounts to the assertion that 'I exist thinking'," an assertion of which Kant says "it is no mere *logical* function, " not theory but basic philosophical fact. It actually "determines the subject (which is then at the same time object) in respect of existence." In other words, it is the basic *ontological* certainty we have.

Of this indubitable existence of self, Descartes wrote: "For that it is I who am doubting, understanding, willing, is so manifest that nothing could occur by which it could be explained more evidently." [17]

This ontological basis was clearly known to Augustine who wrote: "When the mind is told, know thyself, then the very moment the meaning of the word thyself strikes home, the mind does know itself as a self, and for no other reason than that it is present to itself. Therefore let it not try to *become* certain (*cernere*) of itself as if it were absent, but rather take care to *be* certain (*discernere*) of itself as present." [18]

This self-presence is the core point of the *Critique of Pure Reason*. "The proposition 'I think' contains the form of every judgment." And, "the 'I think' must *potentially* accompany all contents of my awareness." [19]

Of this either potential or actual, implicit or explicit 'I think' Kant says it "is an act of *spontaneity*, that is, it cannot be regarded as belonging to sensibility." [20] The world of sense is phenomenal, that is, a world of universal causal interdependence. But since my responsibility cannot have an external cause but is due to my autonomy by which I myself alone can make myself responsible, I am a "subject of freedom" and as such must posit myself "as noumenon." [21] Kant calls the spontaneous act of self-positing "PURE *apperception*, in order to distinguish it from empirical apperception." [21] Of the empirical self-consciousness Kant said, in refutation of idealism: "This consciousness of my existence in time is connected and, in fact, is identical with the consciousness of a relation to something outside me, and it is therefore experience not invention, sense and not imagination; it inseparably connects this outside something with my inner sense." [22]

This proposition of Kant furnishes the clue for the second principle of Fichte's *Wissenschaftslehre* which points out that I cannot be aware of myself as I without distinguishing myself from some Not-I. "A self that posits itself *as* self-positing, a *subject* is impossible without an object." [23]

Now, since objects are conditioned, and since the autonomous subject as such is not, Kant says, we are confronted by "the paradoxical demand to regard one's self, as subject of freedom, as noumenon, and yet from the point of view of nature to think of one's self as a phenomenon," that is, as a conditioned object. "So long as one had no definite concept of morality and freedom, no conjecture could be made concerning what the noumenon was which should be posited as the ground of the alleged appearance."[24] Objectivistic thinking cannot but wind up with a mysterious object called soul or mind. But critical thinking, be it that of Kant or of Augustine, gets rid of that putative object.

However, the problem remains how freedom is possible at all if nature is conditioned throughout. Kant's answer is that objects are phenomena, since the sense world's forms of universal conditionality are the categories of reason. In contrast, we as responsible noumena are supersensuous. Yet, as responsible beings, we live in the world of sense. The Introduction to the *Critique of Judgment* says: "There must be a ground of the *unity* of the supersensible which lies at the basis of nature, with that supersensible which the concept of freedom practically contains."[25] In the words of tradition, the world is God's.

For Augustine, the ontological certainty of self is the only way to our certainty of God. God is not an afterthought which could occur so as to make more certain that I am I. Augustine says, "as the whole life of the body is the soul, so is God the blessed life of the soul."[26] However, since the certainty that I am I is accompanied by the certainty of a Not-I, as Kant and Fichte pointed out, in other words, since I find myself as not utterly alone but as existing in the universe, sooner or later I cannot help asking the question as to the ground of possibility of my existence as a self.

Kant warned us not to ask this question in the form of causation. Objects are caused, by other objects. They are all conditional. If the word God means anything at all, at least it means unconditional. To speak of God as the first cause means to put him in the chain of causes. So we had better distinguish between causation and creation. Kant says, "the concept of creation does not belong to the sensuous mode of conceiving of existence or to causality but can refer only to noumena. Consequently, if I say of beings in the world of sense that they are created, I regard them as noumena. Just as it would therefore be contradictory to say God is the creator of appearances, it is also a contradiction to say that He, as the Creator, is the cause of actions in the world of sense, as these are appearances; yet at the same time He is the cause of the existence of the acting beings (as noumena)."[27]

Here, Kant uses the word cause in a sense distinct from the category cause. However, he does not say *in what way* God is the cause of us, as selves. Aristotle would say, as "loveable," and Thomas could agree though he might feel that more should be said.

Why does man love God? Thomas says, "the vision of the divine substance is the ultimate goal of any intellectual substance."[28] And "the beatitude of any created intellectual nature consists in understanding."[29] Thus, "one can say either that the ultimate goal of man is God himself who is the *summum bonum* as such, or that it is our enjoyment of God which brings with it a certain delight in the ultimate goal."[30]

Psychologically we might say that we experience delight in the degree in which we experience our true self. And in our love for God we experience our true goal. Thomas says, "the true nature of love consists in this that our desire reaches for the beloved as for the one with whom we are one, in a way."[31] We might comment that one cannot truly love whatever is alien, what remains object, *ob-iectum*, which Boehme literally translated as "what is thrown against one", *Gegenwurf*.

The love for God means a return to one's origin. Religion speaks of conversion which means a turning around. The Chassidim call it *Umkehr*.

So the question is, in what way are we one with God? I would answer, in the ontological identity of our own essence and existence. This does not mean any deification of man.

Thomas asserts the identity of essence and existence *in God* as early as his treatise *De ente et essentia* where he distinguishes different ways in which substances have their essence. One of them is as in God, "whose essence is His being itself." (Thomas uses the infinitive "to be" instead of the noun "existence".) He continues saying that "therefore there are some philosophers who say that God has no whatness or essence because His essence is nothing else than His being."[32] In the *Summa contra gentiles* he says that "in God essence or whatness is nothing else than being" or existence.[33] The seventeenth article of the *Summa theologiae* deals with the question "whether essence and being are the same in God?" And Thomas points out that a "thing whose being differs from its essence must have its being caused by another. But this cannot be said of God. Therefore it is impossible that in God His being should differ from His essence."[34]

Since this is the case only in God, we can know it only insofar as by loving God "our desire reaches for the beloved as for one with whom we are one, *in a way*."[31] "Love brings about a certain union of the lover with the beloved."[35]

To be sure, for Thomas this is not a mystic union. He answers the question "Whether God can be known in this life by natural reason?" starting with his axiom that "our natural cognition begins from sense."[36] In this he agrees with Kant. And Kant could agree with the subsequent argument of Thomas: "Hence our natural knowledge can go as far as it can be led by sensible things. But our intellect cannot be led by sense so far as to see the essence of God." Kant would say, because the essence of God is a transcendent entity, and the idea of God is only regulative, not constitutive. Thomas says, "because sensible creatures are effects of God which do not equal the power of God, their cause. Hence from the knowledge of sensible things the whole power of God cannot be known; nor therefore can his essence be seen."

But if those philosophers were right who say "that God has no whatness or essence because His essence is nothing else than His being," then Kant and his followers could point to our existential act of taking our responsibility as to the indisputable fact in which "we are one, in a way," with God. Kant's own religiosity is what he calls "practical", not "theoretical". It is the moral law which "through the concept of the highest good (the Kingdom of God) as the object and final end of pure practical reason leads to religion. Religion is the recognition of all duties as divine commandments, not as sanctions, i.e., arbitrary and contingent ordinances of a foreign will, but as essential laws of any free will as such." [37] "But as concerns religion, i.e. morals in reference to God as legislator, if the theoretical cognition of Him is to come first, morals must be adjusted in accordance with theology, and not only is an external arbitrary legislation of a Supreme Being introduced in place of an internal necessary legislation of reason, but also whatever is defective in our insight into the nature of this Being must extend to ethical precepts, and thus make religion immoral and perverted." [38]

The primacy of practical reason rests on the identity of essence and existence in the autonomous act of conscience. This is my thesis as for Kant.

What is to be discussed, therefore, is the ulterior question how we can even speak of the identity of essence and existence in God, if there is no such identity in ourselves? The very identity would be meaningless and unintelligible, as indeed it is for a mind which, as Kant would say, "has no definite concept of morality and freedom" and which, therefore, could make no conjecture" concerning the noumenon."

My thesis is that Kant furnished the clue and his successors, Fichte, Hegel and Schelling, the proof for the identity of essence and existence in the self, which could not be conceived at all as self except by this identity. My second thesis is that Thomas is right in asserting the identity as basic in a philosophical theology which could not dare to turn God into an unknowable thing-in-itself. In the third place I hold that the basic empiricism of Thomas and Kant logically leads to the doctrine of Thomas that "we have a more perfect knowledge of God by grace than by natural reason," as well as to the doctrine of Kant that God, not being an objective entity, that is, not being conditional, *objectively* speaking is only a postulate though well founded in practical reason.

Kant argues as follows: "since there are practical laws which are absolutely necessary, that is, the moral laws, it must follow that if these necessarily presuppose the existence of any being as condition of the possibility of their *obligatory* power, this existence must be *postulated;* and this for the sufficient reason that the conditioned, from which the inference is drawn to this specific determining condition, is itself known a priori to be absolutely necessary." [39]

Kant is quite right in *seeking* the ground of possibility of our autonomy which alone bestows "obligatory power" on moral laws. Heteronomy can make moral laws only persuasive or at times coercive but never "absolutely necessary." Obligatory necessity springs from autonomous freedom. As free, I am noumenon. Noumena have no *cause*, in the sense of the category of cause. But the question of the *creation* of noumena is unavoidable. And the question "how a *causa noumenon* is possible" [40] cannot be answered by objectivistic thinking. "The concept of freedom alone makes it possible that we must not go outside ourselves in order to find the unconditioned. ...For it is our reason itself which, through the highest and unconditional pratical law, recognizes that reason as well as the being which is aware of the law (our own person) belong to the pure intelligible world and indeed determines the way in which we can act as such a being." [41] However, it is not argumentative reason which lets us recognize that (putting it in traditional language) we belong to God. "No," says Kant, "my conviction is not *logical* but *moral* certainty; and I must not even say, '*It is* morally certain that there is a God, etc.' but *I am* morally certain, etc.'" [42]

Augustine said that, at least, God is truth, the "truth which teaches inwardly" and, in fact, God is "more inward than my innermost." [43]

It is amazing to find Kant equating the "highest Being" with "the thinking subject in us, as pure intelligence." [44] If the empiricist remnants in Kant were to rule he should not even talk about a world of pure intelligence and should not put the highest Being in apposition with the thinking subject in us. He should abide with his mere postulates. However it was precisely Kant's historical mission to open new avenues. Thus there is little wonder that he often uses post-Kantian expressions. At times he may even reopen old highways, perhaps without an explicit intention.

Here I would like to reopen the avenue marked by the doctrine of knowledge by grace. In an age when satellites send us radio messages about the surface of Mars or Jupiter, we should be beyond the temptation to interpret the expression 'revelation by grace' as meaning a message from outer space. We should also remember Augustine who said that, if God were up there, "the birds would beat us to Him." [45]

With regard to the question, "whether by grace a higher knowledge of God can be obtained than by natural reason?", Thomas wrote: "I answer that we have a more perfect knowledge of God by grace than by natural reason . Which is proved thus. The knowledge which we have by natural reason requires two things: images derived from sensible things, and a natural intelligible light enabling us to abstract intelligible conceptions from them. Now in both of these, human knowledge is assisted by the revelation of grace. For the intellect's natural light is strengthened by the infusion of gratuitous light, and sometimes also the images in the imagination are divinely formed, so as to express divine things better than do those which we receive naturally from sensible things, as appears in prophetic visions." [46]

Such medieval language sounds harsh in the ear of a modern who has not learned to look for the kernel instead of biting on the hard shell. We can never completely get rid of our own shell; neither could Thomas. Nor can we flatly replace his terms with ours. Is his "natural light" the same as Kant's *Verstand*? And has the "infusion of gratuitous light" the same effect as Kant's *Vernunft* which critically lifts us beyond the limitations of *Verstand*? It would be naive to expect flat yes or no answers to such casually formulated questions.

What we can say flatly is that empiricism easily overlooks the basic problem of the genesis of images, or what Thomas calls phantasms. This latter word would seem to suggest that images are the product of fantasy, and that the word sensation points at an event but does not explain it. How the senses can produce mental images is a riddle. Kant did not solve it but wrapped it up in his talk about whatever it is that is "given" to our "sensation". What is given to the senses is a physical stimulus. But why a physical stimulus should result in some mental image like red or hot or sweet is precisely the riddle. Only the untutored writers of old textbooks on so-called philosophy of education could make themselves believe they had the solution when they stultified their naive readers with their talk about stimulus and response. What is it that is responding? Kant says it is our intuition or *Anschauung*. *"Anschauen"* means to look at. But why does an image pop up in my mind when my eyes turn to a physical object or when my brain cells are electro-chemically stimulated, as happens even in a dream?

Kant does say we cannot receive the given (which is by definition shapeless) unless we shape it in terms of time and space, the *a priori* forms of our intuition. That still does not tell us what happens and how. Neither does Thomas tell us more than the fact that images do appear and that, in us, there must be a kind of central "common sense which apprehends whatever is sensed by all specific senses."[47]

Consequently those of our images which depend on what Kant calls the *given* are for Thomas *phantasmata ex sensibilibus accepta*, simply "received" images. This would name though not explain the possibility of similarly receiving images infused by grace.

Now Thomas speaks of images "divinely formed" in us rather than received "naturally from sensible things", images such as

142

"prophetic visions", which "express divine things better." Hegel would say the best expression would be the respective concept. But we cannot arrive at the concept unless we learn to take seriously and read clearly the symbolic imagery of religious language. Thomas who so often falls back on Biblical imagery is closer to such philosophical reading than Kant, the child of Enlightenment. But the clues Kant has given can lead us moderns to a deeper understanding of the concerns of medieval thinkers, and also of our own concerns. I repeat the theme of my paper that the identity of essence and existence in God and, with proper restrictions, in man is a link between the views of Thomas and Kant.

I will cast a closing glance at two examples of prophetic vision. Moses desires to see God in His glory, but he must stand in a cleft of the rock while the divine glory passes by and then only can he see God, though from behind (*Exodus* 33:23). What magnificent picture of the fact that all human visions of God are always seen in retrospect, as views and formulations after the event. Yet there is an even more grandiose and, in this case, verbal vision of the inexhaustible divinity and of the ever open future. Moses asks for God's name, and the answer in Hebrew is "ehee-e asher ehee-e" (*Exodus* 3:14) which Jerome translates *ego sum qui sum*. The English translators say "I am who am". But Schelling stressed what Luther already knew, that the form of the verb can mean either the present or the future.[48] And surely the future tense expresses precisely the supertemporal identity of essence and existence in God: "I shall be who shall be."

NOTES

*Signs for quotations from Thomas: ST = *Summa theologiae*, CG = *Summa contra gentiles*. Quotations from the *Critique of Pure Reason*, 1787 ed. = B and page. Other quotations from Kant: Cassirer ed. (1912-18) = Cass. Vol. and page. Translations are mine unless otherwise stated. Author's insertions in brackets [ ].

1 XI,5: *Der Gegenstand der Religion, wie der Philosophie, ist die ewige Wahrheit in ihrer Objektivität selbst, Gott und nichts als Gott und die Explication Gottes. Die Philosophie expliziert nur sich, indem sie die Religion expliziert, und indem sie sich expliziert, expliziert sie die Religion.*

2 XI,15f: *Die Philosophie hat Gott zum Gegenstande und eigentlich zum einzigen Gegenstande. Philosophie ist keine Weltweisheit, wie man sie genannt hat, im Gegensatz zum Glauben. Sie ist keine Weisheit der Welt, sondern eine Erkenntnis des Nichtweltlichen, ... dessen, was ewig ist, was Gott ist.*

3 CG, I,iv: *Quidam autem impediuntur pigritia. Ad cognitionem enim eorum quae de Deo ratio investigare potest, multa praecognoscere oportet: cum fere totius philosophiae consideratio ad Dei cognitionem ordinetur; propter quod metaphysica, quae circa divina versatur, inter philosophiae partes ultima remanet addiscenda. ... Salubriter ergo divina providit clementia ut ea etiam quae ratio investigare potest, fide tenenda praeciperet: ut sic omnes de facili possent divinae cognitionis participes esse, et absque dubitatione et errore.*

4 Norman Kemp Smith translation (St. Martin's Press, N.Y. 1965) 646; B 850.

5 Smith's translation 427; B 498.

6 See my "Faith *versus* Belief" in the *Journal of Religion*, January, 1946.

7 *Critique of Practical Reason*, Lewis White Beck's translation (The Liberal Arts Press, Indianapolis 1956) 125f; Cass. V,131f.

8 Norman Kemp Smith translation 34; B xxxviii.

9 Ibid. 423 and 533; B 493 and 672.

[10] *Critique of Practical Reason*, Beck translation 125; Cass. V,131.

[11] ib.127; Cass. V,133: *ein POSTULAT der reinen praktischen Vernunft (worunter ich einen theoretischen* [meaning: objectivistic], *als solchen aber nicht erweislichen Satz verstehe, sofern er einem a priori unbedingt geltenden praktischen Gesetze unzertrennlich anhängt).*

[12] *Foundations of the Metaphysics of Morals*, Beck translation 44 (Library of Liberal Arts, 1959); Cass. IV,285.

[13] *Eine Vorlesung Kants über Ethik*. Ed. by Paul Menzer (Rolf Heise, Berlin 1924) p.2.

[14] B 611*; N.K. Smith translation 495[a].

[15] N.K. Smith translation 382; B 429: *im Bewusstsein meiner selbst beim blossen Denken bin ich das Wesen SELBST. ...Der Satz aber: Ich denke, sofern er so viel sagt als: ICH EXISTIERE DENKEND, ist nicht blosse logische Funktion, sondern bestimmt das Subjekt, (welches dann zugleich Objekt ist,) in Ansehung der Existenz.*

[16] *Grundlage der gesammten Wissenschaftslehre*, 1794; I,97f: *das Ich setzt sich selbst, schlechthin WEIL es ist. Es SETZT sich durch sein blosses Sein, und IST durch sein blosses Gesetztsein. ...Ich bin schlechthin, WEIL ich bin; und bin schlechthin, WAS ich bin; beides für das Ich.* - Peter Heath translation 98f (Appleton-Century-Crofts, N.Y. 1970)

[17] *Meditatio II: Nam quod ego sim qui dubitem, qui intelligam, qui velim, tam manifestum est, ut nihil occurrat per quod evidentius explicetur.*

[18] *De trinitate X,ix,12: cum dicitur menti: cognosce te ipsam, eo ictu quo intellegit quod dictum est te ipsam cognoscit se ipsam, nec ob aliud quam eo quod sibi praesens est. ...Non itaque velut absentem se quaerat cernere, sed praesentem se curet discernere.*

[19] B 406 and 131.

[20] B 132; N.K. Smith translation 153.

[21] Preface of the *Critique of Practical Reason*, Cass. V,6f: *die Forderung, sich als Subjekt der Freiheit zum Noumen ... zu machen.* Cp. Beck, p.6, who (by mistake I believe) says "subject *to* freedom." - Perhaps one should emphasize the fact that Kant here uses the word noumenon in the critical sense in which we clearly know ourselves as selves, and not in the uncritical sense in which noumenon

is synonymous with thing-in-itself, by definition unknowable.

[22] B xl*; compare N.K. Smith translation 35*.

[23] *Grundlage* of 1794, I,218; Heath translation 195.

[24] *Critique of Practical Reason*, Beck translation 6; Cass. V, 6f.

[25] J. H. Bernard translation 12 (Hafner, New York 1951); Cass. V, 244.

[26] *De libero arbitrio* II, xvi,41: *Sicut enim tota vita corporis est anima, sic beata vita animae deus est.*

[27] *Critique of Practical Reason*, Beck translation 106; Cass. V,111 f.

[28] CG III,58: *Visio autem divinae substantiae est ultimus finis cuiuslibet intellectualis substantiae.*

[29] ST I, Q 26, A 2, resp: *cuiuslibet intellectualis naturae creatae beatitudo consistit in intelligendo.*

[30] ST IaIIae, Q 34, A 3, resp: *ultimus finis hominis dici potest vel ipse Deus qui est summum bonum simpliciter, vel fruitio ipsius quae importat delectationem quamdam in ultimo fine.*

[31] CG I,91: *videtur propria ratio amoris consistere in hoc quod affectus unius tendat in alterum sicut in unum cum ipso aliquo modo.*

[32] loc.cit. VIa: *Invenitur enim triplex modus habendi essentiam in substantiis. Aliquid enim est, sicut Deus, cuius essentia est ipsum suum esse; et ideo inveniuntur aliqui philosophi dicentes quod Deus non habet quidditatem vel essentiam, quia essentia sua non est aliud quam esse suum.*

[33] CG I,22: In Deo non est aliud essentia vel quidditas quam suum esse.

[34] I, Q 3, A 4: *Utrum in Deo sit idem essentia et esse? - Respondeo dicendum ... oportet quod illud cuius esse est aliud ab essentia sua habet esse causatum ab alio. Hoc autem not potest dici de Deo: quia Deum dicimus primam causam. Impossibile est ergo quod in Dei sit aliud esse et aliud eius essentia.*

[35] ST, IIa IIae, Q 17, A 3: *amor importat quamdam unionem amantis ad amatum.*

[36] ST, I, Q 12, A 12: *Respondeo dicendum quod naturalis nostra cognitio a sensu principium sumit.* - The translation of the entire passage is by Anton C. Pegis: *Basic Writings of Saint Thomas Aquinas*, Vol. I, 109 (Random House, New York 1945).

[37] *Critique of Practical Reason*, Beck translation 133 and 134; Cass.V,140.

[38] *Critique of Judgment*, 89, Bernard translation 311; Cass. V,541f.

[39] B 661 f. Translation by N.K. Smith who, on his page 527, renders *"diese bestimmte Bedingung"* as "this determinate condition". However, *bestimmt* can also mean "specific" as, I believe, it does here.

[40] *Critique of Practical Reason*, Beck translation 51; Cass. Vol,56.

[41] Ibid. V,115; Beck 109f has a different wording.

[42] *Critique of Pure Reason*, Smith translation 650; B 857.

[43] *De libero arbitrio* II,xv,39: *iam ipsa veritas Deus est. ib.* II,ii,4: *Donabit quidem Deus, ut spero, ut tibi valem respondere, vel potius ut ipse tibi eadem, quae summa magistra est, veritate intus docente respondeas.*

[44] B 770: *so müsste er es unternehmen zu beweisen, dass ein höchstes Wesen, dass das in uns denkende Subjekt als reine Intelliganz unmöglich sei.* - Norman Kemp Smith protects the reader against the amazement by inserting an *and;* his translation 595: "he must undertake to prove that a supreme being, and the thinking subject in us, viewed as pure intelligence, are impossible." - Kant holds that as thinking subjects we *are* pure intelligence, regardless of any academic views. I would replace the *and* by a *that,* to save Kant's grammatical apposition.

[45] *Enarratio in Psalmus 130,12: Ubi est Deus tuus? Sed intus est Deus, et spiritualiter intus est, et spiritualiter excelsus est; non quasi intervallis locorum, quomodo per intervalla loca altiora sunt. Nam si talis altitudo quaerenda est, vincunt nos aves ad Deum.*

[46] ST, I, Q 12, A 13; Pegis translation - *Respondeo dicendum quod per gratiam perfectior cognitio de Deo habetur a nobis quam per rationem naturalem. Quod sic patet: cognitio enim quam per naturalem rationem habemus, duo requirit, scilicet phantasmata ex sensibilibus accepta, et lumen naturale intelligibile, cuius virtute intelligibiles conceptiones ab eis abstrahimus. Et quantum ad utrumque iuvatur humana cognitio per revelationem gratiae. Nam*

et lumen naturale intellectus confortatur per infusionem luminis gratuiti; et interdum etiam phantasmata in imaginationem hominis formantur divinitus magis exprimentia res divinas quam ea quae naturaliter a sensibilibus accipimus, sicut apparet in visionibus prophetalibus.

[47] CG II,74: *sensus communis apprehendit sensata omnium sensuum proprium.*

[48] Luther wrote, "*Ich werde sein, der ich sein werde.*" Martin Buber translates: "*Ich werde dasein, als der ich dasein werde. ... So sollst du zu den Söhnen Jisraels sprechen: ICH BIN DA schickt mich zu euch.*" (*Die fünf Bücher der Weisung.* Köln und Olten, Jakob Hegner 1968, p.158.)

Schelling XI,171: "I shall be who shall be." Here therefore, where God speaks for Himself, the name is transposed from the third to the first person, and it would be out of place to seek in this an expression of an /alleged/ metaphysical eternity or changelessness of God. Although we do not know the proper pronuncnciation of the name Jehovah, yet grammatically it can be nothing else than an archaic future tense of hawa or, in the later form, of haja, that is, to be.
XII,33: Everything that is a being stands, as it were, under obligation to Being, is liable to it or attached to it. In so far as it is a being, it does not have the choice to be or not to be, to be thus or not thus. ... In this sense God stands outside of Being, or above Being. Furthermore He is not only in Himself free of Being and is pure essence / Schelling should say pure existence / but is also free against being, that is, He is pure freedom to be or not to be, free to assure a being or not to assume it. This is also contained in the expression "I shall be who shall be." One could translate: the one I will be -- I am not what necessarily is (in this sense), but Lord of Being.

XI,171: "Ich werde sein der ich sein werde;" hier also, wo der Gott in eigner Person spricht, ist der Name aus der dritten in die erste Person übersetzt, und ganz unstatthaft wäre es, auch hier den Ausdruck der metaphysischen Ewigkeit oder Unveränderlichkeit Gottes zu suchen. Es ist zwar die eigentliche Aussprache des Namens Jehovah uns unbekannt, aber grammatische kann er nichts anders sein, als ein archaisches Futurum von hawa, oder in der späteren Form hajah = sein.
XII,33: ... alles, was ein Seiendes ist, ist dem Sein gleichsam verpflichtet, vehaftet, es hat, soweit es ein Sein ist, nicht die Wahl zu sein oder nicht zu sein, so oder nicht so zu sein. ... Gott ist in diesem Sinne ausser dem Sein, über dem Sein, aber er ist nicht bloss an sich selbst frei von dem Sein, reines Wesen, sondern er ist auch frei gegen das

Sein, d.h. eine lautre Freiheit zu sein oder nicht zu sein, ein Sein anzunehmen oder nicht anzunehmen; was auch in dem "Ich werde sein, der ich sein werde" liegt. Man kann dies übersetzen: der ich sein _will_ -- ich bin nicht das _notwendig_ Seiende (in diesem Sinn), sondern _Herr_ des Seins.

(This addition to the first five lines of note 48 was not in the Proceedings of the Lewis and Clark Philosophy Conference on Aquinas and Kant, of May 1974. The quoted passages mark a clear distinction between God and man. They also formulate the difference between Schelling and Hegel.)

YOUNG SCHELLING AND KANT

Fritz Schelling—Friedrich Wilhelm Joseph Schelling—was born January 27, 1775, in Leonberg, six miles west of Stuttgart. In 1777, his father moved from the pastorate at Leonberg to Bebenhausen, three miles north of Tübingen, to become a professor at the preparatory school for prospective theologians, in a former Cistercian abbey, still called a monastery. At age ten, Schelling was placed in the fairly famous Latin school at Nürtingen on the Neckar, halfway between Tübingen and Stuttgart. Two years afterwards he was sent home, because he had covered the entire curriculum. Though less than twelve, instead of the required fourteen, he was permitted to attend the classes at Bebenhausen. His first assignment was a paper on the main proofs for the divine origin of Scripture. He handed it in October 20, 1786, embellished by Latin hexameters of his own. Of course he also learned Greek and Hebrew, even some Arabic. In 1787 he wrote a Latin poem of 81 distichs, *Ad Angliam*, in praise of great Englishmen, among whom, though yonder across the Atlantic, he counted Benjamin Franklin, about whom he said:

Illic fulminibus praescripsit et igni
divo Franclinus iura sacrata dedit.[1]

In my limping English:

Yonder, to lightning prescribed, and even to fire
divine did Franklin its sacred laws ordain.

In 1790, at fifteen, notwithstanding the admission rules, he was accepted as a regular student in the theological seminary at Tübingen. After two years he obtained his master's degree in philosophy, with a thesis on the ancients' explanations of the first origins of human evils, in Latin of course. He presented the Genesis story of the Fall as a philosophical myth or a philosopheme expressed in historical form. He followed it up with an essay in German *On Myths, Historical Legends and Philosophemes of the Ancient World*, his first printed publication, 1793. Having started the study of Kant at sixteen, at nineteen he published a short critical treatise on what he missed in Kant, the *Possibility of a Form of Philosophy As Such*. Its preface is dated September 9th, 1794. His two last and more voluminous writings in Tübingen were his Latin

---

Lecture given at Southern Illinois University in Edwardsville, January 27, 1975, the 200th anniversary of Schelling's birth

theological dissertation 'On Marcion, the emendator of Paul' and the systematic treatise *Of the I as Principle of Philosophy or On the Unconditional in Human Knowledge*, both in 1795. In the same year he published his *Philosophical Letters on Dogmatism and Criticism*. The titles of these three philosophical treatises are significant. I'll end these biographic notes saying that Schelling's best friends at Tübingen were Hegel and the poet Hölderlin, both five years older than he.

Where did Schelling stand philosophically? When Hegel had left Tübingen and was in Switzerland, in Bern, as a tutor in the aristocratic house of Carl Friedrich von Steiger von Tschugg, Schelling wrote to him, on the 4th of February, 1795: "Philosophy must start from the unconditional. The question is only where the unconditional lies, in the I or in the Not-I.... It seems to me the real distinction between critical and dogmatic philosophy lies in this that the critical starts from the Absolute I, the dogmatic from the absolute object or Not-I. The latter, if thoroughly consistent, leads to the system of Spinoza, the former to Kant."[2] Schelling's treatise *Of the I* shows clearly that he had Spinoza's *Ethics* before him and almost literally transcribed the decisive propositions of the First Part but used these formulations to describe the I. This explains why, in the same letter, Schelling wrote: "Meanwhile I have become a Spinozist.... You will soon hear how." The treatise *Of the I*, on which Schelling was working, would tell Hegel. The main influence, of course, came from Kant. On Twelfth Night, 1795, January 6, Schelling wrote to Hegel: "At present I live and move in philosophy.[3] Philosophy is not yet at its end. Kant has given its results. Its premises are still lacking. And who can understand results without the premises?"[4]

In 1802, Schelling wrote of the Kantian philosophy, "the very language in which this philosophy has been presented by its author is important for its evaluation, since it is evident that the language is inseparable from the content and that, in order to philosophize with Kant, one must also speak like Kant."[5] In my opinion, it is easy to examine a student on his knowledge of Kant. All that is needed is a list of one or two dozen of the most important Kantian terms. Let the student tell in plain language just what Kant meant by these terms. This will tell you whether your student has understood Kant or is merely repeating what the textbooks say, and what often misses the point.

The shortest examination would ask for the one most important term. It is *the primacy of practical reason*, "das Primat der praktischen Vernunft."[6] And what does Kant mean by practical reason? Surely not shrewd and efficient intelligence, as the ordinary use of language would suggest. In Greek, *práttein* means to act, *páthein* to be acted upon. It is one of the basic distinctions Aristotle made. Kant makes use of the two root meanings when he distinguishes our *practical* actions from pathological inaction. His word *pathological* does not mean sickly[7] and, for Kant, *practical* does not mean pragmatic in the sense of what works.

He says, "by the practical I mean everything that is possible through freedom."[8] You act freely insofar as you are under no coercion. *Practical reason* is reason insofar as it is pure act. In ordinary language it is moral reason.

Thoughtless people believe our actions are moral if we simply do what some code prescribes. Codes say do this and be rewarded, do the opposite and be punished. If we do not mind the punishment, we will ignore the bidding of the code. Yet it is precisely moral reason which asks whether or not the code does apply in the case before us, and whether its bidding has any moral validity. It is the case before me which tacitly raises the question as to what I *ought* to do. And it is I who must decide just *what* I ought to do. Also, I ought to remember that I am not infallible. At best, a code can help me bring the question in clear focus. At worst, it can squelch the question and induce me to throw away my responsibility. Uncritical conformity to a code makes me irresponsible. I then say, "I merely obeyed the boss!" It is *my* responsibility to ascertain in what degree the code conforms to the reality of the case. And nobody can *force* me to be responsible. Responsibility cannot be given, it must be taken. To be sure, society can make it either hard or easy for me to take my responsibility. If easy, we say we have been given our responsibility. Even then, everybody knows he can renege. We *take* our responsibility by a free decision, each time anew, from case to case.

Now, among the cases which confront me there are quandaries of *thought*. Many a pupil knows that it takes courage to think. Thinking is a responsible act. We ought to weigh every proposed answer; does it in truth solve the problem at hand? Serious thinking is a moral act; hence the *primacy of practical reason*. However, Kant reminds us, "if pure reason of itself can be and really is practical as the consciousness of the moral law shows it to be, it is yet always one and the same reason which judges, whether for theoretical or practical purposes."[9] Our practical purpose is to know what we ought to do, from case to case, our theoretical purpose to know what to think, from problem to problem. Neither can be attained if we do not take our responsibility.

We must be on the job even when we seem to be merely passive recipients of the manifold imagery that comes to us through our senses or in dreams. Taking the expression 'I think' in the Cartesian sense of 'I am aware', Kant says in one of the most crucial passages of the *Critique of Pure Reason*: "The 'I think' must *potentially* accompany" whatever confronts me (alle meine Vorstellungen), otherwise it "would be nothing for me"[10]—potentially, because actually my attention may be concentrated on the object which I happen to observe, rather than on myself as the observer. A good driver watches the road and automatically corrects the slight deviations of his car; a beginner is selfconscious and makes a lot of conscious and often late and jerky corrections.

The fact that we do have subconscious reactions induces many thinkers to fashion theories according to which all human action is automatic. Without the assumption of such automatism, biochemistry would be impossible. All his life, Kant was keenly interested in the development of natural science, but he was also aware of the pitfalls of the assumption that all the knowledge we can have is knowledge of objects. Such objectivism led to "a kind of physiology of the human understanding (that of the celebrated Locke)" and eventually to the skepticism of Hume. Kant calls it "the old wormeaten dogmatism."[11] His own system, called Criticism, has the task of finding "the ground of unity"[12] of the world of objects with the world of our moral duties. He was painfully aware that he never quite finished that task. In his seventy-fifth year, on September 21, 1798, he wrote to his friend, Christian Garve: "Being in fair physical health, I am as if paralyzed for intellectual work. The conclusion of my account in matters of the wholeness of philosophy lies before me, yet I can still not see it completed though I am aware of the feasibility of the task. It is the torture of a Tantalus although not without hope.—The task which occupies me now is the transition from the *Metaphysical Foundations of Natural Science* [his work of 1786] to physics. It must be solved; otherwise there would be a gap in the system of critical philosophy. The respective claims of reason do not cease, neither does the awareness of the possibility of a solution. Yet the solution is impeded by repeated hindrances of vitality...to the point of utter impatience." Thus Kant's letter. Half a dozen years earlier, in 1792, Kant had browsed in Fichte's *Critique of all Revelation* and recommended its publication, but he had never read the whole of any of Fichte's works,[13] and he was probably quite unaware of the existence of Schelling though in 1797 the latter had published a *General Survey of the Most Recent Philosophical Literature*[14] in which he dealt with the incompleteness of the Kantian system.

In the same letter to Garve, Kant wrote: "My starting point was not the investigation of the existence of God, of immortality, etc., but the antinomy of pure reason, from 'The world has a beginning—it has no beginning' to the fourth, 'There is freedom in man— there is no freedom but everything in man is natural necessity'. This it was which first awakened me from the dogmatic slumber and drove me to the critique of reason itself, in order to remove the scandal of an apparent self-contradiction of reason." [15]

Still Kant himself left contradictions, even in crucial terms. One of his fundamental distinctions is between *phenomena* and *noumena*. The Greek verb *phainein* can be translated as "to appear". And appearance can mean what is merely apparent and not real. It can also mean the opposite. If somebody is late and finally "puts in an appearance", he is really here, he is no phantasmagoria. When the sun appears on the eastern horizon it is real, not a dream thing. Kant's doctrine that the objects of science are phenomena must be understood critically, in the sense of something manifesting itself, putting in a real appearance. In this sense, Kant has removed the scandal of subjective idealism according to which, as Berkeley says, to be is to be perceived. According to Descartes and Berkeley, it is God who must guarantee that our perceptions, being subjective, have an objective counterpart. But if the idea of God is also one of our perceptions we land in the skepticism of Hume. This is why, in the introduction to the *Prolegomena*, Kant says: "I openly confess that David Hume's reminder was the very thing which first interrupted my dogmatic slumber."[16]

The very purpose of Kant's Critique was to confirm the objective validity of scientific knowledge in which things are manifest to us although the findings of science require unending rechecks. Our knowledge of nature is not illusory; it is phenomenal because it needs rechecking. And when we speak of things in themselves and call them *noumena* we merely remind ourselves that our scientific research never ends. Kant says of the thing in itself, "the concept of a noumenon is thus a merely *limiting concept (Grenzbegriff)*, the function of which is to curb the pretensions of sensibility."[17] Intellectual entities like truth and self are beyond the reach of the senses. They are not objects. Kant warns that "the division of objects into phenomena and noumena is therefore quite inadmissible."[17]

Yet, in contrast to this critical restraint, we find in the *Prolegomena* the puzzling passage that, while "idealism consists in the assertion that these are none but thinking beings," Kant on his part expresses his stand as follows: "I, on the contrary, say that things as objects of our senses existing outside us *are* given, but we know nothing of what they may be in themselves, knowing only their appearances, that is, the representations which they produce in us by affecting our senses."[18] This is as pre-Kantian and uncritical a statement as any that Locke ever wrote in what Kant calls the Lockean physiology of human understanding.[11] Our senses are objects like eyes and ears and noses, and whatever affects them must be some other object like a lightray, a soundwave, a gas. The *critical* Kant classified all objective qualities as phenomenal, and denied any such qualities in the noumena or things in themselves which are not objects. Yet if you go around on academic campuses and ask what a noumenon is, you will still hear it is something that affects our senses, something which only God knows.

The Kantians of Schelling's time cheerfully exploited this uncritical and pre-Kantian nonsense, and even now their exploitation is still fashionable among would-be scholars who are fond of their own misreading of Kant's famous declaration of 1787: "I found it necessary to deny knowledge, in order to make room for faith."[19] They take knowledge to mean all scientific and philosophical knowledge, and faith to mean their own religious beliefs. Kant meant only knowledge of an objective kind, and by faith he meant faith in reason which leads beyond the limits of *objective* knowledge and leads to philosophical insights.[20]

Speaking critically, we can say with Kant that the negative concept of noumenon, the concept of a thing in itself, is limitative; it limits the domain of objects. That does not mean that there is a second and higher kind of object, called noumena, which science dare not touch, objects known only by revelation. Kant did not shackle science. He showed that its legitimate domain is the entire territory of objects, and that all objects are conditional, phenomenal.

What then is noumenal? Verbal answer: The "unconditional"! But, to use the words of the subtitle of Schelling's treatise *Of the I*, is there anything "unconditional" in human knowledge? Kant says yes, at least our moral obligation. That is, our freely taken responsibility. Freedom is the core concept of Kant. And the concept of freedom is what released the so-called romantic enthusiasm in the generation of Fichte and Hegel and Schelling.

It also released the new, that is, the more consistent and more radical departure in philosophy. For, Kant's primacy of practical reason means the liberation of philosophical thought from the servitude of conditional thinking, from objectivism, from the thought-pattern of objective science. It means that metaphysics really has a domain of its own in which it can "come forth as a science" in its own right, as the title of Kant's *Prolegomena* proclaimed. Fichte coined the word *Wissenschaftslehre*, usually translated as Science of Knowledge, but really meaning the discipline (Lehre) of adequate knowing (Wissenschaft) in philosophical matters. Unless there *is* such a discipline which can be learned and must be practiced, Fichte said there is only philosophy in the derogatory sense of that word, only a sentimental fondness of what looks like wisdom,[21] only a hobby. I sometimes wonder in what degree the cultivation of philosophy is only a hobby of some professors and of students majoring in philosophy.

In order that there be a real discipline, there must be some real unconditional knowledge, something comparable to the impersonal verities of mathematics, whose certainty charmed a Plato. This would answer the question implied in Schelling's first systematic treatise *On the Possibility of a Form of Philosophy as Philosophy*. In his own mind, Schelling had reached an affirmative answer which was immediately confirmed when, still a student at Tübingen, he heard that, at the end of February, 1794, Fichte had accepted the chair vacated by Reinhold at Jena, and then heard of and could read the short book *On the Concept of Wissenschaftslehre* which Fichte had written immediately after accepting the professorship and had published in Weimar, so that the students at Jena "could judge whether they wanted to trust him as a guide to the first of the sciences."[22]—On the second page of his own little treatise, Schelling says his conviction was most decidedly "strengthened by the newest essay of Professor Fichte which surprised him the more agreeably the easier he found it, owing to his own assumed answer,"[23] to follow Fichte's thought. On September 26, 1794, Schelling sent his little treatise to Fichte, thanking him for the help he had found in Fichte's book, which had induced him to write the treatise. Fichte then sent Schelling the first fascicles of the *Grundlage* he was writing in installments for his students at Jena.[24]

According to Fichte and Schelling, the first formulation of whatever is unconditional in human knowledge is the proposition 'I am I'. Now, if you had written down 'I am I', and you were going to memorize it so that you could regurgitate it in a test, you would still be confronted with the question of what it means. Let us ask that question seriously. And, in order to be serious, each one of us must take the word I to mean himself or herself. Unless you do that, you will not understand anything that follows, and you might as well stop reading. My only function here is to put before you words and sentences, and I must leave to you the task of finding out whether I am talking sense or nonsense. Nobody can perform that task *for* you. I will borrow my words from Fichte, and I can only hope you find that my sentences do express a truth about your own self.

First sentence: "I am I for myself alone."[25] Is that so? Or can anyone be you for you? Can anyone feel your feelings in your place? Or ask your questions *as* yours? Or say in your stead this is the true answer? "I am I for myself alone." If you find this to be true, is it true as the result of an argument?—Descartes said this truth is "not deduced by a syllogism but is known by a simple intuition of the mind, as a reality known by itself."[26] And long before, Augustine said it is known simply because, as an I, "I am present to myself."[27] It is an old story but ever new. It is the first step into the story of your own philosophy, not as something of mere personal taste, but as a strict and universally valid discipline.

Second sentence: In saying "I am I for myself alone," the word 'alone' marks a distinction between my I and what is not I. In Fichte's more concise formulation: "I am not any Not-I."[28]—Augustine warned: If you want to know what you mean by I, do not seek yourself as if you were something absent but discern yourself as being present to yourself.[29]

Third sentence, and this is a condensation on my part of much that follows in the exposition of both Fichte and Schelling: "The Not-I from which I am distinguishing my own I can be either another I, a you, or else some It." We cannot meaningfully challenge a mere It to become aware of itself. I cannot ask a piece of wood to admit that it is wood, nor ask my sentences to admit that they are sentences. But it is not meaningless to ask *you* to realize that you are a self, an I, not a Not-I. And you can in fact acknowledge that you are neither I who am putting these words before you, nor the chair on which you are sitting. And if you give the matter a second thought, you can also acknowledge that yourself, which you call I, is not flatly identical with your body and your mental endowments, although they are yours alone and not anyone else's.

Our second sentence brings into sharper focus Kant's statement that "the consciousness is at the same time an *immediate* consciousness of the existence of other things outside me."[30] And it confirms the "refutation of idealism" to which Kant gave four not altogether convincing pages in the *Critique of Pure Reason*.[31]

Our third sentence opens the problem of cosmology. The difference between Fichte and Schelling lies in Schelling's keener interest in a real philosophy of nature (*Naturphilosophie*). In comparison, Fichte's system has its center in ethics. In the *Grundlage* he wrote that, if Wissenschaftslehre "were asked, how then are things-in-themselves constituted, it could offer no answer, save, as we are to make them."[32]

The difference between Schelling and Kant lies in Kant's inclination to see the genuine natural science in physics alone, and to consider the undeniable purposiveness of organisms not as necessarily inherent in nature which, he says, "*ought* to be studied according to the principles of the mere mechanism of nature", although our reason, he admits, "is compelled to conceive of a different principle from that of natural mechanism as the ground of possibility of certain forms in nature", the forms of organisms.[33] Even for young Schelling, nature is alive. Later, at the age of thirty-one, he wrote in the *Critical Fragments* of 1806: "Kant says we know nothing but what is in experience. Very true; but that which really is in experience is what is living, the eternal, or God. The existence of God is an empirical truth, nay, it is the very ground of all experience. For him who has grasped this and has come to know it intimately, the sense for *Naturphilosophie* has sprouted."[34] Kant would have called this gush (*Schwärmerei*), but Schelling detested gush as much as Kant or more. Reading passages in Schelling as the one just quoted, it is our task to find their sober meaning and express it in terms which do not sound gushy.

At this point I must confess that, for me, Schelling's *Naturphilosophie* is still a book of riddles. I dare say I do have a sense for it, which makes me feel the need of an adequate preparation for understanding. Trying to speak soberly, I believe the first requirement in a properly prepared student would be an accurate, year by year knowledge of the situation in the natural sciences around 1800. Schelling and Hegel too blithely assumed that their contemporary scientists knew what they were talking about. Both of them took for scientific truth terms like Brown's sensibility and irritability. And they took sciences still in the making, like electro-magnetism, as if they had already matured. They even contributed hunches. Schelling surmised a connexion of electricity with magnetism, and his pupil, Hans Christian Oersted (1777-1851) demonstrated it experimentally, July 21, 1820.[35] If one knew exactly the scientific literature of the time, one could perhaps sort out what in Schelling's *Naturphilosophie* was borrowed or merely copied, and what could be called intuitive anticipations on the part of Schelling himself. But if there are any such anticipations, one would still need a second preparation, demanding more study than the first, that is, a knowledge of the present twentieth century situation in the sciences. I for one never liked chemistry, I missed the boat of physics in 1915, and I am deplorably ignorant of biology. Thus I must toss the ball to younger men. I do believe that Schelling is right in demanding that the natural scientist must have an empathy with things, and that we are wrong when we refrain from looking into his *Naturphilosophie* and reject it simply as romantic gush.

But back to our three sentences regarding the connection between I and Not-I. The title of Schelling's treatise *Of the I as Principle of Philosophy* would seem to make him side with Fichte for whom all philosophy worthy of the name has its principle in the I alone. That would seem to rule out all *Naturphilosophie*. However, Schelling's *Letters on Dogmatism and Criticism* stress not only the possibility but the actuality of dogmatism, *i.e.*, a philosophy whose principle is an It, be it matter or an objectified I, like the monad of Leibniz. Schelling repeatedly declared that the most consistent dogmatism is Spinozism, and he pointed out that Spinoza's concept of substance turns out to have the form of I.[36] Spinoza defined substance as " that which is in itself and is perceived by itself."[37] The Hegelian somersault (Umschlagen), that is, the metamorphosis of one concept into its opposite, here Spinoza's Not-I God into the I, is complete in the 36th Proposition of Part V of the *Ethics*: "The intellectual love of the mind towards God is the very love with which He loves Himself."[38]

Fichte and Schelling call a philosophy which starts from the I criticism, one which starts from an It dogmatism. In the *Letters* of 1795, Schelling says "that both systems have the same problem" of a real starting point, "but that problem cannot be solved at all theoretically, only *practically*, that is, through freedom....Which one of the two solutions we choose depends on the freedom of spirit we ourselves have acquired. We must first *be* what we then theoretically claim to be....we must have worked our way to the point from which we then want to start. Man cannot *argue* himself up to that point, nor be brought to it by the argument of others."[39] Two years later, in 1797, Fichte wrote: "What kind of philosophy one chooses depends on what kind of man one is, for a philosophical system is no dead equipment which one could acquire or discard at will, it is animated by the soul of the man who has it."[40]—However, Schelling also points out "the mighty charm of dogmatism which it exerts inasmuch as it does not start from abstractions nor from dead axioms but (if it is real dogmatism) from something that *exists* and therefore defies all mere words and dead axioms."[41]—In the religious form of dogmatism, this charm issues from the actually existing beliefs which are persuasive for the believer. This is so in all religions, including Marxism, Maoism and McCarthyism.

The It of the dogmatist exists in his firm belief, be it the matter of the materialist or the gods or the objectified spirit of the spiritualist. This is why they both reject the reflective thinking of philosophy as mere verbiage or as dangerous heresy, and why, on their part, they think up argument after argument to bolster their beliefs. The dogmatist does not dare to admit that the reality of the self consists in the sheer intellectual intuition in which, as Augustine says, I am present to myself.[27] For the spiritualist the self is a soul, a ghostly *thing*, and for the materialist it is nothing. And since I as I am *not* a thing, the negative statement of the materialist is stronger than the positive of the spiritualist, as long as the latter does not succeed in his endeavor at converting his fellow man by at least making him *feel* that he is a self. But mere feeling is not enough.

The question which the critical philosopher must face is, to use Kant's phrase, the ground of possibility of an I. How is it possible for me as a creature to realize that I am I? That I am alive, as Augustine would say.[42] Like Schelling, Augustine was a thinker who said that religion need *not* deviate into dogmatism. Yet if you go and merely read and then recite that churchfather's statement that "as the whole life of the body is the soul, so is God the blessed life of the soul",[43] you have a mouthful of words and yet no intelligible meaning. Dogmatists then inform you that Augustine has what they call a theory of illumination. But where is the light switch God turns on, so that you can see? Such theories are nonsense because they talk about things. For dogmatists only things are facts; they ignore the act by which alone I can realize that I am I. To philosophize critically means to gain insight into the reality of that act. Notions like divine illumination, or revelation, are mere theories. So are postulates, in the sense which Kantians read into that word of Kant.

In the letter already mentioned which, three weeks before his twentieth birthday, Schelling wrote to Hegel, he said, here at Tübingen "there are Kantians in abundance. Out of the mouth of babes and sucklings philosophy has prepared its own praise.[44] Through many exertions our thinkers have finally found the point which marks how far one dare to go forward with philosophy, seeing that one cannot progress at all without this vexatious science. They have firmly established themselves on this point, built tabernacles[45] in which it is good to dwell and for which they praise God, the Lord! And who is going to expel them, in the remainder of this century? Once they are firmly settled, only the devil could move them....By now, all kinds of dogmas have been branded with the name of postulates of pure reason, and where the proofs of theory and history do not suffice there the practical reason (of Tübingen!) chops the knot.... I am firmly convinced that the old superstition, not only of positive religion but also of the so-called natural religion, is already combined with the terminology of Kant, in the heads of most. It is a pleasure to see how they can pull the strings which make their moral proof move; before you expect it, the *deus ex machina* jumps out, that personal individual being which sits up there, in heaven."[46]

The old God who sits up there in heaven! I have no evidence that Schelling ever knew the passage in Augustine which says: "where is your God? But God is inside, the way spirit is inward, and he is above, the way spirit has authority over us.[47] God is 'above' not as by intervals of space, the way things are higher. For if we were to look in that kind of height, the birds would beat us to God."[48]

There is a very significant passage in the *Critique of Practical Reason*: "The concept of creation does not belong to the sensuous mode of conceiving of existence or to causality but can refer only to noumena. Consequently, if I say of beings in the world of sense that they are created, I regard them only as noumena. It would therefore be contradictory to say God is the creator of phenomena [or] of actions in the world of sense....Yet at the same time He is the cause of the existence of the acting beings (as noumena)."[49] Obviously here the word 'cause' is not used in the sense of the category of cause. If you ask in what sense it *is* used you may fall back, for the moment, on Aristotle's statement that God acts "as the beloved", ὡs ἐρώμενον.[50] In the *Critique of Pure Reason*, Kant had warned against turning God, "this idea of the sum of all reality, into an object" and finally and quite naturally "personifying" it.[51]

In 1806, in his *Aphorism* 52, Schelling said: "In no kind of knowledge can God occur as known, as object; as known he ceases to be God. We are never outside of God so that we could set him up in front of us, as an object....Knowledge of God means being in God."[52]

This is not a matter of arbitrary choice, nor of taste, nor a psychological need. It is an overruling condition of the human being. And so I must repeat the question of a little while ago: what is the ground of possibility of my being I by free act? And it is this question which induces Schelling, in his treatise *Of the I*, to speak of "the absolute I". What is that?

I trust you realize that the latter question, although asked so plainly and innocently, may be beside the point. For if it were possible to tell *what* the absolute I is, we should have a definition which, as the word *finis* says, would end the matter, setting the term,[54] determining what really has no end. Yet your question is legitimate. And since I must make an end of this too long exposition, I will take the easy way and quote from the letter[2] Schelling wrote to Hegel, February 4, 1795: "God is nothing but the absolute I." And a month later, in the treatise *Of the I*, Schelling repeats: "God, in practical regard, is absolute I, which negates every Not-I. Inasmuch as, in a schematic way, the non-finite I is represented as the last goal of the finite I and therefore *outside* the finite I, in practical philosophy God can be represented schematically as outside the finite, but only as *identical* with the non-finite."[56] Inasmuch as theoretical philosophy in the Kantian sense deals with determinable definite entities, Schelling can say, in the letter just quoted, that for theoretical philosophy God is nothing, $=0$.[56]

You may remember that Paul Tillich wrote: "It is as atheistic to affirm the existence of God as it is to deny it. God is being-itself, not a being."[57]

For Kant, God certainly is not *a* being. *The Critique of Pure Reason* says: "The first error which arises from our using the idea of a supreme being in a manner contrary to the nature of the idea, that is, constitutively [*i.e.* constituting an object], and not regulatively only, is the error of lazy reason."[58] The result is the non-existent God-object.

Young Schelling wrote, in the *Letters on Dogmatism and Criticism*: "weak reason is not the reason which *cannot* know an objective God, but a reason which *desires* to know such a God."[59] Such untutored reason never learned what the word 'idea' means, in disciplined philosophical language.

In the quaint language of moralism, Kant calls God "the ideal of pure reason" and, switching to the more philosophical word 'idea', he says the idea of God "must, as a mere idea, find its place and its solution in the nature of reason, and must therefore allow of investigation."[60]

The investigation never arrives at final formulations. Even the Ecumenical Councils produce only definitions. Yet, at the time of this bicentennial, we may be satisfied with the formulations the older Schelling furnished. In *The Ages of the World,* in 1811, he wrote: "With respect to his highest self, God *is* not revealed, he keeps revealing himself, in order to be manifest as the very freest being."[61] And in the *Account of Philosophical Empiricism,* the name chosen for his own system, Schelling wrote, in or before 1836: "One could very well say that God is really nothing in itself; he is nothing but relation and pure relation, for he is only the Lord; everything we add turns him into mere substance. He really exists, as it were, for no purpose other than being Lord of being. He is the only nature not concerned with itself, rid of itself, and therefore absolutely free. (Everything substantial is concerned with itself, constrained by itself and unfree.) God alone has nothing to do with himself. He is *sui securus,* sure of himself, and therefore rid of himself, and consequently concerned only with other entities. One might say he is wholly *out of himself*, therefore free of himself, and consequently the one who liberates everything else."[62]

NOTES

[1] G.L. Plitt: *Aus Schellings Leben. In Briefen.* (Hirzel, Leipzig 1869) I, 17.

[2] Plitt, I, 76.

[3] Obvious reference to Acts 17:28.

[4] Plitt, I, 73.

[5] Schelling's works edited by his son, K.F.A. Schelling, (Stuttgart and Augsburg 1856-61). Reference will be made simply by volume and page. V, 185.

[6] Kant's works edited by Ernst Cassirer (Berlin 1912-18). Henceforth Cass. Lewis White Beck's translation of the *Critique of Practical Reason,* 124-126 (Bobbs-Merrill, Indianapolis 1956). Henceforth PrR, Beck.

[7] *Critique of Pure Reason,* second edition (1787) 830. Simple page numbers will refer to this Critique. Norman Kemp Smith's translation (St. Martin's Press, New York 1965) 633. Henceforth Smith.

[8] 828; Smith, 632.

[9] Cass., V, 131; cp. Beck's slightly different translation, PrR 125.

[10] 131, Section 16; cp. Smith, 152.

[11] First edition of the *Critique of Pure Reason* (1781) iii-iv; Smith, 8.

[12] Introduction to the *Critique of Judgment*, II; Cass., V, 244. J. H. Bernard's translation (Hafner, New York 1951) 12. Henceforth Bernard.

[13] Fritz Medicus: *Fichtes Leben* (Meiner, Leipzig 1922) 49.

[14] I, 343-452. A second edition appeared 1809 in a collection of Schelling's works, under the somewhat misleading title *Essays Elucidating the Idealism of Wissenschaftslehre.* Students of the history of Philosophy should read it.

[15] Cass., X, 351f., Letter 432.

[16] Cass., IV, 8. Kant wrote "die Erinnerung *des* David Hume", not "meine Erinnerung *an* David Hume" as Beck misread when he translated "my recollection of David Hume", *Prolegomena* (Bobbs-Merrill 1950) 8. Henceforth Prol.

[17] 311; Smith, 272.

[18] Cass., IV, 38; Beck, Prol. 36. Apparently Schelling forgot this passage when, eagerly defending the critical Kant against the pre-critical Kant, he wrote in his *Survey* of 1796: "Kant started by declaring that the first in our knowledge is intuition. This declaration soon turned into the thesis that intuition is the lowest level of knowledge. Yet it is the highest in the human mind, it is that from which all our other items of knowledge obtain their value and their reality. Furthermore, says Kant, what must precede intuition is an affection of our sensibility. He left entirely undecided the question where this affection comes from. On purpose he omitted something which only later was to appear as the last and highest problem of reason. But both adherents and opponents of his philosophy scrupulously picked up what its author had left behind with good reason. And since Kant then proceeded to speak of things in themselves, it was inferred that by all means it must be things in themselves which affect us. However, all one had to do was to read a few pages farther in order to see that, according to Kant's philosophy, everything which for us is object and thing and in contrast to us, has become so only by an original systhesis of intuition." (I, 355).

[19] xxx; Smith, 29.
[20] See Fritz Medicus: *On Being Human* (Ungar, New York 1973) 123.
[21] Fichte, I, 44.
[22] Fichte, I, 30.
[23] I, 88.
[24] Schelling's letter of January 6, 1795, to Hegel. Plitt, I, 73 — Fichte's *Grundlage* has been translated by Peter Heath: *Fichte: Science of Knowledge* (Appleton-Century-Crofts, New York 1970). Hereafter referred to as Heath.
[25] Fichte, I, 98; Heath, 99. Fichte wrote: "Ich *bin* nur für mich." Heath translates, "I *exist* only for myself." But in time and space I am not non-existent for others. Fichte is here not concerned with that existence but with the sheer meaning of I. Hence my insertion: "I am *I* for myself alone."
[26] *Meditations*, Response to the Second Objection: neque cum quis dicit, *ego cogito, ergo sum, sive existo*, existentiam ex cogitatione per syllogismum deducit, sed tanquam rem per se notam simplici mentis intuitu agnoscit.
[27] *De Trinitate*, X, ix, 12; cum dicitur menti, *cognosce te ipsam*, eo ictu quo intelligit quod dictum est *te ipsam*, nec ob aliud quam eo quod sibi praesens est.
[28] Shortened from Fichte, I, 104 (10); Heath, 104 (10).
[29] loc. cit.: Non itaque velut absentem [mens] se quaerat cernere sed praesentem se curet discernere.
[30] 276f.; Smith, 245.
[31] 274-279; Smith, 244-247.
[32] Fichte, I, 286; Heath, 252. It is my conjecture that Fichte's cue for this statement was in the *Critique of Judgment* where Kant says man's existence contains in itself "the highest purpose to which, as fas as is in his power, he can subject the whole of nature, and contrary to which at least he cannot regard himself as subject to any influence of nature." Cass., V, 515; Bernard, 285f.
[33] Cass., V, 465f.; Bernard, 234f.
[34] VII, 245.
[35] Charles Singer: *A Short History of Scientific Ideas to 1900* (Oxford University Press 1959) 359.—Tenney L. Davis: The Faraday Celebrations 1931, *Journal of Chemical Education* Vol. 9, No. 7, July 1932, 1204.
[36] I, 171.
[37] *Ethics*, Part One, Def. III: Per substantiam intelligo id quod in se est et per se concipitur.
[38] Mentis amor intellectualis erga Deum est ipse Dei amor, quo Deus se ipsum amat.—John Wild: *Spinoza. Selections* (Scribner, New York 1930) 392.
[39] I, 307f.
[40] Fichte, I, 434.
[41] I, 290.
[42] *De Trinitate*, XV, xii, 21: qui certus est de suae vitae scientia non in ea dicit 'Scio me vigilare' sed 'Scio me vivere'.

[43] *De libero arbitrio*, II, xvi, 41: Sicut enim tota vita corporis est anima, sic beata vita animae Deus est.
[44] Obviously Psalm 8:2: Ex ore infantium et lactantium perfecisti laudem.
[45] Tabernacles or tents; Matthew 17:4; Mark 9:5; Luke 9:33.
[46] Plitt, I, 72f.
[47] I am trying to render the meaning of *spiritualiter*. Our word 'spiritually' has lost its flavor and should be "thrown out and trodden under foot" like salt that lost its saltiness. Matthew 5:13.
[48] *On Psalm 130*, 12.
[49] Cass., V, 111f.; Beck, PrR 106.
[50] *Metaphysics* 1072b3.
[51] 611*; Smith 495^a.
[52] VII, 150.
[53] 857; Smith, 650.
[54] The conductors shout *Roma Termini* when your train arrives at the end station, in the eternal city.
[55] I, 201.
[56] Plitt, I, 77.
[57] *Systematic Theology* (University of Chicago Press 1951) I, 237.
[58] 717; Smith, 561.
[59] I, 290f.
[60] 642; Smith, 514.
[61] VIII, 308. Cp. Bolman's translation (Columbia University Press 1942) 196.
[62] X, 260. Cp. XI, 571.

THEOLOGICAL EPISTEMOLOGY IN AUGUSTINE, KANT AND SCHELLING

Augustine's *Soliloquies,* written in fall or winter of 387, during his retreat before his baptism, are a dialogue between him and reason. He says what he really wants to know is God and the soul. Reason asks: "And nothing else?" Augustine replies: "Nothing at all!"[1] The year before, in the treatise *On Order,* he spoke of the discipline of philosophy, "whose question," he said, "is twofold, the one about the soul, the other about God. The first lets us know ourselves, the second our origin. The former is sweeter, the latter dearer. The former makes us worthy of the blessed life, the latter makes us blessed. The former pertains to learners, the latter to the learned."[2]

Knowledge of self has methodical priority,* and it is a most certain knowledge. "It is our innermost knowledge by which we know that we are alive. And with regard to it no skeptic can say, 'Perhaps you are asleep and do not know it, and what you see is a dream.' Who does not know that the visions of sleepers are very similar to things seen by those who are awake? But he who is certain in his knowledge that he is alive does not express his certainty saying 'I know that I am awake' but instead 'I know that I am alive.' No matter whether he is sleeping or awake, he is alive. Nor can he be deceived in this knowledge by dreams, because dreaming in sleep also means living."[3]

Dreams can give us a haunted feeling of helplessness. We often escape it by waking up. Is there a comparable escape from the skeptical question whether life itself is but a dream?

If philosophical reflection affords me certainty that I am alive, life is doubly sweet. Still there is the question: Why life? More strictly: Is there a ground or "principle of possibility"[4] of life? Though reason finds the first retort to the skeptic sweet, it still

---
* Schelling: <u>Darstellung der reinrationalen Philosophie</u> (XI,569): nicht Postulat der praktischen Vernunft. Nicht diese, wie Kant will, sondern nur das Individuum führt zu Gott. (Presumably written as late as 1854.)

165

seeks the dearer certainty of that ground or *ratio*. This is what makes man a rational animal.

For, says Augustine in a letter to Honoratus, "the rational creature (being fit to become aware of its ground)... is made in such a way that by itself it cannot be the good by which it becomes blessed. But if, in its mutability, it turns to the immutable good

---

[1] *Soliloquia* I, ii, 7: Deum et animam scire cupio.—Nihilne plus?—Nihil omnino.

[2] *De ordine* II, xviii, 47: Cuius [philosophiae] duplex quaestio est: una de anima, altera de Deo. Prima efficit ut nosmetipsos noverimus; altera ut originem nostram. Illa nobis dulcior, ista charior; illa nos dignos beata vita, beatos haec facit; prima est illa discentibus, ista iam doctis.

[3] *De trinitate* XV, xii, 21: Intima scientia est qua nos vivere scimus ubi ne illud quidem academicus dicere potest: 'Fortasse dormis et nescis et in somnis vides.' Visa quippe somniantium simillima esse visis vigilantium quis ignorat? Sed qui certus est de suae vitae scientia non in ea dicit: 'Scio me vigilare,' sed 'Scio me vivere.' Sive ergo dormiat sive vigilet, vivit.

[4] *Critique of Pure Reason* 813: Prinzip der Möglichkeit.—Compare what Kant says in the preface of 1787, xxvi*: In order to know an object I must be able to prove its possibility (be it from its reality by testimony of experience, or a priori by reason). Einen Gegenstand *erkennen*, dazu wird erfordert, dass ich seine Möglichkeit (es sei nach dem Zeugnis der Erfahrung aus seiner Wirklichkeit oder *a priori* durch Vernunft) beweisen könne.

[5] *Epistula 140* xxiii, 56: Proinde rationalis creatura ...ita facta est, ut sibi ipsa bonum quo beata fiat esse non possit; sed mutabilitas eius si convertatur ad incommutabile bonum fiat beata; unde si avertatur misera est. — Przywara beautifully renders *rationalis creatura* as "die zum Grund hin fähige Kreatur," an expression which I am borrowing, in parentheses. (Erich Przywara: *Augustin. Die Gestalt als Gefüge*. § 63, p. 151. Hegner, Leipzig, 1934).

[6] *De libero arbitrio* II, xvi, 41: Sicut enim tota vita corporis est anima, sic beata vita animae Deus est.

[7] *De vera religione* xxxix, 73: Omnis qui se dubitantem intelligit, verum intelligit, et de hac re quam intelligit certus est: de vero igitur certus est. Omnis igitur qui utrum sit veritas dubitat, in seipso habet verum unde non dubitet; nec ullum verum nisi veritate verum est. Non itaque oportet eum de veritate dubitare, qui potuit undecumque dubitare.... Non enim ratiocinatio talia facit, sed invenit.

[8] *De trinitate* X, x, 14: Vivere se tamen et meminisse, et intelligere, et velle, et cogitare, et scire, et iudicare quis dubitat? Quandoquidem etiam si dubitat, vivit; si dubitat unde dubitet, meminit; si dubitat, dubitare se intelligit; si dubitat, certus esse vult; si dubitat, scit se nescire; si dubitat, iudicat non se temere consentire oportere.

[9] Ibid., X, iii, 5: Quid ergo amat mens cum ardenter se ipsam quaerit ut noverit, dum incognita sibi est? Ecce enim mens semetipsam quaerit ut noverit, et inflammatur hoc studio. Amat igitur. Sed quid amat?... An ei fama praedicavit speciem suam sicut de absentibus solemus audire? Forte ergo non se amat, sed quod de se fingit hoc amat longe fortasse aliud quam ipsa est.... Cur ergo, cum alias mentes novit, se non novit, cum se ipsa nihil sibi possit esse praesentius.

[10] In 1792, Fichte wrote a review of Gottlob Ernst Schulze's anonymous book *Aenesidemus*. His refutation of this skeptic reminds one of passages in Augustine, though there is no evidence that Fichte studied Augustine. The review says that the idea of self "is distinguished from all other ideas by the fact that we realize it by intellectual intuition, by the *I am*. Specifically *I am simply because I am*. All objections to this, raised by

it is blessed, and therefore if it turns away miserable."[5] And in the treatise *On Free Will* he says: "Just as the soul is the whole life of the body, so is God the blessed life of the soul."[6]

Our epistemological inquiry must go step by step. The first question regards the certainty of self and the nature of doubt. The second deals with the intellectual obstacles which bar the way to God. And the third ascertains adequate ways.

The first radical doubt concerns the self. Is the experience of selfhood only phenomenal? And what would noumenal certainty be? In his treatise *On True Religion*, Augustine says: "Everyone who actually understands that he is doubting, understands something that is true, and of this fact which he understands he is certain; therefore he is certain of something true. Consequently everyone who is doubting of the truth has in himself something true of which he does not doubt; and nothing is true except by the truth. Thus, anyone who can doubt at all, must not doubt of the truth.... And ratiocination does not produce what is true but finds it."[7] In the book *On the Trinity*, he writes: "Who can doubt that he is alive, that he remembers, understands, wills, inquires, knows, judges? If he doubts, he understands that he is doubting; if he doubts, he seeks certainty; if he doubts, he is thinking; if he doubts, he knows that he does not know; if he doubts, he judges that he ought not give his consent rashly."[8] In the same book we read: "What then does the mind love when it ardently seeks itself so that it may know itself, while it is still unknown to itself? Behold, the mind seeks itself so that it may know itself, and it is inflamed by its zeal. It does love. But what does it love? ... Has its own nature been pointed out to it by hearsay, the way we hear about absent things? Then perhaps it does not love itself but rather something it merely imagines itself to be, perchance far different from what it is itself." Augustine reminds us that our eyes can see themselves only in a mirror, and by direct sight see only other eyes. Does the mind similarly know other minds first, and itself only as one of that kind? And Augustine goes on to say: "Then why, if the mind knew other minds, would it know itself, since nothing can be more present to itself than the mind?"[9]

Augustine's formula that the mind is present to itself, though using the noun "mind" (*mens*) rather than the pronoun I or the word self, is as vivid as Fichte's statement of 1794 that "the I is *what* it is only *for* the I."[10]

Augustine finds it odd that in the mind there should appear "the disgrace of the error when the mind cannot distinguish the images of sense from itself and thus cannot see itself alone."[11] Fichte was annoyed by the same disgrace he saw in his contemporaries when they were unable to understand what they read about his pure I. In his *Sunclear Report* of 1801 he wrote: "They may have believed that such a pure I is a thing which collapses in itself or returns into itself like a switchblade, a thing which is originally in the mind and can be discovered there, like the waffle iron of the forms among the Kantians. They have busily looked for this switchblade and have found none, and now they conclude that those who claim to have seen it must have been mistaken."[12] In 1794, keenly aware of Kant's crucial concept of autonomy, Fichte wrote: "Most people could be more easily persuaded that they are a piece of Aenesidemus, rest sheerly on his attempt to bestow objective validity (an sich gültig) on the absolute existence and autonomy of the I—a validity nobody knows for whom and how—whereas the autonomy is valid only *for the I as such*. The I is *what* it is, and *because* it is I, *for* the I." (My translation.) Werke I, 16.

[11] *De trinitate* X, viii, 11: Hinc ei oboritur erroris dedecus dum rerum sensarum imagines secernere a se non potest ut se solam videat; cohaeserunt enim mirabiliter glutino amoris.

[12] *Sonnenklarer Bericht*. Werke II, 365: Sie mögen wohl geglaubt haben, dass so ein reines Ich, ein zusammenfallendes und in sich zurückgehendes Ding, ungefähr wie ein Einlegemesser, ursprünglich im Gemüte, so wie das Waffel-Eisen der Formen bei den Kantianern, vorgefunden werden sollte; haben eifrig nach diesem Einlegemesser gesucht, und keins gefunden, und schliessen nun, dass diejenigen, die es gesehen haben wollen, sich getäuscht haben.

[13] *Grundlage der gesammten Wissenschaftslehre*. Werke I, 175★: Die meisten Menschen würden leichter dahin zu bringen sein, sich für ein Stück Lava im Monde, als für ein Ich zu halten. Daher haben sie Kant nicht verstanden, und seinen Geist nicht geahndet; daher werden sie auch diese Darstellung, obgleich die Bedingung alles Philosophierens ihr an die Spitze gestellt ist, nicht verstehen. Wer hierüber noch nicht einig mit sich selbst ist, der versteht keine gründliche Philosophie, und er bedarf keine. Die Natur, deren Maschine er ist, wird ihn schon ohne all sein Zutun in allen Geschäften leiten, die er auszuführen hat. Zum Philosophieren gehört Selbstständigkeit: und diese kann man sich nur selbst geben.

[14] See my translation in METAPHILOSOPHY, Vol. 6, No. 1, January 1975.

[15] *De trinitate* X, viii, 11: Et haec est eis immunditia quoniam dum se solum nititur cogitare hoc se putat esse sine quo se non potest cogitare. Cum igitur ei praecipitur ut se ipsam cognoscat, non se tamquam sibi detracta sit ∧ quod sibi addidit detrahat. Interior est enim ipsa non solum quam ista sensibilia quae manifeste foris sunt, sed etiam quam imagines eorum quae in parte quadam sunt animae quam habent et bestiae, quamvis intelligentia careant, quae mentis est propria. Aquaerat, sed id

[16] *Grundlage der ges. WL*, Werke I, 218: Ein Ich, das sich setzt, *als* sich selbst setzend, oder ein *Subject* ist nicht möglich ohne ein Object. . . . Das Ich setzt sich als bestimmt durch das Nicht-Ich.

[17] *Vom Ich als Princip der Philosophie oder über das Unbedingte im menschlichen Wissen.* Werke I, 177: 7. Wir haben das Ich bis jetzt bloss

lava on the moon, rather than being convinced that they are a self. This is why they have not understood Kant and have not even an inkling of his spirit. And this is also why they will not understand this writing before their eyes, although it starts from the very condition of all philosophizing. He who is not clear about this, in his mind, cannot understand any fundamental philosophy, nor does he need any. Nature, whose machine he is, will lead him, without any initiative of his own, in every business that confronts him. Philosophizing requires the self's own stand, a stand one must gain by oneself." [13] In the same year, young Schelling, at nineteen, wrote his essay *On the Possibility of a Form of All Philosophy* [14] and the following year, 1795, he wrote *About the I as Principle of Philosophy*.

Speaking of how an immature "love glues images of things of sense to the mind," [11] Augustine says: "This is the mind's impurity that, while it strives to think itself alone, it supposes that it is the kind of thing without which it cannot conceive itself." Every teacher of philosophy knows the difficulty students find in refraining from identifying the pure I with their respective empirical I. Augustine continues the passage just quoted, saying: "Therefore, when the mind is bidden to know itself, let it not seek itself as if it had been removed from itself, but let it remove from itself what it had added to itself," namely the images of a Not-I. "For the mind is always inward, not only in respect to those things of sense which are manifestly outward, but even in respect to their images which are in that part of the soul which animals share with us, although they lack the insight which is proper to the mind as such." [15]

Augustine calls the mind's natural trend to identify itself with the empirical I an impurity. In 1794, Fichte explained that "an I which posits itself, *as* positing itself, or as a subject, is not possible without an object.... The I posits itself as determined by the Not-I." [16] A philosophically untutored mind will rashly infer that the I is an object among others, if not a piece of lava or a switchblade at least that elusive thing, an objectified soul.

In 1795, Schelling wrote: "So far we have determined the I simply an that which, *for itself*, cannot be an *object*, and which, for anything outside of itself, can be neither object nor not-object, that is, must be nothing at all. Therefore the I does not obtain its reality from anything outside of its own sphere, as objects do, but singularly and alone *by itself*. This concept of the I is also the only one owing to which it can be called absolute." [17]

It should be obvious that the designation of the I as "the Absolute" is as absurd as it would be to say, in Augustinian language, that the soul is God. But as "God is the blessed life of the soul,"[6] so is absoluteness the ground of possibility of an I. We must remember that, in 1802, Schelling said that "the only true method can be the method of philosophy according to which everything is absolute [i.e., is absolutely] and there is no Absolute."[18] In the *Critique of Pure Reason*[19] Kant had already warned against the objectification of "the I that thinks, as an absolutely simple substance," and he had pointed out (ibid.) that "the I which thinks is at the same time its own object." His great disciples, Fichte, Hegel and Schelling kept stressing this subject-object nature of the I. But long before Kant, Augustine knew it well, saying that "nothing can be more

als dasjenige bestimmt, was für *sich selbst* schlechterdings nicht *Objekt*, und für etwas ausser ihm weder Objekt noch Nichtobjekt, d.h. gar *nichts* sein kann, was also seine Realität nicht, wie die Objekte, durch etwas ausser seiner Sphäre liegendes, sondern einzig und allein *durch sich selbst* erhält. Dieser Begriff des Ichs ist auch der einzige, wodurch es als das Absolute bezeichnet wird.

[18] *Fernere Darstellungen aus dem System der Philosophie.* Werke IV. 406: welches . . . die einzig wahre, d.h. diejenige Methode der Philosophie sein kann, nach welcher alles absolut und nichts Absolutes ist.

[19] B 471: dass der Gegenstand des inneren Sinnes, das Ich, was da denkt, eine schlechthin einfache Substanz sei. . . . weil das Subjekt, welches denkt, zugleich sein eigenes Object ist, . . .

[20] *De trinitate* X, iii, 5: Quo pacto igitur se aliquid scientem scit quae se ipsam nescit? Neque enim alteram mentem scientem scit sed se ipsam.

[21] *Kritik der praktischen Vernunft* (Cassirer edition, 1914) 11f: weil der Begriff einer Schöpfung nicht zu der sinnlichen Vorstellungsart der Existenz und zur Kausalität gehört, sondern nur auf Noumena bezogen werden kann. Cp. Lewis White Beck's translation (Bobbs-Merrill, Indianapolis 1956) 106.

[22] *Kritik der reinen Vernunft* 569: Nach dem intelligibelen Charakter desselben aber . . . würde dasselbe Subjekt dennoch von allem Einflusse der Sinnlichkeit und Bestimmung durch Erscheinungen freigesprochen werden müssen. . . . sofern es *Noumenon* ist . . . Cp. Norman Kemp Smith's translation (St. Martin's Press, N. Y. 1965) 469. Also cp. ibid., 470: "An *original* act (eine *ursprüngliche* Handlung), such as can by itself bring about what did not exist before, is not to be looked for in the causally connected appearances." And ibid., 471: "only as we ascend from the empirical object to the transcendental should we find that this subject (notwithstanding all its causality in the field of appearance) has in its *noumenon* certain conditions which must be regarded as purely intelligible."

[23] Ibid., 429: im Bewusstsein meiner selbst beim blossen Denken bin ich das Wesen *selbst*, . . . Der Satz aber: Ich denke, sofern er so viel sagt als: *Ich existire denkend*, ist nicht bloss logische Funktion, sondern bestimmt das Subject (welches dann zugleich Object ist) in Ansehung der Existenz. —Cp. N. K. Smith transl. 382.

[24] Ibid., 430: um sich als Object an sich selbst nicht bloss durch das Ich zu bezeichnen, sondern auch die Art seines Daseins zu bestimmen, d.i. sich als Noumenon zu erkennen.

[25] Ibid., 857: so muss ich nicht einmal sagen: *es ist* moralisch gewiss, dass ein Gott sei, sondern: *Ich bin* moralisch gewiss u.s.w.—N. K. Smith transl. 650.

present to itself than the mind,"[9] and asking: "By what stipulation could it know that it knows anything at all if it did not know itself? For it is itself that knows, not some other mind."[20]

Having made certain our selfhood we can take our second step and ascertain the obstacles the mind erects between itself and its origin.

Kant gave the clue for that knowledge when he pointed out that the concept of cause pertains strictly to phenomena and therefore that "the concept of creation does not pertain to the sense representation of existence and to causality, but can be applied only to noumena."[21] The Kantians retained the pre-Kantian identification of *noumenon* with the thing in itself, forgetting the radically different and strictly Kantian meaning of *noumenon* as autonomous I. The Kantians forget that a paralogism results if the autonomous act is interpreted as if it were an objective fact. Kant said, "in its intelligible character the subject must be considered to be free from all influence of sensibility and from all determination through appearances... as it is *noumenon*."[22]

Fichte, who was not a parroting Kantian but, in his way, a faithful disciple of Kant, stressed that the noumenal self cannot be caused from without but posits itself.[10] In the second edition of the *Critique of Pure Reason*, Kant himself had said: "in the consciousness of myself, in sheer thought, I am the essence (Wesen) *itself*.... Insofar as the proposition 'I think' means 'I exist thinking' it is not merely logical, but it determines the subject (which is then simultaneously object) with regard to its very existence."[23] And Kant speaks about the "I not only referring to itself as object-in-itself but even determining the mode of its existence, that is, recognizing itself as noumenon."[24]

Since it is the very form of existence of the I which places us in the noumenal world, Kant and his true followers stand on the same epistemological ground as Augustine with regard to the knowledge of God. It is not knowledge of some utterly strange objective entity, material or spiritual, nor is it an illusion produced by or arising within the human mind. The knowledge of God is not a piece of impersonal information. Kant says, "I must not even say, '*It is* morally certain that there is a God,' but '*I am* morally certain'."[25] Thus the *Critique of Pure Reason*. In the *Critique of Practical Reason*, Kant said that it is the very concept of freedom which "enables us to find the unconditioned for the conditioned and the intelligible for the sensuous without going outside ourselves." [26]

1400 years before Kant said we need not go outside ourselves, Augustine wrote his classical warning to every Godseeker. It should hang on the wall of every philosophical and theological seminar. "Do not go outside. Go back into your self. Truth dwells in the inner man. But if you find your own nature mutable, go even deeper, beyond your mere self. Remember, however, that when you transcend yourself, you are transcending the ratiocinating soul. Therefore aim at that by which reason's light itself is lit." [27]

That, of course, is God. But ratiocination can mislead us to objectify God and therefore look for him outside. Unlike Kant, Augustine did not sharply distinguish between ratiocination (Verstand) which thinks conditionally, and reason (Vernunft) which alone moves in the unconditional. However Augustine keenly feels the distinction, and he clearly distinguishes between the images of sense and the awareness of self. Not to make that distinction leads to the "disgrace of that error" [11] which is still so common among the philosophically untutored who objectify both, themselves and God. For them God is a fearsome riddle as long as they have not discovered with the skeptics that an objectified God is an illusion.

In his *Aphorism* 52 of 1806, Schelling said: "In no kind of knowledge can God occur as *known* (as object): as known he ceases to

---

[26] Loc. cit., v, 115: Der einzige Begriff der Freiheit verstattet es, dass wir nicht ausser uns hinausgehen dürfen, um das Unbedingte und Intelligible zu dem Bedingten und Sinnlichen zu finden.—L. W. Beck transl. 109.—The *Critique of Practical Reason* appeared 1788.

[27] *De vera religione* xxxix, 72: Noli foras ire; in te ipsum redi; in interiore homine habitat veritas: et si tuam naturam mutabilem inveneris transcende et teipsum. Sed memento cum te transcendis, ratiocinantem animam te transcendere. Illuc ergo tende unde ipsum lumen rationis accenditur.

[28] *Aphorismen zur Einleitung in die Naturphilosophie* (Werke VII, 150): 52. In keiner Art der Erkenntnis kann sich Gott als *Erkanntes* (als Objekt) verhalten: als Erkanntes hört er auf *Gott* zu sein. Wir sind niemals ausser Gott, so dass wir ihn uns fürsetzen könnten als Objekt.

[29] *Sermo 117*, 5: Ad mentem Deus pertinet, intelligendus est: ad oculos corpus, videndum est.

[30] *De trinitate* VIII, vii, 11: exterius enim conantur ire et interiora sua deserunt quibus interior est Deus. Itaque etiamsi aliquam sanctam caelitem potestatem vel audierint vel utcumque cogitaverint, facta magis eius appetunt quae humana miratur infirmitas.

[31] *In Joh. tract.* 106, 4: Haec est enim vis verae divinitatis, ut creaturae rationali iam ratione utenti, non omnino ac penitus possit abscondi.

[32] In Psalmo 130, 12: Sed intus est Deus eius, et spiritualiter intus est, et spiritualiter excelsus est; non quasi intervallis locorum, quomodo per intervalla loca altiora sunt. Nam si talis altitudo quaerenda est, vincunt nos aves ad Deum.

[33] *Einleitung in die Philosophie der Mythologie* (Werke XI, 186f): Man fragt: wie kommt das Bewusstsein zu Gott? Aber das Bewusstsein kommt nicht zu Gott; seine erste Bewegung

be *God*. We are never outside of God, so that we could set him up in front of us, as an object." [28]

The word object derives from the Latin verb *iacere* which means to throw; *proiectio* is a throwing forth; and *obiectum* is what is thrown toward or against us. Jacob Boehme translated it literally as *Gegenwurf*. And *Gegenstand* is what takes its stand over against us. We can see an object as it stands there. Augustine says we can go around it and see it from different sides, but we cannot by eyesight fully comprehend it. God, however, is not an object. "God pertains to the mind, he is to be understood; a body pertains to the eyes, it is to be seen." [29] Objects are outside ourselves. But those who seek God outside "forsake their own inwardness while God is inward even in them." [30]

"For this is the power of true divinity that it cannot be hidden altogether and inwardly from a creature fit to seek for its ground and actually seeking it." [31] Men call its manifestation conscience. Often they find it too uncomfortably close. So the intellect throws it out, *calling* it God, but meaning by that word a distant entity, "some holy celestial power," [30] a something or Somebody. One function of human religions is to remove the God reality and place it at a safe distance, in heaven, or at least to confine the God in his temple. Then, confessing this original sin, the religions invoke God again, appealing to his mercy and asking for forgiveness. Augustine says: "But their God is inside," not spatially but "spiritually inside, and in spirit above them, not as by intervals of space the way places are higher. For if we were to seek spatial height, the birds would beat us to God." [32]

The obstacles to true religion are man-made but they are natural. The child's mind works by imagination and ratiocination. The mature Schelling writes: "People ask, how does consciousness come to God? But consciousness does not *come* to God; its very first move is away from the *true* God. ... as soon as it moves into awareness, it moves away from Him. There is no other explanation but that God is originally inflicted upon consciousness, or that consciousness has God *in* itself, in the sense in which we say of a man that he has a virtue or, more frequently, a vice, by which saying we mean to express the fact that his habit does not confront him like an object, is not something he really wants, nor even something of which he is aware. ... Man, as soon as he merely *is*, without as yet having *become* something, is consciousness of God. He does not have this consciousness, he is it." [33] In the same vein, Augustine speaks of

"God whom everything that can love at all loves, knowingly or unwittingly."[34]

This brings me to my third question as to adequate ways of knowing God. Our natural way of imagination and ratiocination leads us away to The Fall. Augustine says that, "in order to rise again, a man must push himself up from the spot upon which he fell. Therefore we must use the very forms of the carnal which detain us, so that we may come to know the forms which the flesh cannot reveal."[35] But Augustine warns: "If we cannot yet inhere [in the eternal] let us at least repress our phantasms and throw out of the spectacle of our mind such futile and deceptive games"[36] of our imagination and ratiocination.

---

geht... von dem *wahren* Gott hinweg,... da es, sowie es sich *bewegt*, von Gott hinweggeht, so bleibt nichts übrig, als dass ihm dieser ursprünglich angetan sei, oder dass das Bewusstsein Gott *an* sich habe, in dem Sinn, wie man von einem Menschen sagt, dass er eine Tugend, oder noch öfter, dass er eine Untugend an sich habe, womit man eben ausdrücken will, dass sie ihm selbst nicht gegenständlich sei, nicht etwas das er wolle, ja nicht einmal etwas um das er wisse. ... der Mensch, sowie er nur eben *Ist* und noch nichts *geworden* ist, ist er Bewusstsein Gottes, er *hat* dieses Bewusstsein nicht, er *ist* es,...

[34] *Soliloquia* I, i, 2: Deus quem amat omne quod potest amare sive sciens sive nesciens.

[35] *De vera religione* xxiv, 45: Nam in quem locum quisque ceciderit, ibi debet incumbere ut surgat. Ergo ipsis carnalibus formis, quibus detinemur, nitendum est, ad eas cognoscendas, quas caro non nuntiat.

[36] Ibid., L, 98: Cui [aeternitati] si nondum possumus inhaerere, obiurgemus saltem nostra phantasmata, et tam nugatorios et deceptorios ludos de spectaculo mentis eiiciamus.

[37] *Philosophische Briefe über Dogmatismus und Kriticismus* (Werke I, 290): Schwache Vernunft aber ist nicht die, die keinen objektiven Gott erkennt, sondern die einen erkennen *will*. Weil ihr glaubtet, ohne einen objektiven Gott... nicht handeln zu können, musste man euch, um euch dieses Spielwerk eurer Vernunft desto leichter entreissen zu können, mit der Berufung auf eure Vernunftschwäche hinhalten.

[38] *De trinitate* V, i. 2: Nam quo intellectu homo deum capit qui ipsum intellectum suum quo eum vult capere nondum capit? Si autem iam capit, attendat diligenter nihil eo esse in sua natura melius, et videat utrum ibi videat ulla lineamenta formarum, nitores colorum, spatiosa granditatem, partium distantiam, molis distensionem, aliquas per locorum intervalla motiones vel quid eius modi. Nihil certe istorum invenimus in eo quo in natura nostra nihil melius invenimus, id est in nostro intellectu quo sapientiam capimus quantae capaces sumus. Quod ergo non invenimus in meliore nostro non debemus in illo quaerere quod longe melius est meliore nostro, ut sic intellegamus deum si possumus, quantum possumus, sine qualitate bonum, sine quantitate magnum, sine indigentia creatorum, sine situ praesentem, sine habitu omnia continentem, sine loco ubique totum, sine tempore sempiternum, sine ulla mutatione mutabilia facientem nihilque patientem. Quisquis deum ita cogitat etsi nondum potest omnimodo invenire quid sit, pie tamen cavet quantum potest aliquid de illo sentire quod non sit.

[39] *De doctrina christiana* I, xxxviii, 42: Sed fidei succedit species quam videbimus.

In 1795 Schelling wrote: "Weak is not the reason which *cannot* know an objective God, but the reason which *wants* to know such a God. Because you believed you could not act without an objective God... one had to put you off with the reminder of the weakness of your reason, so that one could snatch away from you that toy of it."[37] Augustine and Schelling point out that objectivistic ratiocination plays childish games with toy gods.

What is needed in the first place is philosophical reflection on the self. Augustine asks: "With what kind of understanding could a man grasp God, who does not yet understand his own intellect by which he wants to understand God?" Certainly it is not an intellect outward bound toward objects, for objects are conditional and God is not. Kant made us understand that our intellect is twofold, ratiocination bent on the conditional and reason seeking the unconditional. Augustine continues saying:

> "If a man already understands his intellect, let him pay diligent attention to the fact that in his own nature there is nothing better, and let him see whether in his intellect he can discover any outline of forms, brightness of colors, spatious bulk, distance between parts, extended mass, any motions through intervals of space, or anything of that sort. Certainly we find nothing of that in the trait of our nature than which we find nothing better, that is, in our intellect by which we attain as much wisdom as we can. Therefore whatever we do not find in what is best in us, we ought not seek in what is far better than the best in us, in order that we may understand God, if we can, and as much as we can, as good without quality, great without quantity, creator without need, present without location, containing everything without any shape of his own, being whole wihout being in any place, eternal without time, making changing things without any change in him, and suffering nothing. Whoever so thinks of God, though he cannot yet find just what God is, will yet take pious heed, as best as he can, not to think anything of Him which He is not."[38]

Logic demands that we state what God is not, but negative statements call for positive insights. Theologically Augustine expects them from faith. "For faith is followed by the splendor we shall see."[39] "When, by seeing, our faith becomes truth then eternity will hold fast our mortality,"[40] having brought out in it what is non-mortal.

Philosophically Augustine finds insights starting from his faith in truth, not from the faith of a specific religion. An early document is the radiant initial prayer of the Soliloquies which expresses nothing specifically Christian. To be sure, philosophical comprehension cannot be exhaustive. In a sermon, Augustine said: "We are speaking of God; is it a wonder if you do not understand? For if you understand, it is not God."[41] Nevertheless, for Augustine God is positively truth, goodness,[42] even beauty,[43] but chiefly truth. "If there is anything more excellent, then that is God, but if not then the truth itself is already God."[44] "And the truth in no way arrives at itself by ratiocination; instead it is what those seek who ratiocinate."[45] Furthermore, "this is our freedom that we yield to that

---

[40] *De trinitate* IV, xviii, 24: Cum fides nostra videndo fiet veritas, tunc mortalitatem nostram commutatam tenebit aeternitas.

[41] *Sermo 117*, 5: De Deo loquimur, quid mirum si non comprehendis? Si enim comprehendis, non est Deus.

[42] *In Ps. 134*, 3: bono suo bonus est. ... Hanc singularitatem bonitatis eius et praeterire breviter nolo et commendare congrue non sufficio. – *De trinitate* VIII, iii. 4: vide ipsum bonum si potes; ita deum videbis ... bonum omnis boni.

[43] *De natura boni*, vii: si obedientiam conservaverint sub Domino Deo suo, ac si incorruptibili pulchritudini eius adhaeserint. — *De quantitate animae*, xxxv, 79: pergit in Deum ... pulchre apud pulchritudinem.

[44] *De libero arbitrio* II, xv, 39: Si enim aliquid est excellentius, ille potius Deus est: si autem non est, iam ipsa veritas Deus est.

[45] *De vera religione* xxxix, 72: cum ad seipsam veritas non utique ratiocinando perveniat, sed quod ratiocinantes appetunt, ipsa est.

[46] *De libero arbitrio* II, xiii, 37: Haec est libertas nostra cum isti subdimur veritati.

[47] *De doctrina christiana* I, xxxi, 34: Diligit enim nos Deus.... quomodo ergo diligit? ut nobis utatur an ut fruatur? Sed si fruitur, eget bono nostro, quod nemo sanus dixerit.... Non ergo fruitur nobis sed utitur.

[48] *De trinitate* V, xiv, 15: Spiritus ergo est dei qui dedit et noster qui accepimus.

[49] *In Psalmo 92*, 1: qui carnaliter sentiebant de Deo, nec intelligebant quia Deus cum quiete operatur, et semper quietus est.

[50] *Confessiones* VII, x, 16: O aeterna veritas et vera caritas et cara aeternitas! Tu es Deus meus, tibi suspiro *die ac nocte* (Psalm I:2).

[51] Ibid., I, i, 1: Tu excitas, ut laudare te delectet [homo], quia fecisti nos ad te et inquietum est cor nostrum, donec requiescat in te.

[52] *Historisch-kritische Einleitung in die Philosophie der Mythologie* (Werke XI, 185): weil im Mensch in seinem ursprünglichen Wesen keine andere Bedeutung hat, als die, die Gott-setzende Natur zu sein, weil er ursprünglich nur existiert, um dieses Gottsetzende Wesen zu sein, also nicht die *für sich* selbst seiende, sondern die *Gott* zugewandte, in Gott gleichsam verzückte Natur.

[53] *Philosophie der Mythologie* (Werke XII, 121): Es ist weder eine *mitgeteilte*, noch eine selbsterzeugte Erkenntnis Gottes, die wir dem ursprünglichen Menschen zuschreiben; es ist ein allem Denken und Wissen vorausgehender *Grund*, es ist sein *Wesen* selbst, durch welches er dem Gott zum voraus und vor allem wirklichen Bewusstsein verpflichtet ist.

[54] *Aphorismen zur Einleitung in die Naturphilosophie* (Werke VII, 149): 46. Die Vermögen aber zur Erkenntnis

truth."[46] For we yield to it not as slavish minds but as autonomous rational beings. Therefore, Augustine asks, "in what way does God love us? To make use of us, or to derive enjoyment from us? If the latter, he would be in need of our good, which nobody would say who is sound. ... Therefore not for enjoyment but for use."[47] And we are not used like dead tools but by our free acceptance of each task. Augustine says of the Holy Spirit that it is "of God who gave it and of us who took it."[48] And this is true even with regard to those who are in error. Augustine says of those "who thought of God in a carnal manner" that "they did not understand because God works quietly, and works always, and is always quiet."[49] Thus Augustine can exultantly exclaim: "Oh, eternal truth, and true love, and beloved eternity! Thou art my God; it is for Thee I sigh, day and night."[50]

It is the quiet presence and accessibility of the truth which underlies Augustine's confession: "It is Thou who movest us to delight in praising Thee; for Thou hast formed us for Thyself, and our hearts are restless till they find rest in Thee."[51] The old Schelling wrote something similar: "Man in his original essence has no other significance but to be the God-positing nature, because originally he exists only as the God-positing being, therefore as not being *for himself*, but rather a nature turned toward God or, as it were, a nature enraptured in God."[52]

With regard to man's knowledge of God, Schelling says: "We do not attribute to the original man any *communicated* knowledge of God, nor any knowledge spontaneously produced by man. Rather there is a *ground* antecedent to all thinking and knowing. It is the very *essence* of man by which he is bound to God, in advance, and long before every actual consciousness."[53] Already in the *Aphorisms* of 1806 Schelling had said: "To seek in oneself the faculties for knowing God, or to count and evaluate them there, is the utmost limit of confusion and of inner obfuscation of mind. Everyone must acknowledge the idea of God as shining by itself in reason." For, "reason does not *have* the idea of God, it *is* that idea, and nothing else. This idea is not an object of contest or discord. In this idea every particularity vanishes from which alone conflict of opinion can come. The inane one who denies it, gives it voice without knowing he does, for he cannot reasonably connect any two concepts except *in* this idea."[54] It is indeed the idea of all-pervading truth.

In 1812, in *The Ages of the World*, Schelling stressed the ever new *life* of truth which always manifests itself in some specific way. "With respect to his highest self, God is not manifest; he reveals himself," ever anew. "He is not real; he becomes real, just that he may appear as the most free being of all." [55] And in 1836, in the *Presentation of Philosophical Empiricism*, Schelling wrote: "God is really quite nothing *in itself*. *He is nothing but relation and pure relation*, for he is only the Lord. Everything we add to that makes him a mere substance. As it were, he is really good for nothing else than for being Lord of being. For he is the only nature not concerned with itself, rid of itself, and therefore is absolutely free. Everything substantial is concerned with itself, caught in itself and constrained by itself. God alone has nothing to do with himself; he is *sui securus*, certain of himself and therefore rid of himself. Consequently he is concerned only with other entities. He is, so one might say, entirely ecstatic, *outside* of himself, hence free of himself, and thus is the one who liberates everything else." [56]

The key word of Schelling is freedom. It is Kant's autonomy. And if I read Augustine right, he too sees in the freedom of God the source of human freedom. He prays God to make him free.[57] He

Gottes in *sich* aufsuchen und zählen oder wägen, ist die äusserste Grenze der Verwirrung und der innern Verfinsterung des Geistes. — 48. Die Vernunft *hat* nicht die Idee Gottes, sondern sie *ist* diese Idee, nichts ausserdem. ... jeder muss die Idee Gottes als an sich leuchtend in der Vernunft anerkennen. — 49. Diese Idee ist kein Gegenstand des Bestreitens oder der Zwietracht; alle Besonderheit, aus welcher allein Widerstreit kommt, geht unter in ihr. Der Unsinnige, der sie leugnet, spricht sie aus, ohne es zu wissen; er vermag nicht zwei Begriffe vernunftgemäss zu verbinden als in dieser Idee.

[55] *Die Weltalter* (Werke VIII, 308): Gott seinem höchsten Selbst nach ist nicht offenbar, er offenbart sich; er ist nicht wirklich, er wird wirklich, eben damit er als das allerfreieste Wesen erscheine. (Bolman transl., N. Y. 1942).

[56] *Darstellung des philosophischen Empirismus* (Werke X, 260): Man könnte sagen: Gott ist eben wirklich nichts *an sich: er ist nichts als Beziehung und lauter Beziehung*, denn er ist nur der Herr; alles, was wir darüber oder ausserdem hinzutun, macht ihn zur blossen Substanz. Er ist wirklich, so zu sagen, zu gar nichts anderem da, als nur um der Herr des Seins zu sein. *Er* eben ist die einzige nicht mit sich selbst beschäftigte, ihrer selbst ledige und darum absolut freie Natur (alles Substantielle hat mit sich selbst zu tun, ist mit sich selbst befangen und behaftet), Gott allein hat mit sich selbst nichts zu tun, er ist *sui securus* (seiner selbst sicher und darum seiner selbst ledig), und hat daher bloss mit anderem zu tun — er ist, kann man sagen — ganz *ausser* sich, also frei von sich, und dadurch auch das alles andere Befreiende.

[57] *Soliloquia* I, i, 1: Deus ... praesta mihi primum ut bene te rogem, deinde ut me agam dignum quem exaudias, postremo ut liberes.

[58] *Confessiones* II, vi, 11: Tu autem eras interior intimo meo et superior summo meo.

[59] Ibid., I, ii, 2: Non ergo essem, deus meus, non omnino essem, nisi esses in me.

says to Him: "You were more inward than my innermost and higher than my highest," [58]—surely not as an incubus nor as a celestial boss. And only a man keenly aware of essential freedom can say with Augustine: "I could not be, my God, I could not be at all, unless you were in me." [59]

EPILOGUE

Before dawn on the last day of November 1977 I had a short, very vivid dream. I stood in a dark space where I could see nothing. Then, fifteen or twenty feet away and at elbow height, hovering horizontally without support, there was a whitehot rectangular iron, about a foot wide and two feet long, almost an inch thick. It may have been a steady white flame, shaped like a board. Without hearing any words nor seeing any inscription, I knew instantly this was a manifest presence of God. I felt no heat but did not dare to step closer, for I knew the tremendous heat would consume (not inflame but rather simply annul) everything, and especially every word ever said or written about God. That knowledge woke me up. Immediately, like an explanation printed under a symbolic picture, the comment came to my mind and I jotted it down.

When I was dressed I put into more explicit language the otherwise no longer decipherable pencil notes. I added nothing but a few quotations which occurred to me while writing. What I wrote was only a fully awake and therefore reflective rendering of the comment which "was there", not of my making. I "saw" the comment the way one sees a picture. When one describes the picture in words, the report looks verbose and like a willful construction. Here is what I wrote.

For Augustine, God - even if nothing more - is at least truth (De libero arbitrio II,xv,39), that truth which, as the highest teacher, teaches inwardly (ib.II,ii,4).

Now the insight into any truth always consumes every verbal formulation. No truth is entrapped in the words that express it. Truth is alive, and its life always demands at least interpretation if not a transposition into new words which make the truth shine in every new mind if blessed with the insight.

Augustine quotes the First Letter of John (1:5) "God is light", and he comments: "not the way our eyes see, but as the heart sees as soon as it hears that there *is* truth" (De trinitate VIII,ii,3). He warns against the fog of bodily imagery and clouds of phantasms. Still, our mind cannot do without corporeal images and forms of fantasy. Furthermore all our words are human and need interpretation and translation. Even when Moses is told that the holy name is "I shall be who shall be" (Exodus 3:14) God is not imprisoned in those words, the way the Egyptian gods are the prisoners of their individual shapes, the one with a hawk's head, the other a jackal's, the third a ram's. Immediately the Hebrew original evokes the question: What do the words mean? And should they be translated as "I am" or "I shall be?"

181

Truth is always a perplexing challenge and will not be nailed down in words, no matter how appropriate the expression. If truth were not this live challenge, it could not set us free. We should be imprisoned in words which would have the haunting appearance of magic incantations. False gods love that kind of language, be it Marxist or Nazi or other totalitarian verbiage. We must take care not to fall into traps when we talk of religion. For it is we who are responsible for our language and our thinking. True, we cannot think without words or other appropriate form of expression. But juggling words is not thinking. Nor are incantations prayers.

As Karl Rahner's beautiful little book, <u>Words Spoken into Silence</u> (<u>Worte ins Schweigen</u>, 1947) reminds us, our prayers are men's words spoken into the silence of God. Among men we can rightly look for somebody with whom we can genuinely converse, but there is no conversation with God. Gabriel Marcel tells never to forget that God is not "somebody who" (Dieu n'est pas quelqu'un qui..<u>Être et Avoir</u>, p. 118; Aubier, Paris 1935).

I had these comments printed in English in a student paper and a German version in a Swiss church monthly. It did not put my mind to rest.

Off and on, for many months, I have asked myself two questions: Why the shape of a board(Brett)? And why did it hover at waist or elbow height?

Carl Gustav Jung advises to take dreams as literally as possible. Since the two questions have been bothering me, I finally started with the key word Brett. There was no association.

Then, in the middle of the afternoon of September 9, while I was thinking about entirely different matters, sudden answers popped up.

In German it can be said of one who is blocked, "er hat ein Brett vor dem Kopf," that is, he has a board in front of his forehead. Now the extrovert tendency in the interpretation of a dream would be to say it really does not concern me but means the behavior of others. It is they who are boarded up by planks of words improperly used about the godhead. The introverted interpretation already came spontaneously last November: The great heat will consume my own words as well. As I have long known, every formulation needs retranslation.

But why the hovering at the height? Ah, another word: "Servierbrett," that is a tray on which a servant brings things; a salver on which a butler brings letters or visiting cards. Extroverted message: Most would-be religious people desire to use God like a butler who brings them whatever they want. True, they couch their orders in the most respectful terms. When the true God appears, it is in the form of a consuming fire. What it consumes is the inadequate and therefore improper and condemnable kind of wording to which they are addicted. Poor things, they have been brought up in it! What God presents to them, as on a salver, is the fiery bill!

So that is why I did not dare to go closer. I stand at a safe distance, as a critic of my misguided contemporaries. Why have I not taught them any better, all these years? Is my own language, though clear for me, an adequate means of communication? That puts the heat on me!

Afterlude in the small hours of the following night: "White hot?" - <u>Argent</u> and <u>or</u> are the papal heraldic colors. Now an iron that is being heated up turns from red to yellow and then white. Secular evaluation would rank gold higher than silver and the church gold higher than the silver of conscience with its small but viable change of dimes.

Furthermore, the next day: White contains all the colors and thus, symbolically, is closer to the truth. - But here the reader will call a halt and say I must not try to squeeze my lemon when it is already all but dry.

Nietzsche who first taught me a bit of selfcritique, confessed he could only believe in a God who could dance. I believe what people who cannot dance lack is a sense of humor. The God whose death Nietzsche proclaimed was the glum God of heartless men and women. But Nietzsche himself admonished us to remain faithful to this Earth. So, if I look around and see the stalking gate of a stick insect or of a praying mantis, or the waddling and hopping of a penguin in his formal dress, even if I look in the mirror, I figure that the Lord who can put up with such creatures must have an undeniable sense of humor.

INDEX OF NAMES

Aenesidemus 166, 168
Anaxagoras 6
Anaximandros 4
Aquinas 84, 87, 125-144
Aristotle 88, 90, 119, 134, 152, 161
Augustine 88, 99, 120, 123, 131, 133, 157, 159f, 165-179

Berkeley 154
Boehme 135, 173
Brown 158
Bruno 24, 25
Buddha 18

Calvin 36
Croce 10
Cusanus 28f, 86f

Descartes 90, 131, 153f, 157

Farrell 50
Fichte 16, 23, 76, 88, 94, 98f, 101, 154, 156-159, 166, 168-171

Garve 154
Gaunilo 87
Goethe 116

Hegel 4, 12, 88, 99, 115, 125, 143, 150, 152, 156, 158, 160, 170
Hitler 30
Hobbes 26
Hölderlin 152
Hume 26, 96, 154f

Jacobi 117
Jesus 54
Joachim of Floris 76f

Kant 26, 39, 83, 88, 91, 94, 99, 119, 123, 125-179
Kroner 20

Leibniz 99, 159
Locke 154f
Luther 15, 121, 143

Mao 159 Mussolini 31
Marx 159
McCarthy 159
Medicus 20, 24, 76, 162f

Nietzsche 18

Oersted 158

Pacher 28
Paracelsus 121
Parmenides
Patterson 39
Paulus 11
Perry 40
Plato 88, 90, 99, 156
Plotinus 88
Przywara 166

Rebec 9
Reinhold 98, 156
Rosenberg 51

Schelling 4-6, 14, 18, 85f, 88f, 96f, 99, 117, 119, 149, 165-179
Schulze 166
Socrates 6
Spinoza 99, 152, 159
Sudhoff 121

Tillich 22, 161

Vico 15, 16
Villers 99

Windelband 101
Wolff 101

Zwingli 121

NOTE

The letter f designates the subsequent page.

The topical index indicates the most important passages by underlined page numbers.

INDEX OF TOPICS

the Absolute 170
the absolute I 152,161,169
the absolute object 152
abutment 52
act 3,157,159f
acts of God 2-4, 88
our age 41
being alibe 165
allegory 23f
Amrica 71
angels 15
antinomy 154
arbitrariness 3
art 118f, 122
autonomy 98,168,171,177

backwardness 120
the beautiful 116
belief 14, 33.44

our calling 35
Calvinism 15
categories 97
cause 84f,95,100f,134,
    139,161,171
Chassidim 135
Christianity 18f,29,51,
    53,54
church 9,29,53
codes 153
coercion 120,153
college 31
commandment 73
common sense 27,28
community 120,122f
conformity 153
consciousness 92
contingency 3,7
creation 2,4,95,100,134,
    139,160,171
creature 16
criticism 152,154,159f
culture 45,49,121

the dead 1
decided past 2-6,5,49,55,
    116
deification 72,76f,79

nature deities 120
determinism 6
devil 28f
disgrace 168
dogma 121f
dogmatism 152,154,159f
doubt 167
dreams 165
duty 79

ecclesiasticism 11
Ecumenical Councils 162
education 10,26f,29,31
empirircism 96,138,141
Enlightenment 71,80f
essence 135
the eternal 5,116
eternity 3
existence of God 90,135f

faith 20,22,31,33-44,78,
    122f,155
faith in absolute truth 118
fate 75
force 72
four supertemporal ideas 116f
freedom 4-6,23,37,42,73,77,
    80f,90,98,100f,121,132,
    139,153,156,171f,178

gift 36f
God 6,83,88-90,92,99,119f,
    134,160f,172f
God as act 87
God is dead 18,91
existence of God 158
knowledge of God 171
presence of God 20
God as Somebody 36
gods 71
Grace 34
ground 84,166

happiness 47,71
height of the time 115f,120
heritage 116
heteronomy 97,101,139
higher religions 120

historical knowledge 115
history 5f
human nature 5, 93

the absolute I 152,161
I am I 157,167
iconoclasm 15,20
idea 90,116,122f
idealism 98
subjective idealism 154f
idolatry 20
illumination 160
images 71
imagery 41
impurity 169
the individual 35f,94
individualism 35
intellectual intuition 98,166
intelligible world 98

the just 118,120f

Kantians 160,168,171

laboratories 7
lava on the moon 169
legitimacy 74f
life 165
life of philosophy 114
Lord 76,162
lords 71
love 116,135,167,169

magic 22,73,80
nature of man 78,_93_,123
Marxism 18,159
mastery of time 5
materialism 159
maturity 115,122
mechanism 2,6
metaphysics 96,156
mind 95,167,169
modern age 25
moral action 93,153
moral law 100,137
moral obligation 95
moralism 162
morality 115
myth _14_,15-21,45,49,_50f_,
_54_f,_79_,91
mythological thinking 7,92,121

nature 3,6
naturalism 11
Naturphilosophie 158
Nazi 17f,23,30
necessity 4
negative philosophy 86f,90
negative theology 86
noumenal certainty 167,171
noumenon 95f,100,138f,_154_f,
160f,_171_

objects 95,97,169,173
objectivism 88,98f,133,
139,156,168,172
objective truth 118
ontological truth 119,122
ontological certainty 131
organization 54
originality 13
orthodoxy

pantheism 90
paralogism 171
participation 115
past 5,2-6,49,55,116
peace 77
personified God 99
philosophy 7,12,_13_,22,_27_,
31,119,123,156,159f,
_165_,_168_
piety 75,81
Platonism 3,24
poetry 14
polytheism 92
positive philosophy 89f
positivism 115
post-Christian 43
postulates 160
practical 152
prayer 20,27
primacy of practcal reason
152f,156
proof 119
phenomenon 154f,171

ratiocination 116-119
reason 87f,96,_99_,117
Reformation 15
rejuvenation 12
religion 11f,29f,56,119,
137,_159_f,_173_

religiosity 2,4,7,49,56
responsibility 115ff,132,
    153, 156
revelation 17,80f,98,156
revivalism 11,31
ritual 10,80

scepticism 97
school (see education)
science 27
scientism 11,26
security 75
self 165,167
sentimentality
Somebody 71,75f,80,119
soul 71-73,76,79,99,130,
    159,167,169f,35
speculation 28
spiritualism 159
subconscious 14,16
subject-object 100,170
superhistorical 115
superhuman order 117
supermundane 94
supernatural 38
supersensuous 76,97,133
superstition 20,22,26f,119
supertemporal 115f,122
symbols 23f,40f,119,121
switchblade 168

teleology 6
theogonic process 93
theology 25
theories 90
thetical judgment 118
thing in itself 96,98,155,171
time 6,80,100
totalitarianism 35f,120f
toy of reason 99
transcendence 38,40,89,100
translation 12,21,114
truth 12,21,117
twofold truth 25

ultimate validity 9
the unconditional 22,26f,35f,
    38f,41,72,95,100,115, 139,
    152,156,172
unconditional certainty 121
United States 71
university 9

waffle iron 168

FRITZ MARTI